MAKING A DIFFERENCE IN COLLEGE ADMISSION

A Step-by-Step Guide for the Secondary School Counselor

Kenneth W. Hitchner
Anne Tifft-Hitchner

THE CENTER FOR APPLIED RESEARCH IN EDUCATION
West Nyack, New York 10995

THE CENTER FOR APPLIED
RESEARCH IN EDUCATION
West Nyack, New York

10 9 8 7 6 5 4 3 2 1

Library of Congress Cataloging-in-Publication Data

Hitchner, Kenneth W.
Making a difference in college admission : a step-by-step guide for the secondary school counselor / Kenneth W. Hitchner, Anne Tifft -Hitchner.

p. cm.
Bibliography: p.
Includes index.
ISBN 0-87628-549-3
1. Personnel service in secondary education—United States.
2. Universities and colleges—United States—Admission. 3. College student orientation—United States. I. Tifft-Hitchner, Anne.
II. Title.
LB1620.5.H55 1989
373.14—dc19 89-710
CIP

ISBN 0-87628-549-3

**THE CENTER FOR APPLIED
RESEARCH IN EDUCATION
BUSINESS & PROFESSIONAL DIVISION
A division of Simon & Schuster
West Nyack, New York 10995**

PRINTED IN THE UNITED STATES OF AMERICA

To Ken and Doug,
who have already been there;
And to Megan and Lynne,
who have yet to go.

About the Authors

Kenneth W. Hitchner is the author of *A Survival Guide for the Secondary School Counselor* (The Center for Applied Research in Education, 1987). He received his B.A. degree in English and social studies from Dickinson College, Carlisle, PA. After doing graduate work in school counseling at Bucknell University, he went on to earn Ed.M. and Ed.S. degrees in school administration from Rutgers University. Mr. Hitchner has had 25 years of secondary school counseling experience and has worked with young people in three different New Jersey school districts prior to his arrival at East Brunswick High School as a counselor.

The author and lecturer spent eight years as director of counseling, first at South River and then at East Brunswick High Schools. In the mid-1970s, he was a member of the Rutgers University coadjutant faculty, lecturing on various affirmative action topics. He is a past vice-president of the New Jersey School Counselor Association and has been published in the *Journal of College Admissions* and the College Board's *College Prep*. In addition to his public school duties, he maintains an independent counseling practice in career and college planning.

Anne Tifft-Hitchner is a recipient of a B.A. degree in chemistry from Georgian Court College, Lakewood, NJ. She went on to earn an M.A. degree in philosophy of science from St. John's University. She has taught in grades 7 through junior college, with the majority of her teaching at East Brunswick High School as a chemistry, physics, and astronomy instructor. She has also taught English at The Peddie School in Hightstown, NJ.

While at East Brunswick, she spent several years as faculty advisor of the student government association, a position she also held at the former Mount St. Mary College in New Jersey. Mrs. Tifft-Hitchner is currently in private practice as an independent counselor in career and college planning, specializing in individual self-assessment.

About This Guide

School counselors are more active and involved than they were 30 years ago. But as society develops, counselors must grow in their ability to best assist their counselees to cope with the challenge—and that is a challenge in itself.

"College counseling" connotes much more than helping a youngster select and apply to a few schools; it also means quality work with related counseling endeavors aimed at personal, academic, and career development.

Making a Difference in College Admission has been designed to serve both as a resource and as an encouragement for you to engage in a bit of self-assessment. As you look over the contents, you can take stock of your current situation and determine how you would like to proceed in the future. You will want to implement some of the practical suggestions and worthwhile field-tested programs in your own school situation.

Before you can be really effective with your counselees and their families, your efforts (no matter how personally stamped they might be) must be conducted within the framework of a well-designed departmental program. And before the establishment of such a program, certain personal skills (which must be continually refined, augmented, and updated) should be in place. The *Guide*, therefore, is divided into three parts:

- Section I, "Enhancing Your Skills," discusses the development and rebuilding of college counseling skills. Chapter 1, "Challenge and Opportunity," supports the premise that the challenge has never been greater for today's professionals to meet the personal needs of their counselees and the opportunities have never been better. At the same time, admission people and secondary school personnel have never needed each other more. Together, they must face significant problems. Chapters 2 and 3 explore the necessity for sharpening the human relations skills of both parties. Chapters 4 through 6 present useful and practical approaches to computers, publications, and workshops that will help the novice to develop important basic skills and the experienced professional to enhance his or her own.
- Section II, "Developing a Well-Designed Program," takes the position that the best college counseling programs are found where there is agreement

among the people as to the goals and objectives to be pursued. In this environment, professionals are free to draw upon their own special talents, interests, and capabilities to serve their clientele better, *but* at the same time there is direction to the overall program. Specific grade-level activities that can be incorporated into a college counseling curriculum are presented in Chapter 7. The many pieces of the admission puzzle are treated in Chapters 8 through 12.

- Section III, "Counselee, Family, and You," shows you that today's high school students are capable of developing a good college and career choice strategy, provided that *conscientious* counselors are afforded the time to show them the way. The development of a sound strategy can become even more of a reality where an *appropriate* amount of concern and support from parents is evident (Chapter 13). For students to present themselves well, they must know themselves well; self-assessment is discussed in Chapter 14. Chapters 15 through 18 explore the role of the counselor in that assessment and presentation. Chapter 19 examines how counselors can improve their efforts to sensitize youngsters to the wide variety of common and unique career possibilities. Chapters 20 through 22 study the involvement of the professional in three critical areas of the admission program: application completion, personal interview, and essay writing. At no time in our history has sound family financial planning been of more significance than today. Where does school counseling begin and end? (Chapter 23 explains.) And who is responsible for assisting students to make the high school–to–college transition as smooth as possible? Chapter 24 takes a look at the stress factors, and at the methods a few secondary schools are using to help students "go with it."

Making a Difference in College Admission is certainly within our potential. We hope this book will help you attain it!

Kenneth W. Hitchner
Anne Tifft-Hitchner

Acknowledgments

We are grateful to the following people for their encouragement and special assistance in the preparation of this book:

At East Brunswick, NJ: The Board of Education; JoAnn Magistro, Assistant Superintendent of Schools; James Sheerin, Principal of the High School; Frank LoPresti, Guidance Department Chairperson; the counselors, especially Curtis Lippincott for his advice and manuscript suggestions, and Robert Sullivan, Dorothy Chard, and Judith Rosenthal for their support and involvement.

Our appreciation to the following colleagues who also provided support for, and valuable input into, the writing of the text: Shelley Brody and Leonard King, The Maret School, Washington, DC; Richard Brown, Williamston High School, MI; Dolores Forsyth, Lyons Township High School, LaGrange, IL; Patricia Henning, The Westlake School, Los Angeles, CA; Cas Jakubik, Westfield High School, NJ; Richard Malley and Henry Milton, Blair Academy, Blairstown, NJ; Allen McCune, Halstead High School, KS; Nancy McGuire, Wyoming Seminary Preparatory School, Kingston, PA; David Siefert, Valley City Multi-District Vocational Center, ND; and Alison Stewart, The Lawrenceville School, NJ.

Many thanks to the more than 200 college admission officers who responded to our survey with their comments and recommendations, especially to Natalie Aharonian, Wellesley College, MA; David G. Behrs, Penn State at Harrisburg, PA; Steven T. Briggs, Dean Junior College, Franklin, MA; John P. Burke, Georgian Court College, Lakewood, NJ; Jack Davies, Glassboro State College, NJ; Richard A. Davis, University of Wyoming, Laramie, WY; Dana Denault, Curry College, Boston, MA; Reverend Harry J. Erdlen, Villanova University, PA; Peter L. Freyberg, Emory & Henry College, Emory, VA; Judith M. Guston, Sarah Lawrence College, Bronxville, NY; Sarabelle Hitchner, Sterling College, Craftsbury Common, VT; Stirling L. Huntley, California Institute of Technology, Pasadena; Richard J. Johnstone, Franklin Pierce College, Rindge, NH; Nancy J. Maly, Grinnell College, IA; William R. Mason, Bowdoin College, ME; Katy Murphy, Whittier College, CA; Jon M. Nicholson, Carleton College, Northfield, MN; Stephanie Norce, Gettysburg College, PA; Jerre C. Pfaff, Southern Illinois University, Carbondale; Shelley Riecke, Brandeis University, Boston, MA; Bobby D. Schrade, Baylor University, Waco, TX; Joseph Slights, Jr., Wesley College, Dover,

DE; Joanne Soliday, Elon College, NC; and James M. Sumner, Willamette University, Salem, OR.

We would also like to acknowledge the cooperation of the following organizations: The United Negro College Fund, The Associated Colleges of the Midwest, and The College Digest.

Particular thanks, too, to Evelyn Fazio, our editor and friend, for her fine counsel and continuous encouragement.

Contents

SECTION I

ENHANCING YOUR SKILLS

Without a doubt the challenge for today's professionals to meet the personal needs of their counselees has never been greater—and the opportunities have never been better. But to meet that challenge, certain personal skills that must be continually refined, augmented, and updated should be in place.

Section I discusses the development and rebuilding of college counseling skills. College admission and secondary school counselors are talking to the same youngsters. Together, they face significant problems and, therefore, should sharpen their working relationships. Practical approaches to computers, publications, and workshops can help the novice develop important basic skills and help the experienced professional enhance his or her own.

Chapter 1

Challenge and Opportunity

So I'm not the greatest counselor. So what!

Dr. Arnold Lazarus, Rutgers University professor and founder of Multimodal Therapy, suggests that there is entirely too much emphasis in today's society on the search for excellence. In a May 1987 address to the New Jersey Professional Counselor Association in Atlantic City, NJ, Lazarus stated: "Everybody is running around searching for excellence. All of this 'searching' has only helped fill psychotherapists' waiting rooms." (Incidentally, society's love affair with excellence can be seen in the attitude of many of today's students: there is an almost joyless concentration on the goal rather than on the journey.)

The author-lecturer continues to suggest that school counselors should be less "uptight" about their own performance and should consider searching for "adequacy," not "excellence." Lazarus believes that a certain amount of excellence is bound to follow.

Are we, then, looking for *adequacy*, which can be defined as "barely satisfactory or sufficient"? Should we instead use the term "fitness," which means "appropriateness or suitability to" the role? In any case, the ultimate question is not "How excellent can I become?" but "Is there any way in which I can do a better job of preparing my counselees for their life after high school?" Or, specifically in this context, "How can I help them make a successful, appropriate choice for their college experience?"

THE CHALLENGE

Counseling, however, can be a hard row to hoe. And acquiring expertise in its operation implies that certain challenges be met.

Long-Range Planning

It seems obvious that the proper counseling of a student, whether it be academic processing or personal issues, involves knowing not only what the youngster was coming from, but also what he or she is going toward. Essentially, counselors are directly involved in the maturation process. The consequence, then, is that counselors need enough time per student to develop probable plans early on, and to work through them to completion. By the time a youngster has finished his high school career, he should be well on the road to success in his postsecondary life.

The challenge? To work toward a systemwide developmental approach which would render greater consistency to the counseling of each student.

Student's Perception and Self-perception

"Over half of the students surveyed [in the state of New York] expressed dissatisfaction with the counseling and advisement available to them in the public schools," according to David W. Chapman et al., in an article published in the fall 1987 issue of National Association of College Admission Counselor's *Journal of College Admissions*. Findings also indicate that the school counselor does not play a major role in assisting students from low-income families in college selection, and many students have difficulty getting individualized attention. Results of a 1985 survey by Chapman and DeMasi show that a substantial minority of students never discuss their college plans with a school counselor, and a substantial number of those who do, are not satisfied with the advisement services they receive.

At the same time, there are conflicting reports about school counselors:

- Many counselors give college advising low priority among their demands. (They spend about 16 percent of their time with it, on average.)
- Many would invest any additional time they would have in other activities.
- Some believe that their college advising is effective and helpful.
- Some overestimate their effectiveness.
- Others believe that they make little or no difference toward their counselees' eventual receipt of acceptance letters.

The challenge? Some authorities suggest that there is a positive correlation between the extent to which one sees oneself as "making a difference" and the amount of personal effort expended in college counseling. Perhaps the correlation between self-perception and the students' perceptions should be further examined.

Insufficient Information

The lack of training and *retraining* opportunities available to counselors presents a major obstacle. The College Board's 1986 *Commission on Precollege Guidance and Counseling* found that only 60 percent of counselor preparation programs in the nation provide graduate degrees or certificates in school counseling. And at those institutions with degree programs, very few (if any) offer specific preparation for counseling students on the transition from secondary school to college.

From the National Association of College Admission Counselors' 1987 project report, *Frontiers of Possibility*:

> Counselors reported to us that knowledge of the college admission process and of the college decision process arises almost completely from on-the-job responsibilities and experience. The haphazard preparation of many school counselors, especially for their college counseling duties, is an area of serious concern. Second, in light of the way counselors are prepared for their duties, it is clear that counselors need to be specially motivated to make serious professional progress in the college counseling area. Counselors related to us that many of their colleagues did not arrive with (nor develop later) any special expertise in this area.

Of course, here lies the *great* challenge: the development of *quality* in-service training programs that address *all* of the gaps in preservice training. Unfortunately, such training programs all too often reflect only the momentary needs of a community. For example, a long-range need to improve the capability of counselors in the areas of academic and college counseling can get continually placed on a back burner, in favor of "hot" topics like drug and alcohol abuse, learning disabilities, and suicide prevention. As counselors, we should press for appropriate programs.

Lack of Agreement on Basic Priorities

One counselor is quoted in *College: the Undergraduate Experience in America*, as telling author, Ernest Boyer, "We don't have that large a staff, and we have all the other problems to take care of. We see the kids for college guidance when they make an appointment. We don't do it automatically."

Many can empathize with these comments, and can well imagine what "all the other problems" are. Possibly Boyer's interviewee is from a school where the counselors are reeling with the numbers. Maybe there is even double trouble: reeling with the numbers in an inner-city situation with its own special problems. Whatever the case may be, the comment exemplifies secondary school counseling's continuing major problems: very heavy caseloads coupled with counselors spread thin in their professional *and* nonprofessional duties.

On the other hand, perhaps the individual works in a setting where ratios are reasonable, but the department's basic priorities differ markedly from the national norm. (There *are* those who believe that advising students on academic, career, and postsecondary matters need not be a high priority.)

If school counseling is to move forward in a big way, then there must be some sort of consensus as to primary functions. *Making a Difference in College Admission* is based on the premise that (1) counselor caseloads *must* be reduced to reasonable levels, with counselors becoming much more proactive about this problem, and (2) although certain counselor functions can and should differ somewhat as to state and local demands, early and continuous advisement of students on academic, career, and postsecondary education concerns (whether it be to individuals or to groups) should be at the top of any list of counselor functions.

One Person

In today's world, a world full of special, never-before-faced problems, youngsters need a primary counselor, someone who will provide stability and a sense of belonging. In truth, there is a considerable interrelation within a counseling program: course selection affects career and college planning, personal problems may forecast academic failure, and so on; and specialists in problem areas will certainly be appreciated. But to make it all hang together, a student needs a "generalist"—someone who will have at least one finger in every piece of the counseling pie.

One such generalist is Wayne Miller, an energetic counselor and key member of the faculty at Katahdin High School in the rural town of Sherman Station in northeastern Maine. Miller, the only counselor for the school's 250 students, does it all! By the end of their junior year, Miller has guided and goaded most of his counselees into deciding whether (and even where) they will apply to college. (In 1987, some 80 percent of Katahdin graduates went on to college.) As Miller states in the February 23, 1987, issue of *Time* magazine, "Everyone could do it if they had a small caseload." Amen to that, Wayne!

THE OPPORTUNITY

Most students who enroll in college intend to leave with a degree in hand, but about half of them don't make it. Even for some 25 percent of the "finishers," the degree-granting school is their second stop, sometimes the third. Virtually all of these young people—the contented, the transferees, and the washouts—start in our offices. They've been there at one time or another.

Yet there are students who rarely, if ever, show up at our doors. Some of these infrequent visitors go on to graduate, but, regrettably, others "fall through the cracks" along the way. The latter don't get the opportunity to wash out of college—they wash out of high school first.

The opportunity is: Could we, *should* we, be making a greater difference for all these people?

Perhaps we could cause the contented to become even more satisfied with their situations, or we could spend additional time on self-assessment activities with potential transferees. We could help probable college washouts to hone their study skills better, or we could make a greater impact on the underadvocated and nonadvocated, by intensifying our efforts to make college a reality for more of them.

Most counselors would agree that "making a difference" means much more than just supporting a student with a well-written recommendation. It means *advocacy*: helping a person get to know herself better so that she can make a better choice, getting yet another youngster to see the practicality of beginning collegiate life at the local community college, or "going-to-bat" for a wait-listed counselee.

But how many of us think we would "make a difference" if we were to:

1. Make a commitment to further improve our professional status by joining state and national organizations.
2. Whisper words of encouragement as colleagues assert themselves regarding their excessive caseloads.
3. Develop and then present a single-topic program for parents (e.g., a seminar on stress factors).
4. Conduct a financial aid workshop in three different languages, with interpreters stationed in several corners of the room.

Ah yes, "differences" are there—and they are being made every day!

But we're too busy to notice the differences we make. We plunge ahead, barely treading water at times, seeing one student after another—even after the last bus has pulled out. As concerned counselors, though, we *must* find the time to be more reflective: Am *I* making a difference? Is my *department*? How and where could we be making a *greater* difference? *This* is the opportunity!

CONTENDING WITH CRITICS

People continue to hammer away at the mediocre (or even poor) job done with that big piece of the pie: precollege counseling. It is important to remember that even in schools where but 30 percent of the seniors go on to college, the "slice" *does* represent one-third of the student body—a full third of our efforts. Are we spending the proper proportion of our time with precollege counseling activities? Or are we, as the counselor stated to Boyer, "too busy doing other things"?

Admittedly, of all the things we do in working with our counselees, college counseling has got to be the most controversial. We are either spending too much time with this task or not enough; overly involved with recommending schools or not into it enough; too influential about students taking the "right" courses for college or too passive. It's probably the most "damned if you do and damned if you don't" aspect of our total role. Yet it is a most important function. There *is* life after high school—and we have the potential to provide each of our counselees with a terrific start!

SUGGESTED READINGS

BOYER, ERNEST L. 1987. *College: The Undergraduate Experience in America*. New York: Harper & Row.

CHAPMAN, DAVID, AND MARY DEMASI. 1985. "College Advising in the High School: Priority and Problems." *NASSP Bulletin* (National Association of Secondary School Principals, 1904 Association Drive, Reston, VA), 69, no. 484.

CHAPMAN, DAVID, CYNTHIA O'BRIEN AND MARY DEMASI. 1987. "The Effectiveness of the Public School Counselor in College Advising." *Journal of College Admissions* (NACAC, 1800 Diagonal Road, Alexandria, VA), no. 115.

"Frontiers of Possibility: 1986 National College Counseling Project." Sponsored by the National Association of College Admission Counselors, Instructional Development Center, University of Vermont, Burlington, VT.

Chapter 2

Human Relations with College Representatives

Every youngster in America is affected by some or all of the significant problems in college admissions: skyrocketing attendance costs, dwindling numbers of potential college-bound youths, continued lack of attention paid to certain minority problems, and unrealistic counselor caseloads. The solutions to these problems are in part the responsibility of both the secondary school and the college—a cooperative effort by both parties to amplify the educational development of young people.

Because of the special position college representatives occupy, school counselors receive their support on such issues as caseload reduction and the strengthening of curriculum. Reps look to school counselors to help solidify the partnership by making it a warmer and more productive one for *all* concerned.

Cooperation could be further strengthened if counselors and college representatives would take the time to sensitize themselves further to the role and function of the other party. Both groups *should be more fully informed* of the options and restraints inherent in the work of the other.

SO WHAT DO REPS DO?

Secondary school counselors are at times unaware of all the background preparation that goes into high school visitation by a college representative. It is more than taking to the road for several months of the year and holing up in hotel rooms—or forever lugging boxes of admission literature around. Some admission counselors are away from their families for weeks on end; others merely during the week, returning home on weekends. Life on the road has its pleasant moments, but living out of a suitcase or returning to one's motel room in late afternoon to stare at the walls or flip on a TV set are not some of them!

Even in those rooms, reps spend time boning up on a particular high school prior to stepping through the front door. This can take the form of reviewing the school profile, or familiarizing themselves with certain statistical information, or reviewing data sheets to see which students are presently attending the college.

Some institutions take pride in keeping tabs on which students are enrolled from which high schools. Some of these same colleges expect that the host counselor will have a working familiarity with this kind of information as well. Therefore, it might be important for you to have done some homework prior to any meeting—the same kind of basic research you ask your counselees to do prior to *their* meetings with representatives.

An admission counselor is an *individual* human being who represents an institution. She is not the institution itself. Although there appears to be some difference of opinion as to just how much the reps embody their colleges and universities, they certainly do represent their special concerns. And this is where you, in hopes of improving both your own personal and your school's relationship with a particular institution, should be sympathetic to these special concerns.

Consequently, as you sit eye-to-eye with your visitor from one of the nation's selective, private, liberal arts and sciences colleges, you might be especially sensitive to those issues that might be running through the back of her mind: having to deal with a declining population of 17-year-olds; contending with the fact that some 35 percent of college-bound youth within her market choose to enter engineering or business schools; the fact that the cost of a high-quality education at most private schools is rising much faster than is the national inflation rate, and almost everyone is uptight about it; the fact that her school is one of the holdouts on "enticement" scholarships, and she knows that you're probably wondering why. (After all, everyone else is doing it.)

No college or university is free from imperfections, and a rep must deal with them—but should she be *blamed* for them? She *represents* the school; she is not solely responsible for its development. Indeed, often she has nothing to say about it. In any case, an admission counselor is a human being with a specific job: to present to you and your students the best that her school has to offer.

AS FOR THE SCHOOL COUNSELOR . . .

Of course the proverbial shoe can be on the other foot. You sit next to your high school principal, who has come along with you to a meeting sponsored by one of the state colleges. Midway through the presentation, the admission officer blithely touches upon the on-site admission program (college conducts interviews at *certain* secondary schools and then renders immediate "admit" or "deny" decisions) in which some of the public and private colleges in the state participate.

As you leave, your principal says in a rather accusing voice, "How come we don't have this program?" You don't know quite how to respond. One thing you *do* know is that the speaker gave the topic a very cursory treatment and that you intend to explore the matter more fully.

Tossing off underdeveloped statements at mass functions without carefully weighing the impact of one's remarks can be problematic, to say the least. It illustrates the insensitivity that can sometimes exist on the part of admission representatives toward school counselors. At this particular gathering, the speaker in question had not bothered to mention that the *few* participating colleges were only interested in setting up shop at relatively large high schools. It wouldn't be at all productive for them to be at your school of 750. The speaker ignored the fact that such an on-site program might possibly be discriminatory. And could it be that you and your principal were not well informed about the program because the publicity to secondary schools left something to be desired?

On another front, school counselors also have to wrestle with certain public-versus-private issues. Private college people, particularly those in states with extensive public university systems, believe that on occasion they get the short end of the stick. One western admission officer feels that because of overburdened school counselors, it has become all too easy for them to extend state university officials special treatment with things like the dissemination of information materials. According to this representative, private colleges are largely ignored.

Public university officials have special concerns as to how well informed school counselors are about curricular programs and changes within their own state systems of higher education. Such lack of information can result in counselors not sufficiently encouraging students to explore carefully the "endless number of in-state options." These same officials go on to argue that where counselors have limited curricular knowledge, especially about honors programs, public institutions are often overlooked in favor of prestigious private ones. There are those who adamantly believe that counselors should have at least a working knowledge of programs of both public and private institutions within their own states. This can become an especially difficult task with a state like Pennsylvania, where there are more than 100 institutions of higher education.

As for students making appropriate selections, there seems to be no end to the debate over who should apply to what. And the question remains: What should be the role of the school counselor in this process? How much influence *can*—and should—the counselor exert? These questions will be explored in Chapters 15 and 16.

Although developing greater sensitivity toward each other's position must be a principal goal, admission officials need to understand that when the "chips are down," the school counselor is going to go with his or her counselee. Students are school counselors' first priority!

THE SECONDARY SCHOOL VISITATION

There is a deepening concern on the part of secondary school folk as to the value of the school visit by admission representatives. Is such visitation sufficiently worthwhile to students and counselors to justify the expenditure of time and effort on the part of secondary schools? Some schools have "thrown in the towel" and will receive no reps. Others feel that half a loaf is better than none. They continue to support this endeavor, but have cut back to a more manageable number of visitations, for example, to two a day.

The arrangement does have its avid supporters who firmly believe in the importance of keeping counselors and students continually updated as to new and ongoing programs and facilities. And, in their determination to preserve this aspect of the college planning process, these supporters don't hesitate to vocalize their positive feelings to anyone who will listen. They see the development of meaningful and productive relationships as yet another opportunity to "make a difference" in the lives of young people. For these school counselors, the college representative is a vital link in a four-way communication scheme: students, parents, counselors, and college admission officers. Consequently, in these high schools the visitation program can be a controlled and well-managed affair. Care is exercised to receive only those whom they can do a good job of hosting. Pride is taken in the *quality* of the reception given to *all* visiting officials.

Who Is Heard?

But some of the "all" would like to see a bit more effort. Katy Murphy, director of admissions at Whittier College in California, writes that "Public school counselors don't give enough time and attention to college people visiting from distant states." Even if there are only one or two students who might be interested in going that far away, "these students should be prepped *beforehand* for the visit so that they can speak directly to the representative."

In their visitation request letters, admission counselors will sometimes specifically ask to speak with a guidance counselor. Students are important, but many colleges regard the school counselor/admission representative contact to be of equal importance. Consequently, when there are no students to be seen, being asked to "just leave materials" does not sit well with some colleges. In one instance, an admission rep pressed so hard for an interview that the reluctant counselor agreed to sit for a few minutes. The counselor became so intrigued with the college that she begged the rep to stay even longer. Spending a few moments of human contact *can* further "turn you on" to a particular school.

And "Paraprofessionals have their role, but not as people to meet with admission representatives," says Joseph Slights, Jr. (dean of admissions at Wesley College, Dover, DE). "In most cases, it is the school counselor who meets with students and parents regarding the selection process. That is why the school counselor/admission representative contact is so important."

Quality Reception Defined

At a regional conference, an admission officer from an eastern college was heard to remark that he was experiencing better receptions at secondary schools. He went on to say, "But then again, maybe it is because we are doing more minifairs and carefully selecting high schools where we know we will get a quality reception." When pressed to define what he meant by a quality contact, the officer responded, "One: a visit where there is a genuine interest shown in what I have to say; where I don't feel rushed—the counselor is not continually looking at his watch. Two: where the dialogue between the counselor and myself is straightforward with a certain amount of give and take. And, three: where the counselor sits with the students, prepared to raise important questions that, for varying reasons, might not otherwise be raised by the students."

One official spoke about the "off-the-wall" behavior she occasionally encounters, particularly in settings where no counselor sits in on the session. "It is a shame for those serious students who would like to listen and absorb, but can't because of the misbehavior of others."

Another official noted that counselors could make a greater difference if they would use a screening technique for students wishing to hear college representatives. "Too often we visit, and half the students waiting to see us just wanted out of class; consequently, they fail to pay attention and are disruptive."

On the other hand, control *can* go to the extreme, as exemplified by one school counselor who, in a rather loud voice, told a young lady to tuck in her shirt. In this kind of rigid atmosphere, would students be relaxed enough to probe important nonacademic issues that relate to collegiate living?

To Sit in or Not to Sit in

For some departments, rep visitation is very much an updating of counselor skills, so the hosting responsibility is rotated among the staff. Even where there is a college specialist(s), other counselors are encouraged to sit in whenever they feel the need to do so. At the very least, the assigned counselor or college specialist takes notes and then shares his findings with his colleagues; that is, the notes are photocopied, then kept in a college file in the College and Career Center or in a ring binder by each counselor.

In terms of student and counselor learning, it appears that the most beneficial visitation programs are those where *both* counselor and students join together for the presentations.

Consider the following:

1. The presence of a counselor helps keep the rep on his or her toes.
2. A counselor can often ask revealing questions that might otherwise be missed by the students.
3. A counselor "taking notes for his department" sends a positive message to the attending students concerning the department's attitude toward the whole admission process.
4. Hearing a college rep speak can be a broadening experience for a counselor. She learns many things not contained in catalogs and anthologies.
5. The presence of a counselor means a continual monitoring of student participation, for example, numbers in attendance, student behavior, and the worth of questions asked. (It also sensitizes departments to the kind of fa-

cilities they provide visiting reps: some reps report they have to meet with students in hallways.)

6. Contrary to the thinking of those who believe that the gifted and talented can "go it alone" and do not need the presence of a counselor, many of these kids are so immersed in things academic and so short on the practical that they fail to explore important nonacademic issues.

If it is impossible for the counselor and students to be together, the next best approach is for the rep to meet first with the students and to sit with the counselor later.

The least effective approach is for *no one* to meet with the representative. A counseling department might want to think twice before remarking, "We're too busy to sit in or to say 'hello,' because counseling students comes first." Twenty students were just left alone with a college rep! Besides, if this is a school with heavy ratios, this is *not* the way to get ratios reduced! Ratios are reduced by struggling to do all the things you *should* be doing within the *normal* school day, and then raising the roof about overloads and poor working conditions.

If you cannot free up at least one counselor to do a good job of hosting, then maybe you should be "upfront" about the whole thing *in advance of the rep's visit*. In that way you don't come off looking like an unfeeling bunch, which can only have an adverse affect on a department's role and image.

While a few colleges couldn't care less about touching base with a counselor, most college reps welcome the adult human touch. You do, too.

Special Considerations in Hosting the Visiting Rep

"When they welcome us with, 'Here's your table, some kids will be along in a minute,' we never go back; or if we do, it's many years later." So commented an admission official about her treatment at a few secondary schools. Another college representative bemoaned the fact that he was greeted at one school with, "Hey, college, come over here!" Still another stated that she had gone a whole week on the road without seeing a single counselor, talking only to secretaries. (Of course that's possible in some high schools where there are no counselors. In several states, reps meet with parent hosts.)

An undesirable location, upon which admission folk appear to be in complete agreement, is the school cafeteria. As one rep put it, "It's either tuna salad on your dress or butter patties on your shoes."

Then there's the story of the admission director from a highly selective college, arriving at a high school only to find an empty meeting room. A counselor, aggravated by the fact that all 12 of his applicants had been denied admission the previous year, had not bothered to announce the director's coming. "You drive us crazy," the counselor yelled. "We can never predict who's going to get into your school." (At times the "highly selectives" do drive us crazy with the unpredictability of it all. Still, a professional should be a professional.)

Although the vast majority of counseling offices welcome reps with a warm, friendly, and efficient manner, informal surveys seem to indicate that admission people are indeed running into a certain amount of coldness and disinterest on the part of school counselors. *The manner in which counselors treat these representatives cannot help but convey a message about the importance of this college to the students of that school.* One gentleman, traveling for a small selective college, was greeted with considerable indifference at several high schools. Two years later, as a representative of a very prestigious university, visiting the same schools, he was greeted with great warmth.

You and your department might want to review your policies and procedures regarding college rep visitation. If no *written* guidelines exist, you might want to consider developing them. One question that should be addressed is the purpose(s) for this kind of visitation. Is it just for the kids? Or is it to update counselors as well?

THE LYONS TOWNSHIP APPROACH

Lyons Township High School (LaGrange, IL) continues to believe in the worth of direct visitation by college representatives. Its students can find written guidelines concerning such visitation in their *College Planning Information* booklet. As you read the extract in Figure 2-1 (shown here with permission of Dolores Forsyth, Lyons Township High School), you can see the school's solid support for this type of endeavor. Note the effort to involve parents in the process, too.

GATHERING INFORMATION ON COLLEGES

A. College Representatives

Over 200 representatives from colleges visit this high school each year. Second only to a student interview on the campus itself, the representative is the student's best means of getting information about specific colleges. Representatives who will visit L.T. the following week are announced by a special guidance bulletin each communications period. This bulletin will give a brief description of each college sending a representative that week. You should read these carefully and share them with your parents. Then, make arrangements to visit with the representatives of colleges that interest you. Parents are also invited to visit with representatives.

Figure 2-1

NOTES OF APPRECIATION

Once they have been well received, representatives don't forget easily. Figures 2-2, 2-3, and 2-4 are three revealing thank-you notes sent to a high school in the East.

Dear ...

As you might imagine, after thirteen years of visiting high schools, my days are often routine, save getting lost, arriving late, and occasionally meeting an outstanding counselor. You made my day on Thursday, December 18.

I enjoyed the high school visit very much. I felt welcome and comfortable. Your enthusiasm, energy, and knowledge of Grinnell puts you among the top counselors with whom I've had contact. If all my stops were like your stop, my life would be a delight.

Nancy J. Maly
Grinnell College, Iowa

Figure 2-2

Dear ...

Thank you for the cordial welcome you extended to me during my recent visit to your school. I know what a hectic time of year this is for you, and consequently greatly appreciate the time you gave to Gettysburg College.

While there is some question about the value of school visits, I am still convinced that our responsibilities as counselors are made easier by these opportunities to discuss college admissions on a more personal basis with both you and your students. As a result, I feel that I now have a closer association with your school which I hope will in turn promote even greater contact.

Stephanie Norce
Gettysburg College
Pennsylvania

Figure 2-3

Dear ...

Now that my travel schedule has slowed down, I wanted to take the opportunity to let you know how much I appreciated the time given and interest shown during my visit to your school.

Having been in college admissions for ten years I have visited more guidance offices than I care to remember. In recent years I have cut back dramatically the number of guidance visits and replaced them with college fair programs. The reason is a combination of scheduling in light of the proliferation of admission events and, in many cases, the decline in effectiveness of the individual school visit. Overtaxed counselors, the unavailability of students, and the nonguidance volunteer seem to have become the norm.

Your school is one of the exceptions. I have come to your school numerous times over the years and have always had a very positive reception. You and your colleagues always show a genuine interest in any updates or changes in programs at our college. As a result, those students who attend Franklin Pierce are well informed from the beginning.

Richard Johnstone
Franklin Pierce College
New Hampshire

Figure 2-4

AS CLOSE AS A PHONE?

"We have here a picture of too often or too little, with not much in between," responded one panelist at a national conference. The discussion centered on the appropriate use of the telephone by admission representatives and school counselors. "Too often" refers to the fact that a few school counselors make pests of themselves with their constant telephoning; "too little" means that others rarely, if ever, reach out to advocate further for their counselees. In listening to the interaction between panel and audience, one couldn't help but feel that it is indeed a case of too often or too little, *but,* as Lola in *Damn Yankees* sings, "with an emphasis on the latter."

So—reach out and call someone? There *are* plenty of admission officers who would like to see both an expansion of, and an improvement in, the quality of personal contact between reps and school counselors. Greater use of the telephone is one way to go about it.

The best bet is to pick up the phone and call the director of admissions, and ask for: (1) a straight-forward answer; (2) what does he/she recommend. *Nothing* is more effective than a *call* to the office.

— John P. Burke
Director of Admissions
Georgian Court College, NJ

Communicate to the admission office more! Call us! Give a profile of a prospective student to us over the phone. It may save a lot of heartache later on.

— Steven Briggs
Director of Admissions
Dean Junior College, MA

I'd like to think that the counselors I know and who know Carleton wouldn't hesitate to pick up the phone and call me about a prospective student. It might be to say, "This lad seems to me to be a good bet for Carleton, but his academic stats don't fit your profile. Let me tell you why I would like to recommend Carleton to him. . . . Would he be a reasonable candidate?" Another time it might be, "I have a young woman who is a superb candidate academically, but she has some special needs (or problems). Could you accommodate her? Would Carleton be a good place for her?"

These are examples of counselors who can make a great difference by taking the simple extra step of picking up the telephone.

— Jon M. Nicholson
Associate Dean of Admissions
Carleton College, MN

Appealing a Questionable Decision

Each April, the air is filled with their agonizing cries: students who have had their hearts set on a particular school suddenly discover a rejection letter tucked between *Time* and the electric bill. It's usually a "target" or a "reach" school that drops the bomb.

Some students get ready as early as the spring of the junior year, as they unfortunately focus on the negative aspects of the entire admission process with their "I'll never get in" attitude. And when they *don't* get in, they feel vindicated, and then you hear, "I knew it." The situation is further exacerbated by their seeing kids they think less deserving getting into "better" schools.

Of course, if your counselee did her homework, she knows the odds of her making it into any of her "reaches." (Some are more difficult than others.) But no amount of bracing oneself can totally fortify a young person against the disappointment he feels as he opens that thin envelope. Tears are usually shed at home, not in counseling offices. Some swallow the denial pill more easily than others. Some take it too personally: I've been accepted, therefore, I'm acceptable; I've been rejected, therefore, I'm a reject.

Looking into a wait-listed or rejection decision is an area where telephoning your professional colleague, the admission counselor, *can* be very much in order. Changes in rejection decisions are rare, but talking to an admission counselor might provide you with additional insight into assisting a counselee over the rough spots, and more effectively helping future clients.

Yes, "person to person, counselor to counselor" can pay great dividends when it comes to your students and the college admission process.

Some suggestions:

1. Know the selectivity level/applicant pool of the institution you are calling. A smaller or less sought-after college will often be able to give you more time than will a school deluged with applications.
2. Know the time of year. January, February, March can be the busiest months for many admission counselors: they are behind closed doors, working to form a class. Be sensitive to that issue. They might be more receptive if you can do your advocating before or after this time period.
3. Your telephone conversation might warrant a short follow-up note to the person with whom you spoke.
4. Use of the telephone can be an excellent means of settling misunderstandings and clarifying issues, policies, and programs.
5. Your specific concerns should be well thought out before you pick up the phone. Unless the admission counselor prolongs the conversation, be brief and to the point.

OTHER WAYS YOU CAN STRENGTHEN THE RELATIONSHIP

- You can certainly visit local colleges.
- You can take the time to look at audiovisual material produced by various colleges. Or are they only for kids?
- You can get out to professional meetings, even if only for a portion of the day.
- You can participate in college nights, thereby helping to ensure that the *entire* counseling staff is present for this occasion.

Chapter 3

College Visitations

To acquire a real sense of an institution's personality, and a greater understanding of the applicant/institution "fit," get out to and onto the particular campus. Whether you visit independently or as a member of an organized tour, such visitation can be extremely beneficial to you—*and* to your colleagues back home, if you can share your findings with them.

CONSORTIUM TOURS

All aboard a college consortium tour bus! What a great way to get in-depth knowledge of the academic programs, student social life, and facilities of individual colleges and universities!

All over the country, collegiate institutions within reasonable distances of one another have formed consortiums, among whose myriad purposes is to better acquaint counselors with all the programs and facilities. Established consortium tours continue to be a popular (waiting lists are not at all uncommon) and practical method for school counselors to see things firsthand. Specific tours can last from two to six days, depending somewhat on the number of institutions to be visited. The cost to you (if any) is usually minimal. Some consortiums charge a nominal registration fee and/or expect you to absorb the cost of getting yourself to the bus pickup point or headquarters hotel. Most of the consortiums conduct their tours in the springtime (a far less hectic time of the year for admission officials).

One drawback of group touring is that you are afforded little or no time to get away and explore on your own. When on a given campus, it *is* important to speak randomly with students and faculty members, to check out counseling services, and to drop in on career placement offices. This kind of probing can be especially difficult to accomplish on tours that move with Amtrak-like speed, for example, those that have you visiting a dozen or more schools in four or five days. A word of advice: Always be concerned about what you are *not* being shown.

Some added words: (1) First, select those tours that include colleges and universities popular with your students. Then participate in tours that enable you to "expand your horizons." (2) At the end of the tour, encourage the tour leader to send a note to your principal and/or superintendent, thanking him or her for encouraging this kind of communication. Such a move by a college official can be very good politics for you and can keep the door open for you and your colleagues to indulge in more of the same activity. Consortium trips are exceedingly beneficial to both the experienced and the inexperienced counselor.

Usually the colleges do the inviting. (Their letters of invitation will often go out to a specific locale or region.) But many schools are receptive to inquiry, and might in fact note your interest by placing your name on their mailing list. Figure 3-1 gives a list of college tours available across the country.

TOURS

California (fall) The Decemberfest Colleges: California Institute of Technology, Claremont McKenna College, Harvey Mudd College, Occidental College, Pitzer College, Pomona College, Scripps College, University of Redlands, and Whittier College. By invitation only.

Connecticut (spring) Connecticut Association of College Admission Officers (CACAO): Central Connecticut State University, Eastern Connecticut State University, Hartford College for Women, St. Joseph College, Trinity College, University of Hartford. Contact: Susan J. Lewandowski at Hartford College for Women.

District of Columbia (spring) National Capital College Admissions Program (NCCAP): American University, Catholic University of America, George Washington University, Mount Vernon College, and Trinity College. Contact: Michael O'Leary at George Washington.

Maine, Southern (fall) Bates College, Colby College, Portland School of Art, Saint Joseph's College, Thomas College, University of Maine at Farmington,

University of New England, University of Southern Maine, and Westbrook College. Contact: Gretchen Bean at Colby.

Maryland (spring) Mount St. Mary's College, Hood College, Western Maryland College, Goucher College, Johns Hopkins University, Loyola College, and Notre Dame College of Maryland. Contact: Kip Darcy at Western Maryland.

Massachusetts (spring/fall) "Private Colleges of Greater Springfield": American International College, Bay Path Junior College, Elms College, Springfield College, and Western New England College. Contact: Private Colleges of Greater Springfield, c/o Bay Path Junior College.

Minnesota (spring) Carleton College, Macalester College, and St. Olaf College. Contact: Dean of Admissions at Carleton.

New Hampshire (fall) Colby-Sawyer College, Daniel Webster College, Franklin Pierce College, Hawthorne College, Keene State College, New England College, New Hampshire College, Notre Dame College, Plymouth State College, Rivier College, St. Anselm College, and the University of New Hampshire. Contact: New Hampshire College and University Council, 2321 Elm Street, Manchester, NH 03104.

North Carolina (spring) Guidance Counselors' Tour of North Carolina's Independent Colleges and Universities—Eastern Tour: Atlantic Christian College, Campbell University, Chowan College, Duke University, Louisburg College, Meredith College, Mount Olive College, N.C. Wesleyan College, Peace College, St. Augustine's College, St. Mary's College, Shaw University. Contact: N.C. Center for Independent Higher Education, 1300 St. Mary's Street, Raleigh, NC 27605.

North Carolina (spring) Guidance Counselors' Tour of North Carolina's Independent Colleges and Universities—Western Tour: Bennett College, Brevard College, Gardner-Webb College, Greensboro College, Guilford College, Lees-McRae College, Lenoir-Rhyne College, Mars Hill College, Montreat-Anderson College, Salem College, Wake Forest University, Warren Wilson College. Contact: N.C. Center for Independent Higher Education, 1300 St. Mary's Street, Raleigh, NC 27605.

Ohio (spring) Miami University of Ohio and the University of Dayton. Contact: Myron Achbach at Dayton or Randy Trostel at Miami.

Ohio (fall) "Ohio Colleges": Denison University, Kenyon College, Ohio Wesleyan University, Wittenberg University, Oberlin College, and Wooster College. Contact: Maura Condon Umble at Wittenberg.

Oregon (spring) "Oregon Private Colleges": Reed College, Lewis & Clark College, University of Portland, Linfield College, Willamette University, and Pacific University. Contact: James Sumner, Dean of Admissions at Willamette.

Pennsylvania (spring) Bucknell University, Juniata College, Lycoming College, and Susquehanna University. Contact: Any admission director.

Pennsylvania (fall) Bucknell University, Franklin and Marshall College, Johns Hopkins (Maryland). Contact: Any admission director.

Pennsylvania (spring) Dickinson College, Franklin & Marshall College, and Gettysburg College. Contact: Stephen MacDonald at Dickinson.

Pennsylvania (spring) "Lehigh Valley Association of Independent Colleges, Inc.": Allentown College, Cedar Crest College, Lafayette College, Lehigh University, Moravian College, and Muhlenberg College. Contact: Galen Godbey at Moravian.

Pennsylvania (spring) "Pittsburgh Council of Higher Education (PCHE)": Case-Western Reserve, Allegheny College, and Carnegie-Mellon University. Contact: Susan Garrity or Gayle Pollock at Allegheny.

Rhode Island (spring/fall) "RIAAO Counselor Tour": Bryant College, Johnson & Wales College, Salve-Regina College, Providence College, Rhode Island College, University of Rhode Island, and Roger Williams College. Contact: Nancy Parchesky at Bryant.

Vermont (spring) "The Vermont Colleges": Bennington College, Castleton State College, Champlain College, Goddard College, Green Mountain College, Johnson State College, Landmark College, Lyndon State College, Marlboro College, Middlebury College, New England Culinary Institute, Norwich University, Saint Michael's College, Southern Vermont College, Sterling College, Trinity College, University of Vermont, and Vermont Technical College. Contact: Kathy Segar at Vermont College.

Virginia (spring) "Virginia College Tour": Hampden-Sydney College, Lynchburg College, Randolph-Macon Women's College, Sweet Briar College, and the University of Virginia. Contact: Director of Admissions at one of the small schools.

Virginia (spring) "Virginia Capital Area Consortium": Mary Washington College, Randolph-Macon College, and the University of Richmond. Contact: Conrad Warlick at Mary Washington, John Conkright at Randolph-Macon, Tom Pollard at U. of Richmond.

West Virginia (fall) "West Virginia Consortium of Independent Colleges and Universities": Alderson-Broaddus College, Bethany College, Davis & Elkins College, Salem College, University of Charleston, West Virginia Wesleyan College, and Wheeling College. Contact: William Johnston at West Virginia Wesleyan.

Figure 3-1

A STATE LENDS A HAND

Occasionally, a state government will get involved in enhancing college counseling skills. Such is the case with the state of New Jersey. Its Department of Higher Education supports an annual counselor visitation program entitled, "New Jersey College Tour for New Jersey Counselors." This particular tour project is part of the department's program to increase counselor awareness of higher education opportunities in New Jersey. Two tours, northern and southern, are scheduled each April. Counselors can visit a total of seven colleges in each of the three-day programs. All expenses, other than transportation to and from the tours' designated departure points, are covered by the Department of Higher Education.

As a state, New Jersey is not alone in sponsoring this type of activity. Perhaps a similar opportunity exists—or could exist—in your own state. If it doesn't, you might want to explore this issue with your state department of higher education and your state counselor association.

ROLE OF THE LOCAL SCHOOL DISTRICT?

Touring for counselors should by no means be left only to colleges and state departments of education. School administrators and local boards of education should exert greater leadership in awarding released/reimbursed time for counselors to engage in *self-designed* campus visitation programs.

The Mini Travel Sabbatical

Jerre Pfaff (director of admissions, Southern Illinois University at Carbondale) proposes a novel and worthwhile idea: since administrators are often agreeable to granting counselors three to five professional days for consortium touring, perhaps on occasion they could be talked into extending the tour to four weeks—a minisabbatical.

Pfaff says: "Your last question asked about ways in which counselors could make a greater difference in the admission process. It seems to me that one of the things that should be considered is to allow counselors leaves of absence similar to those of other faculty members . . . something like a mini travel sabbatical. . . . I don't think we have a problem related to counselors understanding admission procedures and mechanics as much as we do about their understanding of particular programs of study in which students might be potentially interested. These mini sabbaticals, which could be of a month's, semester's, or even a year's duration, would certainly place counselors in a better position to advise students as to programs of study for which they could be requesting information."

SUMMERTIME: A GOOD TIME TO VISIT

Dana Denault's response to the issue reflects the feelings of many admission counselors about summertime visits by counselors. The director of admissions at Curry College in Massachusetts states, "We are always pleased to have counselors visit our campus and tour our facilities. During the summer we are able to spend more time with visitors and have them join us over lunch."

In their invitational letter to school counselors, Mitchell College, a leading two-year institution in New London, CT, is forthright in presenting its rationale for such summertime activity: "Our motives are obviously selfish ones—we are interested in attracting more of your students. Nevertheless, we think that opening the campus to counselors when accommodations are unused is a very legitimate function—we hope a welcome one, at a time when travel budgets are limited. And to live on a campus—to know its people and programs—is an invaluable experience for the counselor who is expected to help high school students with college plans."

Virtually every college and university in the nation will welcome you in July and/or August. Some will be able to accommodate you overnight or to provide a meal, but even those that cannot do so will nevertheless take the time to chat and offer you a tour.

Like Denault, there are numerous admission counselors who would be downright enthusiastic about hosting you. For example, the Birmingham-Southern College people in Alabama would love to have you visit their attractive 185-acre wooded campus. They will not only feed and house you, but pick you up at the airport if necessary. Hope College, in the heart of beautiful western Michigan and Dutch country, publishes an attractive fold-out brochure entitled, *Ready for a Getaway?*

If you are on an 11-or 12-month contract, there is the possibility of combining vacation and professional leave to visit institutions. If you are on a ten-month contract, you could select a spot in the nation, and then plan a vacation around a series of campus visitations. Now this is where Jerre Pfaff's minisabbatical concept makes even greater sense: if being away from your desk for a period of time during the school year is a problem, your board of education might be more receptive to underwriting a 30-day *summer* travel program. The fact that this type of touring is partially tax-deductible can be an additional incentive for you to take to the road.

Important Points to Consider:

1. Give the college or university at least two weeks' advance notice of your arrival.
2. Request a copy of the institution's visitation policies and procedures. Policies and procedures *do* vary from school to school.
3. Be aware that a few institutions charge a modest sum for overnight accommodations. Usually this charge includes guest house or apartmentlike quarters. Some schools require a nominal registration fee, refundable at the time of checkout.
4. Go prepared! Just as you would expect your counselees to have done some homework prior to their meeting with an admission representative, so too should you do a little advance research. Be ready to pose a half dozen or so questions. You might reflect on what messages you'd like to take home to your department. Remember, *you* are interviewing the admission counselor. (Admission folk find this opportunity to respond to a series of questions, as opposed to their having to give a structured presentation, a refreshing change of pace.)
5. If there are no plans to house and/or feed you, then having a prior appointment is not a critical issue. Some school counselors find their trips to be less

pressured situations when they do not make previous appointments. If you take this route, *do not* assume that an admission person will be free to speak with you. On the other hand, if you approach the situation with words like, "I realize that I don't have an appointment . . . I'd be happy to just pick up some literature. However, if you do happen to have a representative free . . ." often the admission secretary will try to accommodate you. A key person in all of this *is* the secretary. The manner in which you present yourself to him or her is most important.

Figure 3-2 is a *sample* list of colleges and universities throughout the United States that would be delighted to host you for one or more days during the summer months. These institutions will provide food and lodging.

INSTITUTION	STATE	INSTITUTION	STATE
Alfred University	NY	Hiram College	OH
Allegheny College	PA	Johnson & Wales College	RI
Birmingham Southern C.	AL	Northeastern University	MA
Campbell University	NC	Rochester Inst. of Tech.	NY
Colorado School of Mines	CO	Rockhurst College	MO
Denison University	OH	Russell Sage College	NY
Drew University	NJ	Southern Illinois U.	IL
Elizabethtown College	PA	U. of Southern California	CA
Emory & Henry College	VA	University of the Pacific	CA
Florida Southern College	FL	University of Wyoming	WY
Franklin Pierce College	NH	Wabash College	IN
Green Mountain College	VT	West Virginia Wesleyan	WV
Guilford College	NC	Wheaton College	IL

Figure 3-2

THREE TRIPS YOU CAN TAKE

Trip 1, A Swing into New England

Never mind the autumn foliage—New England is lovely in the summertime. So let's go to Massachusetts, Vermont, and New Hampshire. (See the map in Figure 3-3.) Your first stop could be Williams College, in Williamstown, MA. If there is a production at the Williamstown Theatre Festival, take it in. They do an

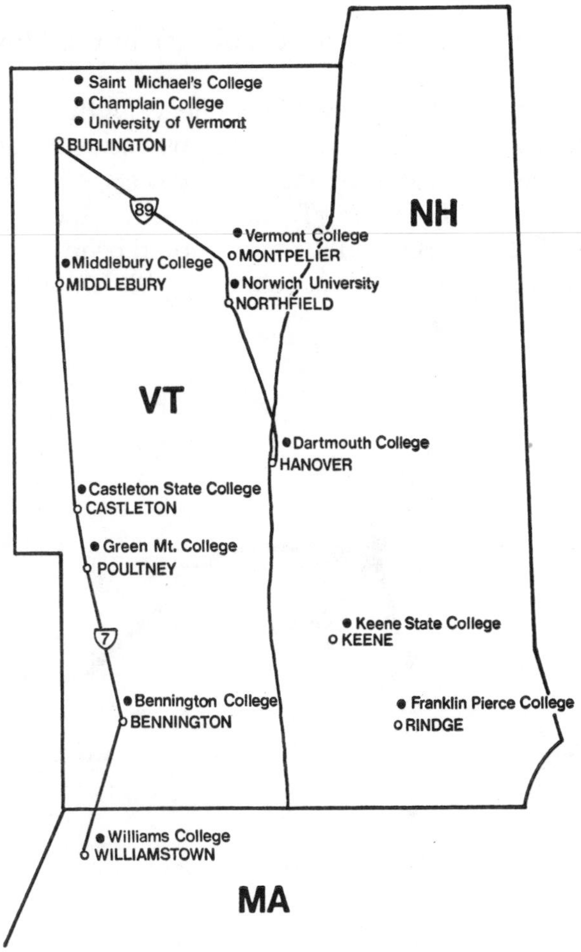

Figure 3-3

excellent job. From there you might work your way up to the colleges of Bennington, Green Mountain, and Middlebury in Vermont. Green Mountain maintains its own inn (former home of Horace Greeley) and would be happy to accommodate you. Further up in the city of Burlington you will find Champlain College, St. Michael's College, and the University of Vermont. Champlain will house you while you are visiting it and the other two schools.

As you breeze down Interstate 89, you can easily swing over to Dartmouth in New Hampshire. But before doing so, don't miss Vermont College in the capital city of Montpelier and Norwich University, the oldest private military college in the nation, in nearby Northfield. When in Hanover consider splurging a bit and staying at the handsome Hanover Inn on the Dartmouth campus. Now it's down again and slightly east to the beautiful Mt. Monadnock region and Keene State College at Keene and scenic Franklin Pierce College at Rindge. Franklin Pierce will take good care of you.

Trip 2, A Loop Tour of the Associated Colleges of the Midwest

The 13 members of the Associated Colleges of the Midwest (ACM), a group of small, private liberal arts colleges, invite you to visit them. During your vacations, long weekends, or extended summer travels, they hope you will stop by one or more of the ACM schools. To do the entire loop (see Figure 3-4) would probably take the better part of ten days, but you'd be in a position to see six states, including Nebraska. (To reach Colorado College it is necessary to travel through Nebraska.)

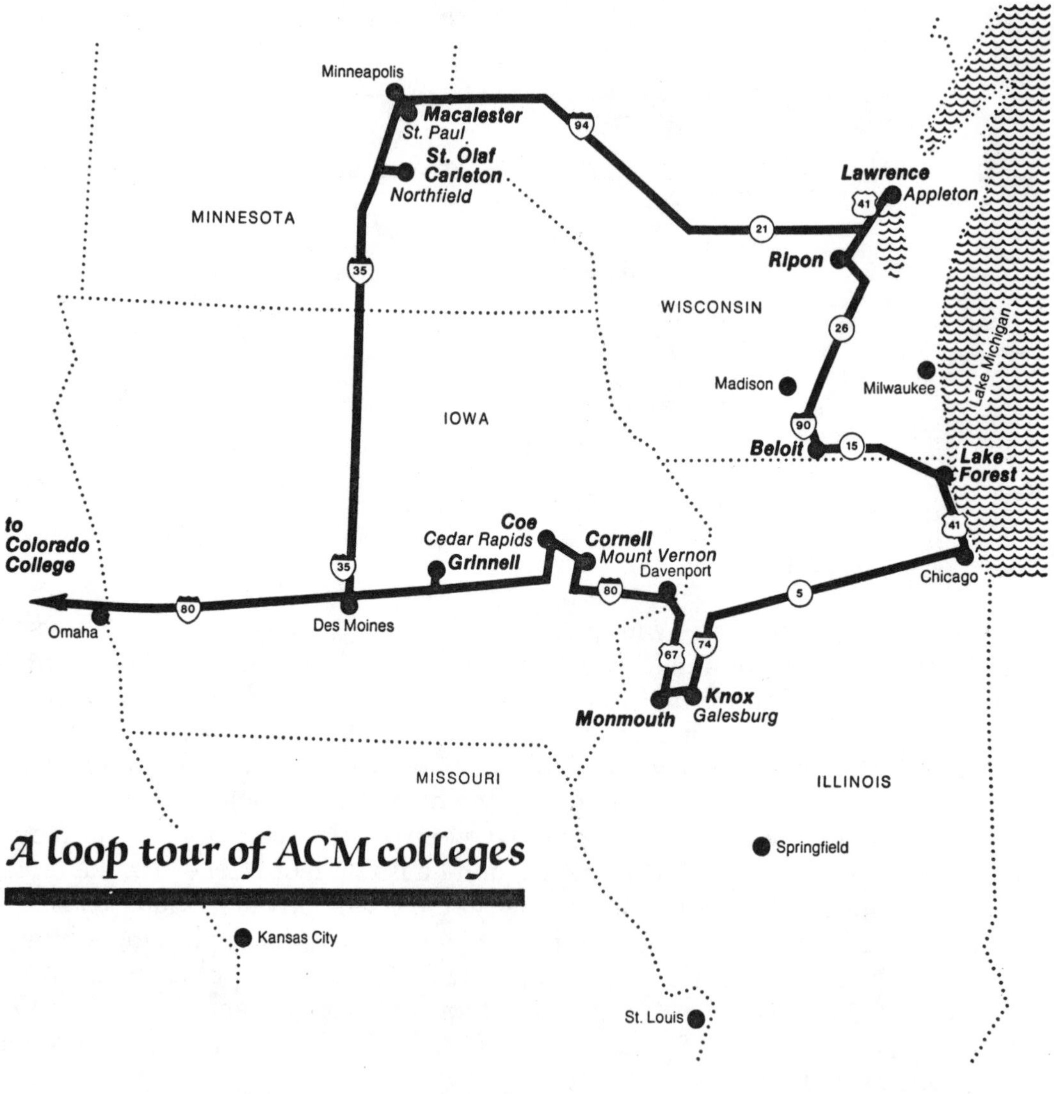

Figure 3-4

Since you would be concentrating solely on small colleges, this trip should vividly demonstrate that not all liberal arts and sciences colleges are the same. The schools share at least one similarity: they are all selective as to admission, some even more so than others.

An added bonus to doing the entire loop would be the opportunity to visit four great cities: Chicago, Minneapolis/St. Paul, and Denver.

Trip 3, The Great North Carolina Curve

Like Pennsylvania, North Carolina is loaded with colleges and universities—some 100 schools of all sizes and shapes. You could see 18 of them (see Figure 3-5), including three historically black institutions, in a two-week sweep from Raleigh in the East to Charlotte in the South, via Durham, Greensboro, Winston-Salem, and Salisbury. Of the 7 North Carolina schools listed in Fiske's "Best Buys," 6 are on this tour. If you are from the North and are concerned about the heat of the summer in the Carolinas, don't be. It's no worse than the dog days of New Jersey and New York.

In addition to visiting the virtual smorgasbord of schools, you might want to take in the following attractions: the museums of art and history in the state capital of Raleigh; the Research Triangle—a 5,200-acre wooded tract of land seven miles south of Durham; the town of Chapel Hill—rated by some authors as the number one college town in America; Guilford Courthouse Military Park—a perfect late afternoon self-guided drive through a lush 220-acre setting where you can step back in time to one of the closing battles of the Revolutionary War; Old Salem—a restored eighteenth-century section of Winston-Salem; Tanglewood—a stunning

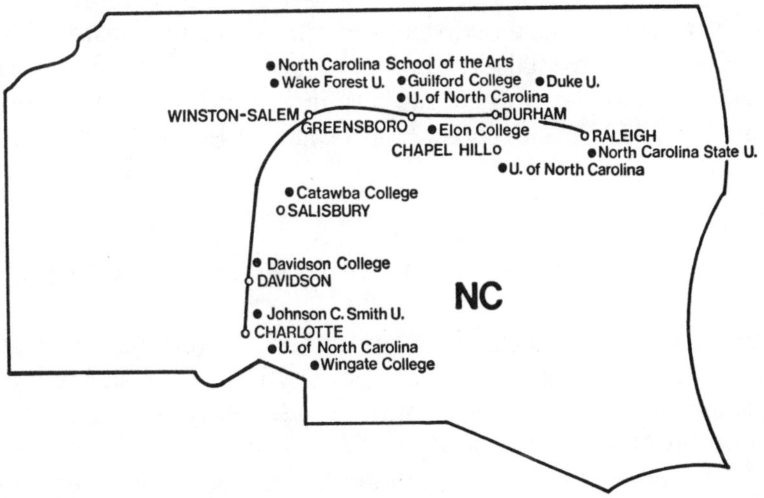

Figure 3-5

1000-acre park ten miles outside of Winston-Salem; Lake Norman near Charlotte; and the beautiful Carowinds Theme Park ten miles south of Charlotte. Travel brochures can be ordered from the North Carolina Travel and Tourism Division, Dept. of Commerce, Raleigh, NC, 27611.

A BIG TRIP YOU CAN TAKE

One of the best kept travel secrets has been Lou Elgart's annual tour of college campuses. Now in its fifteenth year, the tour, which originates in Ohio, includes an unbelievable variety of colleges and universities. It is a "best kept secret" because it has been only recently that Elgart, a former public school counselor and registered Ohio travel agent, opened the program up to counselors in states other than Ohio. The two-week Summer '87 Tour featured almost 30 institutions located in New York, Pennsylvania, Maryland, New Jersey, and Connecticut. Elgart usually selects different regions of the nation to visit each summer. And it's not all work and no play, either. The '87 Tour advertised Philadelphia and New York City sightseeing, sunning on the beaches of Long Island, and shopping at Baltimore's colorful and historic Inner Harbor. The '87 Tour carried a per person cost of $299. Two semester hours of graduate credit are available through Kent State University, Kent, Ohio. Interested counselors can contact Lou Elgart, 4097 Washington Blvd., Cleveland, OH 44118.

NACAC'S MAP OF COLLEGES AND UNIVERSITIES

A two-dollar bargain is the National Association of College Admission Counselors' map of two- and four-year colleges and universities in the United States. This 25″ × 36″ fold-out, with institutions east of the Mississippi on one side and west of the Mississippi on the other, can assist you in planning a trip. Plastered to a wall (the two sides can be joined to make a complete map), it is also a useful visual as you work with your counselees on geographics and locale. Copies of the map can be ordered from NACAC Publications, 1800 Diagonal Road, Suite 430, Alexandria, VA 22314.

UNCLE SAM WILL SHARE *SOME* OF THE COST

As an educator, don't be bashful about writing off nonreimbursed costs when you attend local, state, or national conferences or when you visit businesses, industries, or colleges and universities. Naturally you will want to do so within the bounds of the Tax Reform Act of 1986.

The 1986 Act still allows deductions for educators who engage in professional activities. Yes, things are tighter. But don't let it scare you. For example, educational expenses are deductible as ordinary and necessary business expenses only if the education (1) is required by your employer, by law or regulation, or (2) maintains or improves skills required to perform your present occupation. If attending conferences and visiting college campuses cannot be covered by criterion 1, such activities can certainly be covered by criterion 2.

Beginning with December 31, 1988, business-related expenses for food and beverage can only be deducted at 80 percent. To deduct a "business meal," it must meet two criteria: (1) the meal must be directly related to the "active conduct of business," and (2) the meal must directly precede or follow a business discussion. Under the new regulations the IRS is carefully scrutinizing excessive expenses for food, beverage, and entertainment—all in the name of "doing business." They do not look favorably on meals costing much more than $25 per person.

Expenditures for travel as a form of education are deductible only to the extent that such expenditures are attributable to a period of travel that is directly related to your duties as a counselor. (No more deducting expenses for "general" educational travel, that is, travel itself as a form of education.) "Period of travel" is considered directly related to your job only if the *major* portion of the activities during such period directly maintains or improves your counseling skills. (Note the word "major" as opposed to "all.") Under the new tax law, you are supposed to put in a full work-related day in order to claim 100 percent deductions for travel expenses. A dip in the lake at midday will excite no one.

FOUR SEASONS UNIVERSITY
Vista, Orizon 06743

Office of Undergraduate
Admissions

August 6, 19xx

To Whom It May Concern:

I wish to confirm that Robert Watkins visited Four Seasons University on Wednesday, August 5, and Thursday, August 6, 19xx to tour the facilities and gather information.

Sincerely,

Renee Rowlands, Secretary

Figure 3-6

Travel expenses such as lodging, automobile usage, and airfare will continue to be deductible at 100 percent. You will want to keep track of all automobile mileage and save all lodging and highway toll receipts. Using a charge card is ideal in that it provides you with an automatic record of expenses.

To make it all legal, you'll want to obtain a letter from the institutions as evidence of your visitations, as shown in the sample in Figure 3-6. (If plans call for visiting more than one college, use your first letter as a sample for the next college's receptionist. It will save you explanation time, and the receptionist, construction time.) Posing for a picture next to an entrance sign makes sense, as well.

Considering that most school counselors (1) earn a modest income, (2) are encouraged to visit college campuses, and (3) often receive little, if any, reimbursement from their local boards of education for doing so—go for it! Claim every last penny! Counselors aren't exactly on the IRS's "most wanted" list.

Chapter 4

The Increasing Role of Computer Software

There you are, sitting at the strange-looking keyboard, thumbs caught between keys, and hating yourself for not having taken that high school typing course. But think of it this way: pushing keys is sometimes easier than pushing paper.

Fortune has indeed smiled on you if you have access to a mini- or microcomputer. As you work with the college admission process, you can blissfully and instantaneously store and retrieve information; conduct research; track the effectiveness of specific programs; provide your publics with information on colleges, careers, and financial aid; write letters of recommendation; and record postsecondary placements—among other things!

THE WYOMING SEMINARY APPROACH

Requesting that a college acknowledge the receipt of a student record by way of a return postcard is nothing new, but what *is* new is using the computer as a companion to such a program. Wyoming Seminary Preparatory School, Kingston, PA, has adopted a computerized tracking system for those student records submitted to colleges and universities. Prior to mailing, Seminary's college placement office assigns each record a number and then logs the number into the computer. A self-addressed stamped postcard bearing the student's computer number accompanies the record. Figure 4-1 shows a modification of the postcard. It is used with the permission of Wyoming Seminary Preparatory School. When the college returns the postcard, it is so noted in the computer. At any given time, a scanning of the computer-stored information can quickly reveal which postcards have not been returned. The placement office can then telephone the college to see whether or not the material was received.

PLEASE COMPLETE AND RETURN Computer # ________

We have received for ______________________________

☐ Secondary School Transcript and Test Record

☐ School Statement

☐ Application

☐ Application Fee or Fee Waiver

Date:

Signature:

Position:

Institution:

THANK YOU!

Nancy H. McGuire
Director of College Placement
Wyoming Seminary

Figure 4-1

FIRST STEPS

Students aren't getting their thumbs caught between keys these days. Most of them take a semester typing course as early as grade 8 and become quite proficient in keyboard mechanics. Nonetheless, far too many youngsters are banging away at terminals in meaningless fashion while reams of computer paper spew forth from printers.

Students Helping Students

The presence of computers in a counseling department offers all kinds of possibilities for peer guidance activities. Indeed, several high schools train volunteer seniors to assist their peers to handle both computer hardware and software effectively. These schools have discovered that such a corps of "student aides" has significantly increased student use of software materials.

Before students engage in a computerized college search, two things should have been accomplished: (1) they should know themselves well as the result of self-assessment activity, and (2) they should have made tentative decisions on typical selection characteristics based on their knowledge of themselves. What *are* the consequences of my choosing either characteristic 132, "four-year colleges with no graduate work," or characteristic 134, "universities and four-year colleges with graduate work," on a Peterson student worksheet? What *are* the implications of my selecting a college that does not require a foreign language for entrance or one where the number of black students is less than 10 percent? (More of this in Chapter 16.)

Your Role

It can be very profitable for your counselees to have reviewed such selection characteristics with *you* prior to their inputting certain information into a computer. Utilizing the worksheets from any one of the several service corporations that supply them, you can lead a discussion on the effect that variables such as selectivity level, enrollment, and community composition can have on the student's collegiate experience.

SOFTWARE FOR HOME AND OFFICE

What rational, systematic, and rapid design system will allow you to (1) conduct college and/or career searches, (2) streamline office management procedures as they apply to the college admission process, (3) assist families to do some initial financial aid planning, and (4) help your counselees sensibly evaluate their admission testing results? Answer? A computer. Most counseling departments that have access to minis and micros are quite vociferous in praising their worth. Oh yes, you do have to give considerable attention to the quality of the software you intend to purchase, and you often have to put up with school district business office red tape, but the aggravation is well worth it in terms of time saved and results achieved.

As for financial aid, a reputable and all-inclusive computer-based software program can be a fine planning tool to provide *early* indications of whether or not a family will need financial help to be able to attend one or more colleges of their choice. Parents should understand that use of such software is a confidential matter. (Most packages are designed so that the entered figures provided by parents are automatically wiped out of the computer the moment the program has been completed. For those reluctant to divulge information, several of these programs carry a home-use purchasing option.)

Some counseling departments eagerly encourage parents to make use of their computer facilities. Aside from presenting an open and helpful appearance, such encouragement is politically astute in that delighted parents can be supportive of a department's budgetary efforts to acquire additional hardware and software.

The following are worthwhile, easy to use, and relatively inexpensive software packages, appropriate for career and college planning. Purchase of one or more of these popular programs would be an excellent starting point for any department moving toward computer-assisted counseling.

The Guidance Information System

One of the first computer-based information systems on the market (1976), the *Guidance Information System (GIS)* is now moving toward its fifteenth edition. The system can deliver a wide variety of informational services, including data on occupations (both civilian and military), two- and four-year colleges, and graduate and professional schools and sources of scholarships and financial aids. Although the *GIS* program is relatively easy to operate, first-time users will want to work with a counselor or paraprofessional familiar with the system.

To make optimum use of *GIS*, students should utilize both the *GIS User's Guide* and the *GIS Resource Kit*. The *Guide* contains all the information and instructions needed to operate the system. The *Resource Kit* is a comprehensive manual that outlines implementation techniques for a variety of counseling settings and offers practical information to help ensure successful use of *GIS*. A training guide is also included in the kit. Available through the Houghton-Mifflin Company, Box 683, Hanover, NH 03755. Cost: About $1,100 if part of a 100-member consortium, $1,900 for single-site hookup. Twenty-five states have contracts with Houghton Mifflin and offer the service to their schools.

College Selection Service

Peterson's *College Selection Service* is a computer-based search program to help students and their parents uncover colleges and universities that have specific characteristics in which they are interested. The data used in *College Selection Service* come from Peterson's *Guide to Four-Year Colleges*. The data base covers accredited U.S. and Canadian institutions that grant baccalaureate degrees and the few colleges abroad that are accredited by recognized American accrediting associations.

As with other computerized search packages, the Peterson program works by a process of elimination. The user starts with a pool of over 1,800 four-year colleges and universities and numerous characteristics to use as criteria for selecting appropriate institutions from this pool. The characteristics are divided into 20 general categories, such as geographic location, competitiveness of admission, and size of enrollment.

From each of these categories, the user selects the characteristics that are important to him or her. Every time the the user makes a selection, the computer eliminates from the pool all the institutions that do not have all the characteristics selected. The final pool will contain only those institutions that possess the combination of qualities the user is searching for. Available through Peterson's Guides, Inc., Princeton, NJ 08540. Cost: About $160.

College Explorer

College Explorer is the College Board's search program that permits families to investigate quickly an authoritative, annually updated file of 2,800 two- and four-year colleges and universities. The following are some of the program's more important features:

- Easy-to-use pull-down menus, and an on-line tutorial to help students make the best use of the program.
- A college file that contains some 500 options, thereby permitting students to search such categories as special programs, enrollment size, on campus housing, and religious affiliation. Note: The College Board does not include "cost factor" as a category in the program.
- The package also includes Advanced Placement Explorer which permits you to examine the advanced placement (AP) policies of some 1,800 colleges and universities. (See description below.)

College Explorer comes complete with a copy of the Board's *College Handbook* and a counselor's manual. Available through the College Board, 45 Columbus Avenue, New York, NY 10023. Cost: About $50.

Advanced Placement Explorer

Also published by the College Board, this particular microcomputer-based information source can bring to you and your families the *advanced placement (AP)* policies of some 1,800 colleges and universities. The user can search the program's data base to find out which colleges generally award credit and/or placement for a specific AP examination and then go on to determine what minimum grade is generally required.

Advanced Placement Explorer (APE) is highly flexible and can be used in conjunction with the College Board's complete search package, *College Explorer. APE* users can also:

- Learn about the policies of colleges in which they are already interested.
- Do a preliminary search of colleges to locate, for example, all schools that accept AP results in the state of California or all schools that offer sophomore standing in New England.
- Acquire a list of all institutions in the nation that honor a grade of 2 in specific AP subjects.
- Look through an on-screen list of every college in the country with specific AP policies, select the ones that interest them, and then find out about their policies for all current AP examinations.

- Procure highly specific information about a particular institution, for example, whether the University of Iowa awards placement and/or credit for a grade of 3 on the Latin (Vergil) examination.

Note: The information in *Advanced Placement Explorer* is updated frequently, but as you know, college policies can change rapidly. Moreover, AP policies may vary with individual departments within institutions. The families you advise should check with the admission offices of individual colleges to confirm the policies they see in the APE program. Available through the College Board, 45 Columbus Avenue, New York, NY 10023 Cost: About $48.

College Search Program

Yet another "search" package—this time by the American College Testing (ACT) Program. The *College Search Program (CSP)* uses current information on about 1,400 two-year and 1,700 four-year colleges and universities. These institutions provide updated information directly to ACT each year. Changes in this information enable ACT to revise annually the characteristics used by students as they search for colleges that meet their needs. Because of the changeable nature of such important information as cost and level of admission selectivity, ACT would like you to buy the latest version of this program each fall. At the very least, this type of package should be purchased every other year.

Students can use the *College Search Program* with minimal assistance, since all instructions for its use appear on the screen. With a printer, students can make a copy of specific displays by following simple instructions on the screen. The user moves forward through the two-phased program by adhering to the directions at the bottom of each display. After a brief program introduction, the student is asked to select either the two- or four-year college file to search. Once this selection is made, the concise two-phased process begins.

The American College Testing Program is, and always has been, most sensitive to the needs of secondary school counselors. It's *College Search Program* is no exception. With three models, the program's manual shows you *how to prepare your students for the acquisition of computerized information and how to appropriately handle it afterward*. Available through the American College Testing Program, 230 Schilling Circle, Hunt Valley, MD 21031. Cost: About $125.

ACT's Discover

A superb career planning service, *Discover* software, is available from the American College Testing Program. The software has been refined through a series of enhancements and redevelopments over the past two decades. With this particular computer-based program, you will be able to focus on the specific career planning needs of your counselees.

Interestingly, ACT offers a wide number of career planning software packages. At one end of the continuum of programs is a version of *Discover* for middle and junior high school students. This program is ideal for doing some initial career exploration with your counselees, and for helping them make a successful transition to high school. At the other end, ACT has a program that can be utilized by corporations and government agencies to help their employees manage their careers more effectively.

The high school version of *Discover* is intended for use by the full range of students. It is a very easy system to operate regardless of a student's previous experience with computers. Since your counselees can function independently, you will be able to concentrate on helping them make certain important decisions.

What is *Discover*? Simply put, it is a career planning program that can help students better assess their abilities, interests, and values and, then with this increased knowledge, continue on to uncover occupations that might be appropriate for them. The program will also inform students as to the kind of preparation needed for these occupations and assist them to locate appropriate postsecondary schools for proper training. ACT's College Search Program is an excellent companion piece to Discover. Available through the American College Testing Program, 230 Schilling Circle, Hunt Valley, MD 21031. Cost: About $1750.

ScoreSense: Understanding Your SAT Scores

It's down the tubes with this one. The College Board stopped publishing this excellent and illuminating software piece because secondary schools were not buying it. A limited number of the 1985 edition are available for under $50. Perhaps a number of counselors could press the Board to reproduce this confidence-building program, which was designed to help students understand and interpret their SAT scores.

ScoreSense enables your counselees to compare their scores with those of other students (all high school seniors, college-bound seniors, students of a particular college, and students within a particular high school) and to identify institutions that accept applicants with similar scores. Students can also determine their chances of increasing or decreasing their scores if they repeat the SAT.

In addition, this easy-to-use package seems to calm student apprehensions about testing results. Available through the College Board, 45 Columbus Avenue, New York, NY 10023. Cost: About $48. Well worth the price!

Peterson's Financial Aid Service

Peterson's *Financial Aid Service* is a comprehensive microcomputer-based program that can help families plan for financial aid. The program encompasses six different topics:

- Estimating your family contribution toward college costs
- Calculating college costs and estimating your need
- Average costs of colleges by type
- Federal and state aid programs
- Financial aid from private sources
- No need scholarships from colleges

As you can see, the first two topics have estimating and calculating functions that allow families to approximate what their expected contribution will be at any college in which their youngster is interested. The calculations are modeled on the system used by the federal government, most states, and most colleges in determining need. The last four topics are informational in nature.

With the Peterson program, if parents provide their youngsters with a complete set of financial figures, they can receive a full *Financial Aid Service Report*. However, if parents elect to tell their youngsters only which ranges to use for income and assets and do not wish to reveal specific figures, the report will contain the tools with which the parents can do the calculations and come up with the estimates themselves, *but* the report will not contain any finished calculations. If parents are not comfortable with giving their youngsters any financial figures, the report will contain only the informational components of the service. Regardless, by utilizing the table in *The College Money Handbook*, a publication that accompanies the service, parents can get a rough estimate of their required family contribution. So, the greater the amount of supplied information, the more comprehensive the report. Available through Peterson's Guides, Inc., Princeton, NJ 08540. Cost: About $195.

College Entry

Now here's a time-saver—an innovative, powerful software program published by the College Board that will help you stay on top of the admission process by eliminating paperwork. *College Entry* will assist you in monitoring application flow, tracking submissions, as well as assisting students to gather and organize admissions information. Key features include:

- *Senior Class Profile*, which tracks the number of college applicants, average number of applications per student, percentage accepted and denied, and distribution of SAT and ACT scores—all of this by class, sex, and total group.
- *College Summary*, which generates two basic reports: one lists students' names and application status by college, the other compares students' characteristics with admission decisions and prepares a summary by institution.
- *Reminder List*, which alerts counselors to students with applications still to be filed.
- *Class List*, which compiles one list of students' personal and score data and another of their college planning information.

The beauty of this program is that it allows for the quick and accurate creation, updating, and maintenance of students' college planning records. Available through the College Board, 45 Columbus Avenue, New York, NY 10023. Cost: About $140.

WHEN TO COMPUTERIZE A COUNSELING TASK

The first step in deciding whether or not a task should be computerized is to analyze it. In the December 1987 issue of *The ASCA Counselor*, Lance Huffman, Manitou Springs High School, Manitou Springs, CO, presents 11 questions that can assist you in your analysis. In the article, Huffman states that "The issue of time commitment is critical to making a wise decision about computerizing a task. If the task under consideration will be reused a number of times without major revisions, then it is possible the task deserves to be computerized. . . . The road to enhanced counseling services can be made smoother by including the micro in the process of planning. But counselors will need to keep the usefulness of the microcomputer in proper perspective. Because a task CAN be computerized does not mean it SHOULD be computerized."

IT IS NOT WITHOUT ITS PROBLEMS

Schools that presently use computers have been quick to discover that this "wonder technology" has its own special problems:

- It can have a negative impact on public relations. Students and parents get the idea that the "answer" is somehow going to emerge from the computer, like the good genie from the bottle. Computers tend to have an "aura of infallibility," but, as a matter of fact, sometimes they don't "produce." Students are still being heard to exclaim, "They screwed up my schedule" (hesitant, of course, to use the second person singular). Or when a computerized college selection program is employed, "I'm more confused than ever."

  Historically speaking, counselors have not done much in the way of explanation of the student scheduling process to their publics. But now, with the advent of computer technology, departments are learning that such orientation can pay off. Tired of hearing the surprise and disbelief in parental voices that "the computer" hasn't given their children what they wanted, counselors are conducting evening sessions to explain the strengths and weaknesses of the entire scheduling program. Where appropriate, the use and abuse of computer technology in college and career planning is also covered at these sessions.
- As a department rushes toward computerization, the *extent* of involvement with this technology needs to be addressed. In some departments, counselors pushing excessive paper has given way to counselors pushing an excessive number of keys—and the youngsters are still not being seen. Was not the intent of implementing computer technology to free the counselor to do more listening? This is not to say that counselors should not be pushing terminal keys. What is needed, however, is a conscious effort on the part of

a counselor to know when he should be pushing them. If you find it easier to start a college recommendation at a computer terminal rather than on a yellow legal pad, so be it. But you might not want to punch in SAT scores, class rank, and other information in lieu of one-to-one counseling. An aide could do it as well, or better.

- Confidentiality of student records should continually be a high-priority concern. The preservation of confidentiality can be especially threatened where networking (organizations tied together to a central servicing agency) is involved.
- Whatever you do, *don't* use computers to replace your own inadequacies. Computers as a second opinion—fine. You, personally well versed on *all* aspects of the college admission process—a must!
- In utilizing a computer, the student reads a screen. She does not hear the spoken word, nor can she react vocally. No other *person* is there. Therefore, students and educators need to be alert to the dangers of self-diagnosis and self-treatment. As the counselor, you must stand ready to help your clients. With you, they can hear and react to a variety of stimuli, including a computer printout. Your point of view should interact with the student's point of view. A counselee can feel unwanted if you limit your interview on postsecondary plans to saying, "*Discover* will help you figure things out." You should use whatever information gathering programs you can get hold of as a *supplementary* device, but young people *need the human touch*. They need a human being who cares about their plans and development.

THE HUMAN RELUCTANCE FACTOR

Has computerization been slow to take hold in school counseling because terminal-shy counselors are more "people oriented" than "things oriented"? One researcher likens the restraint to the advent of the pocket calculator—time takes care of things.

A California admission counselor wasn't at all hesitant to describe what *he* thought was the problem: "Counselors are often timid about incorporatimg new technologies in their work, i.e., computerized tracking of college choices, software designed to estimate financial need, and videotape equipment for early searches. They do themselves and their students a great disservice by neglecting to develop these kinds of support, so that their time can be best used in real, solid counseling. They need to become much more sophisticated, and employ mechanisms that are now a matter of course in colleges and universities."

But with numerous secondary schools, it is more than a "neglect" issue. Budgetary restrictions is a prime reason why computer technology has been slow to take hold in many districts. Nonetheless, after initial exposure to the numerous possibilities of this wonder technology, most reluctant professionals do become ardent supporters of the process. To reach that stage, a department needs an open mind, well-constructed and -presented in-service workshops, *and* a proactive stance with the powers-that-be, once the department is convinced of the necessity of implementing the technology.

P.S. A word of advice: If your typing skills are rusty, start practicing. Computers are here! Practice especially for word processing, which is the best thing that's happened to writing since the paper clip.

SUGGESTED READINGS

HUFFMAN, LANCE. December 1987. "When to Computerize a Counseling Task." *The ASCA Counselor*. American School Counselor Association, Alexandria, VA.

Chapter 5

Enhancement Through Publications

Recent studies indicate that college planning publications rank at an all-time high as a source of information for families of college-bound youngsters. This interest exists in spite of two problems with the information: it continues to be somewhat biased, since the content material is provided by the institution, and it is often out of date, because it takes a year or more before a particular work hits the bookstores.

In spite of these drawbacks, publication pieces (especially those produced by corporations that make a serious effort to publish quality materials) can be a fine planning source for your counselees.

They can be an equally good source to help *you* enhance and update your counseling skills if you use these publications as effectively, productively, and creatively as possible.

GUIDES, GUIDES, AND MORE GUIDES

The increased popularity of guidebooks can be attributed, in part, to the marketing of a variety of readable specialty guides. Just when you thought you had seen them all, still more began to appear: everything from "quality-for-less" publications, for example, Edward Fiske's *Best Buys* and Richard Moll's *The Public Ivys*, to Lisa Birnbach's "tell-it-like-I-see-it" *College Book*.

Experienced counselors tend to "rest easy" with their favorite books, but this can be problematic. Sometimes these veterans fail to notice that a new and potentially helpful publication has appeared or that a new section has been added to their favorite work, for example, the sports index the Lovejoy people put into their sixteenth edition.

Everyone is guilty, from time to time, of failing to read the fine print of important documents. Counselors should take the time, however, to read the "fine print" of a given guide—the introductory remarks. By perusing the introduction, you will not only learn how best to use the work, but you will also grow professionally by ruminating over the philosophical statements and editorial comments of the author(s). The introduction of the Fiske and Michalak guide, *The Best Buys in College Education*, and the opening material of Cass and Birnbaum's *Comparative Guide to American Colleges* are especially informative and purposeful.

It might be helpful to have a "guide to the guides": this is an analysis of *some* of the more popular and substantive guidebooks on the market, as well as tips on how they can be used more effectively in college counseling. No attempt has been made to review these publishers' regional editions.

A GUIDE TO THE GUIDES

Peterson's Guide to Four-Year Colleges

In their introductory remarks, the Peterson people state, "This guide contains a wealth of information for anyone interested in American and Canadian colleges and universities" (Peterson's Guides, Inc.). Indeed it does, although its jam-packed pages seem to necessitate the use of tiny print, which could cause the reader a certain amount of eye strain. Besides—one could get back strain in lifting the work: it is thicker than many big-city telephone directories.

One major section, entitled "College Profiles and Special Announcements," contains detailed and factual profiles of some 2,000 institutions. At the end of some of these profiles are boxed special announcements from the colleges regarding new programs or special events. This feature can be of timely benefit to you, as the Peterson people update their guide annually.

Another section carries the rather interesting title, "Messages from the Colleges." Here 700 or so colleges and universities pay some $800 for the privilege of displaying an additional two-page, in-depth description of their institution. Some schools have even supplied campus photographs to accompany their text.

On one page, there is an alphabetical listing of those institutions that have recently closed, merged with other institutions, or changed their names or status since the previous edition. This is a fine idea, and a most helpful inclusion for the counselor. The fact that the guide contains a two-page map of the United States, including a display of major metropolitan areas, can assist you in working with your counselees on distance and travel time criteria. (See Chapter 15.)

If your department is fortunate enough to have a copy of Peterson's popular and excellent computer software program, *College Selection Service*, you will want to have several copies of the *Guide* available. The software program has been cross-referenced to the *Guide*.

Rugg's Recommendations on the Colleges

It appears that several years ago Frederick Rugg stumbled onto a good thing. He decided that the time had come to match quality departments with quality institutions. Does it really matter that he goes on the say-so of some 10,000 collegians, whose opinions he gathers by calling dormitories and visiting campuses? Possibly.

Now in its fifth edition, *Rugg's Recommendations on the Colleges* (Ruggs Recommendations) is a handy reference to which you can turn, especially when working with a counselee who knows what major she wants to pursue. As a counseling tool, the work can be of some help in today's career- and quality-conscious society.

Frederick Rugg has selected 500 supposedly "quality" four-year colleges and universities and then determined with his research staff what departments are especially strong at these institutions. Under each major program heading, the author places a recommended institution according to one of three levels of admission selectivity: "most selective," "very selective," or "selective."

Unfortunately, the guide is of limited value because it contains a limited number of majors (39), some of which are not subdivided, such as engineering and foreign languages. However, the book seems to be growing "like Topsy" with each new edition. Obviously, there are many solid institutions with solid majors that have not been included in the guide, and the author does not pretend to have them all.

Even if you have doubts about how "on the mark" Rugg is on some of his selections, the guide can serve as a sensible beginning point for further in-depth inquiry by you and your counselee. And you can always use your expertise to recommend a few schools on your own. Incidentally, it is possible for a not-so-selective school to have a dynamite major, as you know—but do your analysis carefully. As Rugg wisely states, even weak departments at the "ivy" types might be equal to, or better than, the strongest departments elsewhere.

A cross-reference approach would be of considerable help to counselors. All recommended departments, with corresponding page numbers, should be listed next to the names and addresses of each of the 500 colleges and universities. Harvard appears to have the greatest number of strong departments; a cross-reference approach would enable the reader to see the "famous 17" at a glance. This kind of indexing would be advantageous to those who want to see which of the author's recommended departments are given for a particular institution.

Lovejoy's College Guide

The granddaddy of them all, the first of its kind on the market, the *Guide* was compiled in 1940 by Dr. Clarence E. Lovejoy and published under the title, *So*

You're Going to College (Monarch Press). The editors have nicely carried through on the original title, using it as their Section I heading.

Without a doubt, the great strength of this particular work is that it doesn't attempt to be all things to all people, but what it does, it does well!

In its top-notch career curricula (Part I of Section II), you can find all kinds of majors—everything from accounting to zoology. In presenting the material, however, the editors exercise a certain amount of control over the inclusion of institutions. For example, with many majors, the editors list only those schools that carry special private accreditation along with the expected regional one. Let us take "Nursing" as an example. To be included in the guide, the institution's program must have been approved by the National League for Nursing. With other majors, the editors will not list an institution unless it awarded a prescribed number of degrees in a given year. Take "French": only those institutions that awarded ten or more undergraduates degrees in a given year are mentioned. This type of inclusion control could be considered a middle ground between the considerable restrictions exercised by Rugg and the "anything and everything" approach the College Board takes in its *Index of Majors*.

This design can be most helpful to the experienced counselor, one who has a good familiarization with colleges and is searching with her counselee for a relatively strong major program. Utilizing her broad-based knowledge, the counselor should be able to "pull it all together." However, it is important to remember that there *are* excellent programs at schools that, for one reason or another, choose not to seek private accreditation or graduated but nine French majors in a given year, instead of the requisite ten. Nevertheless, the Lovejoy editors' careful yearly monitoring of the material in this section, and their clear and meaningful presentation, makes this particular publication an extremely valuable counseling tool for working with the college bound. The editors' decision to publish a work that does not include every "whistle stop" school and major should be applauded.

In Part II of Section II, you can find 27 special programs—things like 3–2 forestry, ROTC information, colleges serving kosher meals, and sea/sail semesters.

The brevity of the Section III title, "The Colleges," is a forecast of what is to come—that is, a concise description of each of the 2,500 colleges and universities, listed alphabetically within each state. There are those who would criticize the Lovejoy summaries as being too brief. Yet such brevity might well be another one of the publication's strengths, for, as you counsel, you can readily flip from the guide's career curricula section to these brief summaries to acquire just enough information to make some tentative selection decisions with your counselees. Within each summary, important basic statistical information is *not* hidden in the body of the text. The editors have wisely placed these data at the top of each summary where the reader can locate it quickly, and the data have been printed in extra-dark, easy-to-read ink.

One drawback of this publication is that the useful (but brief) "Non-Sports Activities" area is tucked behind the "Sports Index" section. A greater problem: the editors don't change the running head at the top of the page; consequently, the area is not properly advertised.

Another weakness of the work is in the design of the main index. It simply lists the state for each of the institutions mentioned. There is no question that the reader can note the state and then turn and scan the listings to find the desired institution, but how much better it would be to have appropriate page numbers listed! One could find a particular school more rapidly.

Comparative Guide to American Colleges

A most readable and worthwhile work by James Cass and Max Birnbaum (Harper & Row), this particular publication is an interesting combination of objective and subjective material.

In Section I, "Description of Colleges," the written material comes from original research and information supplied to the authors by campus leaders, college presidents, and deans of students. The comments, particularly the subjective ones, can be of special benefit to you in your effort to do some sophisticated research; each edition of the book is updated as the authors tap into changing student interests and aspirations. The material in the "Campus Life" and "Academic Environment" subdivisions is decidedly purposeful. Even though the comments are subjective, they are a far cry from those that tell you where you can get a good pizza at midnight. Two other subdivisions, "Graduates Career Data" and "Academic Environment," can assist you in working with your counselees on undergraduate and graduate paths to careers.

Like the Lovejoy guide, Cass and Birnbaum's "Comparative Listing of Majors," tucked away in the back of the book, provides some sense of the strength of individual departments as well as the extent of student interest in particular programs. Unlike Lovejoy, the authors organize their material in a different fashion. For example, to the right of each college or university is the number of actual degrees conferred in a given year. In their thirteenth edition, the authors use 1983–1984 data (the most recent year for which data were available for this particular edition) procured from the U.S. Department of Education. Even with such dated information, you should have little trouble making certain rudimentary, but informed, deductions concerning program strength.

Again, let us take "French" as an example. In perusing the listed schools under the heading of French, you see that Michigan State University, a school of some 30,000 undergraduates, awarded 9 degrees in this language in 1984. Middlebury College in Vermont, with about 1,900 students and a national reputation for strength in foreign languages, conferred 20. And you can find similar strength at similarly sized colleges such as Colby in Maine (16), Dickinson in Pennsylvania (17), and Smith in Massachusetts (28).

Taking yet another example, "Physics," and scanning the same comparative listing, you learn that Oberlin College in Ohio conferred 17 degrees; Reed in Oregon, 23; Carleton in Minnesota, 26; and Ohio State, a university of some 35,000 students, 15. Do such statistics reveal anything about the relative strength of Oberlin, Reed, and Carleton in the physical sciences? Better yet, do they reveal anything about the exceptional program quality that can be found within many small colleges?

It appears, therefore, that another method of your learning about the popularity of particular majors, and also estimating departmental strength, is through the comparison of numbers of degrees conferred annually with the consideration of institutional size. In their explanation of this section, the authors are careful not to use the word "strength," but rather opt for the phrase "relative size of program." No matter what, whether experienced or inexperienced, by proceeding with caution, you should be able to utilize the Cass and Birnbaum listings as an excellent initial source for uncovering high-quality major programs. Then you can move on to college catalogs, looking for such things as numbers and titles of course offerings and size of teaching faculty.

The authors' "Admission" subdivision is an appropriate place to refer to when advising counselees on "reach," "target," and "safety" schools. Here you can quickly zero-in on selectivity level, class rank data, and average SAT scores. What is even more helpful is to have the distribution of SAT scores from responding institutions. Unfortunately, some schools elected not to supply the authors with any SAT and/or class rank data.

The fact that colleges and universities appear in strict alpha sequence is certainly convenient when you want to turn quickly to particular institutions—that is, if you can keep all your Saint's and University of's straight.

Actually the *Lovejoy* guide and the *Comparative* guide can be great companion pieces. You can check under a major heading in Lovejoy, and then turn to the *Comparative* guide to see the number of degrees granted.

The Best Buys in College Education

Edward Fiske and Joseph Michalak tie academic quality to the American dollar by identifying "bargain" schools in a book entitled, *The Best Buys in College Education* (Times Books).

Quite frankly, every counselor should possess a copy of this most unusual and worthwhile publication. From the authors' "upfront" comments on why the book and how the research, through the dramatically and separately presented price indexes for public and private schools, through the enlightening, and very readable treatments of each of the 200 some selected schools, to the rather humorous back cover statement, "At last a weapon to fight the soaring cost of college education . . . ," you will find this much needed publication to be a valuable supplemental resource. Within the table of contents, the authors have listed their schools by states, enabling you to see at a glance just where these "relative bargains" are located. The guide contains an unbelievable variety of higher educational institutions within 46 states. (There appear to be no bargain schools in Alaska, Hawaii, Nevada, Montana, and Washington, DC.)

By spending time with this publication, you can acquire a real feel for what is out there as to quality and reasonable cost. And, quite honestly, it *is* important that we develop a greater sense of the importance of these schools, to be of genuine assistance to an increasing number of parents who find themselves pressed to the wall financially.

Besides—as you pick up *Best Buys*—you can't help but be pulled in with such first edition opening lines as, "The University of South Carolina, once cited by *Playboy* . . .," or "Anyone who believes that Kansas is just one flat, waving wheatfield, has a lot to learn about the University of Kansas." Fiske encourages browsing. Therefore, as you lean back in your chair with this manageable book of 200 schools, you can become educated with schools of which you may never have heard. In the L's alone, are LeMoyne, Linfield, Loras, and Luther.

Barron's Profiles of American Colleges

In their preface the Barron's editors use such dubious phrases as "extremely exciting" to describe student preparation for college and "the road to paradise" to depict the application process. This, and the fact that the guide weighs in at about five pounds, aside, *Profiles of American Colleges* (Barron's Educational Series, Inc.) is a most valuable reference work on which you can hone your skills.

Barron's maintains that the work is the "most comprehensive, easy-to-use guide available." Most comprehensive—maybe; easy-to-use—not so. The book has a crowded look and, because of its bulk, is cumbersome to use. (The reader has to flip through 1,119 pages to get to special information sections.) New material on completing application forms, selecting schools, financial aid, and choosing a major, topics that one could easily and more suitably find elsewhere, have been unnecessarily packed into the fifteenth edition.

Especially helpful features:

- *College Admissions Selector* The "Selector" groups all of the colleges and universities listed in the guide according to degree of admissions competitiveness. A definitive and useful explanation of the criteria used to rank the schools introduces *each* "Selector" level. (Incidentally, a less obvious benefit for studying a selectivity index is acquiring a feel for institutional geographic location within the various levels of selectivity.)
- *Special* Here we have a one-page separate listing of institutions with specialized programs: professional schools of art, music, and theater arts.
- *College Locator Maps* A great idea! Instead of one map of the United States, each state is pictured separately. This enables you not only to find the general (only principal towns and cities are included) or specific location of a particular college or university, but also to work with your counselees to calculate distance and travel time.
- *The College Entries Section* The section opens with a well-written and instructive three-page explanation of use of this 1,119 page *long* section. In addition to the typical topics characteristic of this kind of publication, Barron's addresses other less typical issues such as facilities for the handicapped, opportunities for transfer, campus visitation policies, and availability of computers. At the beginning of each profile is a "capsule" area where you can see at a glance basic information, including a map code referenced to the proper college locator map.

- *Part III—An Overview of Specialized Data* The editors consolidate and place all of the essential data about the four-year schools that they profile in chart form. The schools are recorded by states for easy geographic reference. Topic headings include enrollment figures, in-state and out-of-state costs, and SAT and ACT data, both median scores and the distribution of scores.
- *Religious Institutions* Four-year accredited schools, whose specialized programs of study prepare students for the clergy and/or church related vocations, can be located in this section.
- *Advice and Basic Information for International Students* Barron's offers informative and all inclusive information for international students who contemplate studying in the United States.
- *A Look at Career Services and Placement* Perhaps a one-of-a-kind guide inclusion, this section is an effort to illustrate how each institution is attempting to meet the career needs of young people.

PUTTING A PROFESSIONAL LIBRARY TOGETHER

It is far more understandable for a department to lack sufficient travel funds than it is for it to be missing the funds necessary to equip *all* its counselors with the proper publication tools to do a competent job. It is sad to hear that many counseling offices do not have adequate varieties of, and copies of *updated* guides. (See Figure 5-1.)

CATEGORY I: "MUST" PUBLICATIONS FOR ANY COUNSELOR'S LIBRARY

Either Barron's Profiles of American Colleges or Peterson's Guide to Four-Year Colleges

Lovejoy's College Guide

Comparative Guide to American Colleges

The College Handbook by the College Board

Index of Majors by the College Board

Total cost: Approximately $75 for the set

Total cost for a department of five counselors: $375. If the school has 1,500 students, 50 percent college bound, the cost per college bound student would be 50 cents.

CATEGORY II: OTHER USEFUL PUBLICATIONS

The Best Buys in College Education

The Black Student's Guide to Colleges

The Insider's Guide to the Colleges

The Public Ivys

Rugg's Recommendations on the Colleges

Either Lovejoy's College Guide for the Learning Disabled or Peterson's Guide to Colleges with Programs for Learning Disabled Students

Peterson's National College Databank

Any of the regional editions published by the major guide corporations

Figure 5-1

ERIC/CAPS: A RICH RESOURCE

Hardly a household word; nevertheless, this clearinghouse system for counseling information offers a variety of services to facilitate your job and enhance your professional growth. ERIC/CAPS (Counseling and Personnel Services Clearing House of the Educational Resources Information Center) is a nationwide information system funded by the Office of Educational Research and Improvement (OERI), U.S. Department of Education.

You should find this type of service extremely helpful when you want to improve knowledge and skills within a specific area. An "ERIC SEARCH" can provide you with an extensive bibliography, *and* a brief resume is furnished on each entry. There is a fee for this particular service.

One- and two-page annotated minibibliographies are free. There are 22 timely titles available from the ERIC data base.

ERIC/CAPS also publishes handy one- and two-sheet digests (monographs) on such topics as "Counselors and Computers," "Selecting a College: A Checklist Approach," and "Multicultural Counseling." Single copies are free. You can then reproduce as many copies as you want for any of your publics.

For a complete list of available publications and services write to: ERIC/CAPS Publications, 2108 School of Education, University of Michigan, Ann Arbor, MI 48109

Chapter 6

Workshops, Conferences, and Fairs

Attending a state, regional, or national conference is a superb way to enhance one's skills. Journal articles can come alive as you listen to any one of a number of panel presentations. You have the chance to communicate on all levels with colleagues from your locale, or even from across the country. For the practiced professional, such attendance can be akin to being reborn: you have an opportunity to rethink many aspects of the counseling and admission process. For the inexperienced, it can mean practical exposure to the basic problems and issues that will confront you in that operation.

The National Association of College Admission Counselors (NACAC), based in Alexandria, VA, is the largest national organization of its kind. Beginning its second 50 years, the NACAC mission is to develop the professional competence and to meet the professional needs of individuals involved in the college admission process. One way in which it fosters professional growth is through the sponsorship of an annual national conference. (See Figure 6-1.)

SUMMER INSTITUTES

Summer institutes bring together both new and experienced secondary school and college admission counselors for intensive, experientially based conferences. The

NACAC NATIONAL CONFERENCE SCHEDULE

Year	Dates	City	Location
1989	October 5–8	New York City	New York Hilton
1990	October 2–5	Louisville, KY	Galt House
1991	October 2–5	New Orleans, LA	Marriott
1992	October 1–4	Long Beach, CA	Hyatt Regency
1993	October 5–8	Pittsburgh, PA	Vista International

Figure 6-1

associations that conduct these three- to six-day programs sometimes try for an equal balance of participation by school counselors and college admission folk. Some institutes even try to achieve participation representative of different types of institutions, that is, according to ethnicity, gender, and geographical location. Most, but not all, of these programs are sponsored by state or regional ACACs and carry the endorsement of the National Association of College Admission Counselors. A few have been around for a long time; for example, the Ohio institute has existed since 1967.

The following is a *sampling* of various state and regional ACAC summer programs that have been endorsed by NACAC. For additional information you might want to write to the contact college or university.

Illinois ACAC Summer Institute

Location: DePaul University
Eligibility: Secondary school and college admission counselors
Enrollment Limit: None
Cost (Approximate): $200
Credit: Available
Contact: Summer Institute Director
Elmhurst College
190 Prospect Avenue
Elmhurst, IL 60126

Missouri ACAC Summer Workshop

Location: Rockhurst College
Eligibility: Secondary school and college admission counselors
Enrollment Limit: 40
Cost (Approximate): $150
Credit: Not available

Contact: Fontbonne College
6800 Wydown Blvd.
St. Louis, MO 63105

New England ACAC Summer Workshop
Location: St. Michael's College, VT
Eligibility: Secondary school and college admission counselors
Enrollment Limit: 75
Cost (Approximate): $285
Contact: Champlain College
P.O. Box 670
Burlington, VT 05402

Ohio ACAC Summer Institute
Location: University of Toledo
Eligibility: Secondary school and college admission counselors
Enrollment Limit: None
Cost (Approximate): $150
Credit: Available
Contact: Senior Admission Specialist
Clark Technical College
Springfield, Ohio 45501

Pennsylvania ACAC Summer Institute
Location: Bucknell University
Eligibility: Secondary school and college admission counselors; also graduate students in counseling
Enrollment Limit: 70
Cost (Approximate): $350
Credit: Available
Contact: Director, PACAC Summer Institute
Springside School
8000 Cherokee Street
Philadelphia, PA 19118

Texas ACAC Summer Workshop
Location: Rice University
Eligibility: Secondary school and college admission counselors
Enrollment Limit: 100
Cost (Approximate): $450
Credit: Licensure credit for Texas counselors
Contact: Dean of Admissions
Rice University
Houston, TX 77251

Wisconsin Association of Secondary School Counselors Summer Program
Location: Not permanently based. Classroom on wheels that includes in-depth visits to a cross section of Midwestern colleges and universities.
Eligibility: Secondary school counselors and graduate students
Enrollment Limit: 40
Cost (Approximate): $350

Credit: Available
Contact: WASSCAC Institute Coordinator
St. Norbert College
DePere, WI 54115

New York State ACAC Summer Institute

Location: Hamilton College
Eligibility: Secondary school and college admission counselors
Enrollment Limit: 60
Cost (Approximate): $350
Credit: Not available
Contact: Co-director, ACAC Summer Institute
Guidance Department
Rye High School
Rye, NY 10580

The following is a *sampling* of summer programs that are not directly sponsored by a state or regional ACAC but do carry NACAC endorsement.

Northwestern University College Counselors Workshop

Location: Northwestern University
Eligibility: Secondary school counselors
Enrollment Limit: 25
Cost (Approximate): $510
Credit: Not available
Contact: Associate Director of Admissions
Northwestern University
1801 Hinman Avenue
Evanston, IL 60201

Counseling for College Institute

Location: Santa Clara University
Eligibility: Secondary school counselors
Enrollment Limit: 24
Cost (Approximate): $400
Credit: Available
Contact: Dean of Admissions
Santa Clara University
Santa Clara, CA 95053

Summer Institute on College Admissions and School Relations

Location: Colorado College (Program includes tour of Colorado colleges.)
Eligibility: Secondary school and college admission counselors
Enrollment Limit: 40
Cost (Approximate): $325
Credit: Not available
Contact: The College Board
4155 East Jewell Avenue, Suite 600
Denver, CO 80222

NATIONAL FAIRS: A BROADENING EXPERIENCE

As your department develops its annual program of goals and objectives, one activity that you will want to consider including is the National College Fair Program. But what is a national fair?

The project had its inception in 1972, when, after a National Association of College Admission Counselors conference in San Antonio, TX, the membership put together a one-day "College Day" for area students and their parents. Since 1973 NACAC has sponsored 200 some fairs in 30 cities; so, what began as a modest local endeavor has since expanded to a nationwide effort. To date, these events have attracted millions of families and thousands of counselors.

If you are lucky enough to counsel near a fair site, go! Such attendance can be professionally rewarding. Fair participation provides you with the opportunity to:

- Visit and confer with colleagues from neighboring school districts.
- Speak directly to admission counselors from a wide range of states as you expand and update your knowledge and skills.
- Grow professionally by donating a few hours of your time to help ensure that a fair is a successful venture.
- More efficiently schedule the release time needed by students to meet with admission representatives.
- Institute a busing program whereby your school transports students to the fair site, making it possible for certain students to attend this function who otherwise could or would not do so.

As for your counselees, the experience can be more fulfilling than one of simply receiving literature from reps who smile out from wallboard booths. They (counselees) will have the opportunity to speak openly with these reps, attend special seminars and workshops, and even receive individual advisement from school counselor volunteers.

"Prepare for the Fair" Videocassette

NACAC has produced a ten-minute videocassette entitled "College Fair Is Coming." The content material, written with both counselors and students in mind, features interviews with college admission and secondary school counselors, as well as with students who have attended one of the National Fairs. The video can serve as a fine instructional device, as it also includes steps that students can take to prepare properly for a fair. Copies may be ordered from College Fair Video, NACAC, 1800 Diagonal Road, Suite 430, Alexandria, VA 22314.

National College Fair Sites

According to NACAC, the following areas hosted a National College Fair during the 1986–87 school year:

Baltimore, MD
Boston, MA
Chicago, IL
Cleveland, OH
Hartford, CT
Long Island, NY
Los Angeles, CA
Middlesex County, NJ
Milwaukee, WI
Minneapolis, MN
Montgomery County, MD
New York City, NY
Philadelphia, PA
Orange County, CA
Pittsburgh, PA
Portland, OR
St. Louis, MO
San Diego, CA
San Francisco, CA
Springfield, MA
Seattle, WA
Washington, DC

If you would like to explore the possibility of having a National College Fair in your area, or just learn more about this program, you can contact the National Association of College Admission Counselors, 1800 Diagonal Road, Suite 430, Alexandria, VA 22314.

SECTION II

DEVELOPING A WELL-DESIGNED PROGRAM

Before you can be really effective with your counselees and their families, your efforts—no matter how personally stamped they might be—must be conducted within the framework of a well-designed departmental program.

Section II takes the position that the best college counseling programs are found where there is agreement among the people as to the goals and objectives to be pursued. In this environment, professionals are free to draw upon their own special talents, interests, and capabilities to serve their clientele better, *but* at the same time there is direction to the overall program. Specific grade-level activities that can be incorporated into a college counseling curriculum are presented in this section. The many pieces of the admission puzzle are also treated.

Chapter 7

A Developmental Approach to College Counseling

> We have two extremes: those counselors who stress preparation so intensely and so early that students become over-stressed and terrified about getting into college; and those counselors who leave preparation to the senior year, thereby leaving capable students stranded without proper coursework and with no realistic understanding of the college experience. Surely there must be a middle ground!
>
> — A Southern admission counselor

In its 1986 report, *Frontiers of Possibility*, the National Association of College Admission Counselors speaks of schools with exemplary college counseling programs: "Over and over, we heard counselors say, 'Have a plan and start it early.' "

Evidently the most crucial factor in any successful precollege counseling program is the existence of a *written* curriculum: a well-defined sequence of activities spanning grades 7 through 12 that becomes an integral part of the total guidance and counseling curriculum.

Since the formal education of our young people has always been appropriately developmental in structure, doesn't it follow that an important facet of this education, precollege planning, should be developmental in design as well? Unfortunately, this is not always the case. Nevertheless, an increasing number of schools are putting their "hit or miss" approaches behind them and are developing sequential and substantive college counseling programs.

In their introductory remarks at junior parent meetings, for example, department chairs can be seen wisely recapping the activities and accomplishments of previous years. And, of course, the key figure in all this curriculum evolution *is* the department chair, for it rests with him or her to ensure that all the sequenced activities are effectively implemented.

MIDDLE/JUNIOR HIGH YEARS

Could it be that the middle/junior high years are those during which a young person can get on base or strike out forever?

Suffice it to say that the growth of today's middle or junior high school students is most complex! Their development involves four major areas (intellectual, emotional, physical, and social) that teachers and counselors must address. *What transpires at this level is crucial toward making a successful transition to high school and beyond.*

School systems attempt to handle the intellectual, and to some extent the physical, areas of development, but the emotional and social continue to be somewhat neglected. Insufficient time and attention are paid to establishing individual and group programs that deal with issues within these areas. Since you specifically deal with the development of these young people, you can work some emotional and social growth into their intellectual development—into their "life plans."

And for intellectual development, these are important years! Here we see an expansion of conceptual thinking and a reduction of concrete thinking. Youngsters begin to see beyond the literal meaning of things and become more reflective thinkers. They are much more independent, but cannot yet stand alone, so they need your encouragement and support. Middle or junior high school education has a lasting effect on postsecondary and career possibilities.

Simultaneously, students need to know where they stand as to their academic strengths and weaknesses in order to make informed decisions; they must know themselves *well*! Good knowledge includes periodically *seeing* standardized test results and having them *interpreted* by the counselor. All too often, students' cumulative records are underutilized, just gathering dust in file drawers and closets.

Elementary teachers encourage their pupils to explore anything and everything within reach, so youngsters enter the middle years wide-eyed and wide-optioned. It is vital to continue the "options-open" thinking of the elementary years with even greater intensity. Your students, especially those from low-income and/or minority groups, should be encouraged to stretch academically and try out various subjects. Again, the whole idea is to keep all options open!

Students should be provided with accurate and concrete advice on course selection. And, most important, they need *early* and complete information about postsecondary school choices. The home cannot always be counted on to carry its weight. You must pick up the slack from the low-expectation-and-support home—

the home that should have played its crucial role in the development of your counselee's sense of self-worth and competence, but could not and/or did not.

Grades 4–8: Critical Years for Minorities and Females

The elementary and middle school years are crucial for females and minority students in mathematics, science, and computer science. This is when intervention is most needed to prevent them from losing interest, according to a group of Educational Testing Service researchers. Funded by the Ford Foundation, the ETS people found that girls perform as well as boys do in mathematics during these years, but do not do as well in certain aspects of science. Girls do not get involved in as many extracurricular science or computer science activities as boys.

The researchers also discovered that black, Hispanic, and Native American youngsters record substantially lower rates of participation and performance in both mathematics and science. The findings are significant because (1) the differences that begin to emerge during the middle school years continue to widen as students move through the higher grades, and (2) at the end of the middle school period, students are called upon to make important decisions concerning future coursework in these areas. It appears that once in high school, many minority students and young women choose to avoid the more advanced math and science courses, thereby cutting off opportunities in the technical fields that include better paying positions.

In your counseling capacity you can *actively* encourage minorities and girls to pursue mathematics, science, and computer science activities, both in and out of school.

MIDDLE/JUNIOR HIGH SCHOOL ACTIVITIES

Some specific activities that can be incorporated into a college counseling curriculum that are well suited to the middle/junior high school level:

1. Individual and small-group guidance activities related to the building of useful study habits and skills.
2. Activities associated with the clarification of personal interests, abilities, values, and career aspirations. The introduction of decision-making exercises is also appropriate at this level.
3. Seventh-grade day and evening family conferences that address such issues as the suitability of pursuing a foreign language and/or Algebra I in eighth grade, standardized testing history, and local and state graduation requirements.
4. An eighth-grade program for parents, hosted by counselors with high school department chairpersons as guest speakers. Purpose: to orient parents to curricular offerings and options available, prior to the scheduling of students into ninth grade.

5. A second program (late spring) for eighth-grade parents devoted to the examination of career and postsecondary school possibilities. Such a meeting might include a presentation on both financial aid and financial planning.

THE "PAVING THE WAY" PROJECT

At last an early college planning program! *Paving the Way* is the first such program intended for national distribution and specifically developed for parents with youngsters in grades 7–10. Sponsored by the National Institute of Independent Colleges and Universities, the *Paving the Way* kit, which assists parents to do some long-range planning, contains a 23-minute videotape and companion booklet on academic and financial preparation for college. The material is especially appropriate for use at evening parent programs at the middle or junior high school level. The kit carries PTA endorsement and is inexpensive to rent or purchase.

You can rent or purchase this material by writing to *Paving the Way*, 1430 Broadway, 9th floor, New York, NY 10018.

COUNSELING STUDENTS ON COURSE SELECTION

One has only to read national commission reports to understand that postsecondary options apparently close out early for thousands of American youngsters. If it is true that of the high school freshmen who claim they are headed for college, 45 percent are not even taking college preparatory work, then we have a most serious problem that educators, especially counselors, must confront and resolve.

Critics continue to charge that counselors are nothing more than "schedulers," implying that they are wasting their counseling abilities—or that scheduling is all that they are capable of. Wrong on both counts! The counselor *must* bring all his or her expertise to bear to set up academic programs that will ensure the inclusion of:

1. Requirements for high school graduation.
2. Entrance requirements for postsecondary education.
3. Curriculum to be covered prior to admission testing.
4. The student's abilities and interests.
5. The student's values and career aspirations.
6. Growth that might alter interests, values, and aspirations.
7. Family expectations.

Placing students in appropriate courses is one of your most serious and vital responsibilities. It is an essential element of a developmental college counseling program. The ramifications of incorrect placement of the student include failure, extreme frustration, depression, *adverse effects on career and college planning*, and loss of self-esteem. (This loss can come from two sources: if the course is too difficult, the student feels inadequate; if it is too easy, the student feels undervalued.) It is most important, then, to evaluate carefully the student's abilities and interests, comparing them to the content and real demands of the course.

Humanizing the Process

There are those who say that a clerk or a computer could do it as well. A clerk makes some sense: at least you can talk to a clerk, but you can't talk to a computer—yet! Still the *magic* word in the course selection process is counseling! That's something clerks and computers *can't* do, and counselors can, and many do it well. Even those counselors with horrendous caseloads magically become available for counselees who request a bit of time. As a caring, creative, and energetic counselor you could:

1. Encourage a college-bound student to explore Accounting I, knowing that such exploration might open a career door.
2. Suggest to an aspiring automotive engineer that she try a practical course in small engine mechanics.
3. Mention to a potential elementary teacher the school's semester course in child growth and development as an interesting and worthwhile undertaking.
4. Propose to an exceptionally able young woman who did not begin her college prep math program in eighth grade that she "double up" (study both Geometry and Algebra II) in her sophomore year.
5. Listen to a counselee who was "passed by" for honors English tell you that his present English level is too easy and help him resolve the problem.

These are but a few placement problems you might have to face. Each course selection has its consequence, so take your experience and talents and "go with it!" Humanize the course selection process as much as possible.

"LEFT AT THE GATE"—BY TRACKING?

One of the lines in John Davidson's poem, *War Song*, reads, "The race is to the swift." That is, provided that one can at least get out of the gate. Without a good start, there is little or no chance of catching up.

Increasing numbers of both average and academically talented youth, especially minorities, are not getting a good start toward postsecondary educational opportunities. Some never even *reach* the gate—they are scratched from the race beforehand.

Could a major factor in all this be the inflexible "general tracking" systems (homogeneous grouping and consequent assignment of students to a curricular track) found in some of our secondary schools today? The very term is upsetting to some people, who see general tracking as a confining, options' closing, vision binding, and elitist—good for the institution, but not for its students.

Do we really need tracking and labeling? Is it not sufficient simply to have "academic" courses of a preparatory, honors, or advanced placement nature? Is it not wise for the student who can't quite make up her mind about secretarial or college preparatory subjects to enroll tentatively in both types of courses without having to commit herself to a single track? Must we tell students who take minimal college preparatory work, and then enter a cooperative education program in their junior year, that they'll never get into college?

How does this "pigeonholing" influence today's young people? It has its greatest effect at the seventh- and eighth-grade levels, where general tracking and group labeling (college preparatory, business, general, etc.) take on a full head of steam. Once students are tracked, choice is gone, and yet our youth, *as they continue to grow*, should be afforded the chance to experiment and eventually to find themselves.

One adverse effect of tracking is the *increase* in the number of academically talented students who are now dropping out of school. This is especially evident in our urban institutions. Most schools watch out for the "honors" kids, but what about the bright youngster who performed poorly in seventh grade and is consequently a junior in the "general" track? Suppose that he has matured and is now ready to use his intelligence. Where shall he go? What should he do? Or what about the student with exceptional mathematical skills but weak verbal aptitude—to which track is she assigned? A student cannot continue to function on a path where he or she does not fit.

What is really stupefying is seeing secondary schools installing brand-new tracking systems to accommodate the increased academic course requirements of *public* colleges and universities. One high school now requires *all* its "college prep" students to take four years of preparatory English, four years of preparatory math, three years laboratory sciences, three years of social studies, and two to four years of foreign language *just to graduate*. It's as if there were no collegiate institutions that would settle for a bit less. It must be disheartening for an average eighth grader to look down the long line and know that, if he wants to go to college at all, he'll have to push a ball-bearing cart down a physics lab table in his senior year.

(Interestingly, we see a mutation of the tracking concept at the collegiate level in the "pre" form—prelaw, premed, etc. Young people acquire the mistaken notion that to enter medical school, one has to be accepted into a "premed" program.)

It can be more convenient for a school system to set up a tracking system, to be sure. Many more labor-hours are needed to monitor students continually and place them in proper subject levels, and some districts are hard-pressed to find sufficient staff and funds. But the question remains: What programming modifications should be made for the education of our young people?

To solve their programming problems, some secondary schools offer preparatory and honors *courses*, not preparatory and honors *tracks*. In recognition of the fact that numerous "honors types" are not both verbally and mathematically talented, counselors in these schools might encourage certain of their counselees to pursue honors math, but carry regular preparatory English, or vice versa. Also, in these settings counselors readily acknowledge that not all students "come alive" simultaneously. Consequently, the counselors can *genuinely* work with individual differences!

It must be noted, however, that these same schools are not so liberal as to make the election of an honors course a carte blanche affair. A potential student might be required to meet certain minimal criteria: standardized test scores and/or grades in prerequisite courses.

What we have here, then, in contrast to general tracking, is a system with open doors and well-greased pathways that enables students to move readily in or out, up or down, guided by *caring* counselors who *fully encourage* students to reach for their potential.

Oh, there is much to be said for long-range planning, which could all too easily lead to general tracking. But there is much to be said for day-at-a-time planning as well. Day-at-a-time counselors are often the "options open" ones. They are often creative, energetic, proactive types—not afraid to make a few waves. Helping young people realign their paths can be a crusade with some of these professionals, even if it means expending an inordinate amount of time to do so.

You *do* have a role here! As your counselees proceed from semester to semester, grade to grade, you could be continually on the lookout for promising "diamonds in the rough," so to speak, and welcome them to the fold of the collegebound. If there has to be a race, then young people should have the opportunity of *entering it at any point on the course*! And, as counseling professionals, if we do not heighten our efforts to help make this more of a reality, increasing numbers of young people will be "left at the gate."

FRESHMAN YEAR

"Being a freshman" no longer has the novelty that it used to have—and it sometimes doesn't mean "going to the high school." If precollege planning starts at the middle/junior high levels, young people don't *begin* their programs; they *continue* them. And if there is a junior high (grades 7 through 9) and senior high (10 through 12) set-up, the youngsters even stay in the same building!

(Therefore, there are two kinds of freshmen: those in a 9–12 high school, who have made a transition, but are at the bottom of the social ladder, and those in a 7–9 situation, who are on the top of the heap, but who have not yet "moved up." There are definite sociological differences!)

Whenever movement occurs, however, the facility will be different, and, more important, the counselor will be different. Educational continuity assumes the existence of careful, accurate communication, both on the programs available in the school district and on the status of the individual himself. An important objective of that first year will be your getting to know your students and helping them to know you.

While the change might cause some youngsters to experience adjustment problems, the official "moving up" of a class seems to minimize the difficulties. But students who have to "go it alone" need more attention.

Keeping an Eye on That New Transfer Student

Naturally, students can transfer to a school at most any point in time. And transferring schools can be an unsettling experience. To keep a more watchful eye on her new students, counselor Judith Rosenthal at East Brunswick High School in New Jersey designed the worksheet shown in Figure 7-1, which the department later adopted.

The Pass/Fail Option

In those secondary schools where pass/fail programs exist, counselors find that effective advising on the option can become rather sophisticated. Because some parents regard this special option as nothing more than a "cop out," communication with them must be precise with regard to the pros and cons of a pass/fail program. You can be instrumental in properly interpreting this particular option to your publics.

Some high schools allow little or no time for such reflection; others are most generous in their declaration deadlines. A school usually adopts a pass/fail option commencing with the freshman level, and for one or more of the following reasons:

1. To encourage its students to "stretch" academically by pursuing challenging work that they might not otherwise pursue, for example, a semester of calculus or the fourth year of a foreign language.
2. To encourage its students to take courses outside of their strength areas.
3. To relieve grade pressures in certain nonacademic and/or skills courses.

Switching to pass/fail is not always an easy decision for many youngsters. Case in point: student is doing poorly in Spanish III. Is it better for him to switch to pass/fail or to drop the course? In other words, is it better to show the course on the transcript even if it has been taken on a p/f basis or not to show it at all? Many counselors *and* college admission officials would agree that it is better to show the course.

Counselors need to advise their counselees carefully about the p/f option with respect to college admission requirements. Many colleges don't get "hyper" over the taking of one pass/fail course yearly. However, they don't appreciate a student taking a college preparatory foundation course on a p/f basis. Nor are they too happy when a student, intending to major in mathematics, takes some of her upper-level math work p/f.

Some colleges and universities permit their own students to take a certain

EAST BRUNSWICK HIGH SCHOOL
GUIDANCE DEPARTMENT

Date ______________

Dear ______________________________

I am following up on the placement level and performance of __________, the new transfer student that I recently placed in your class. Would you please circle the most accurate response to the following questions:

1. Subject-Level Placement

   Appropriate   Not Appropriate
   Too easy   Too difficult

2. Interaction with Classmates

   Excellent   Good   Poor

3. Approximate Average to Date

   A   B   C   D   F

4. General Attitude and Behavior

   Excellent   Good   Poor

5. Please Feel Free to Add Any Other Appropriate Comments

Thank you for your time. Please return this form to the Guidance Office.

Sincerely,

Counselor

Figure 7-1

amount of course work pass/fail. Therefore, the high school pass/fail option affords your counselees the opportunity to have an early experience with this kind of program.

FRESHMAN YEAR ACTIVITIES

Some specific activities that can be incorporated into a college counseling curriculum that are well suited to the freshman level are:

1. Conducting a family meeting at midyear at which you explore adjustment problems associated with the new high school setting, respond to questions on the curriculum, clarify the consequences of eventually selecting particular coursework, advise on study skill habits, and *generally* orient parents as to college admission requirements.
2. Familiarizing freshmen with the facilities and materials contained in a College and Career Center and providing an opportunity for *all* students to have a hands-on experience, however brief, with available computer software directed at college/career planning.

SOPHOMORE YEAR

As your department moves toward establishing a college counseling curriculum, consider including activities that speak to the issue of nontraditional careers. The fall of the sophomore year is an ideal occasion to present such programs. At this point many young women have not made a final decision on the pursuit of higher mathematics and advanced science subjects. Many young men have not considered nursing or professional dance or elementary education. Putting together a panel of successful professionals and nonprofessionals who are currently engaged in nontraditional occupations—role models—is an excellent way to go with it. Sophomores are sufficiently mature to benefit from a series of presentations on this topic.

Numerous studies seem to indicate that parents are the chief determiners of their children's career selections. Yes, parents—especially fathers—are most influential in career development, with this influence being felt as early as preschool and continuing through high school.

Both counselors and parents can be great encouragers, but, regrettably, both can also be great discouragers. Researchers cite that one reason for not finding more girls sitting at computer terminals is that fathers may not be giving their daughters the same amount of encouragement with the family Apple as they give their sons.

Society looks to you to help turn things around. But to be of effective assistance, you need to (1) sensitize yourself to the many factors which prevent young women and men from entering nontraditional careers and (2) familiarize yourself with intervention techniques potentially useful in helping counselees surmount career barriers. "Youth and Nontraditional Careers" is a fine topic for an in-service workshop.

SOPHOMORE YEAR ACTIVITIES

Here are additional activities that can be incorporated into a college counseling curriculum:

1. Use small groups to discuss a variety of college selection characteristics and have students evaluate each one from their own perspectives. This activity

is seldom employed in secondary schools. The positive consequence is a better understanding of the options available, which results in more meaningful use of publication materials and computer software, and an improvement in the quality of time spent with counselors.

2. Students accelerated in mathematics (geometry taken prior to tenth grade) should take a sophomore PSAT. If nothing else, it will serve as a practice shot for the junior year PSAT/NMSQT program.

JUNIOR/SENIOR YEARS

The relative freedom of college can pose great difficulties for a youngster who has spent his secondary school years buttoned up to the neck with regulations. Young people need to stand on their own feet, to test their own judgments. The junior and senior years can offer opportunities for "practice shots," as students try to enhance their self-determination skills in preparation for collegiate life. School administrators can encourage students to take ever-increasing charge of their lives by extending such privileges as going out to lunch, having a "senior park," and using honor passes. Counselors can help in decision making by working with their counselees to choose appropriate courses, enhance extracurricular participation, and assume personal responsibility. And if some young people happen to fall on their faces, at least Mom and Dad and school personnel are around, during these years, to help cushion the fall—and to show them a way to get up.

JUNIOR/SENIOR ACTIVITIES

Here are some specific activities that can be incorporated into a college counseling curriculum and that are well suited to the junior and senior levels:

1. These are pivotal years for students with regard to academic performance. Therefore, plenty of one-on-one academic counseling is called for within this time frame.
2. It is essential that any junior student even vaguely interested in attending college take the October PSAT. Counseling departments need to have proactive mechanisms in place to ensure that as many juniors as possible sit for this important examination.
3. Publish and distribute a college information and planning booklet. It is imperative that this particular publication is (a) attractively formatted; (b) updated annually; (c) placed in the hands of juniors at *midyear* in a group session, where the importance of the piece can be emphasized; and (d) promulgated at all subsequent student and parent conferences as a significant prime source of college planning information.
4. Enlist the cooperation of a subject area department (such as English) to enable you to visit classes for the purpose of orienting students to basic col-

lege admission topics. The completion of such a program can take a department some time and is best accomplished during the winter months.

5. Present an evening orientation program during the winter months for junior parents. Content material should be similar to that presented to junior students. A midyear meeting, as opposed to the more common springtime one, permits families to do a certain amount of long-range planning with such items as achievement testing and financial considerations.
6. *All* college-bound juniors should take either a May or June SAT. May is certainly more appropriate for those who plan to take one or more Achievements. (Students generally don't complete their coursework until mid-June.) Furthermore, the May date offers you the possibility of doing some further counseling prior to your students departing for summer vacations. As with the junior PSAT program, a counseling department might have to "beat the bushes" to ensure that all its college-bound juniors take a spring SAT.
7. Spring of the junior year is a great time for conducting small-group "special topic" sessions. Such topics as application completion, essay writing, and athletic eligibility lend themselves well to the formation and conduct of groups.
8. Put on hold until September of the senior year orientation programs that relate to office procedures and the college admission process. Students tend to forget procedural material if it is presented to them too early (spring of the junior year). (One department takes over senior gym classes in September and presents a tightly scripted program that covers such essentials as how to order a transcript and how to handle teacher recommendations.)
9. Late September is a good point at which to hold a final parent meeting. You might want to devote a small portion of the program to the discussion of procedural matters and then turn the meeting into an open forum so that you can respond to questions. You've been talking "at" them for the past several years, including urging them to engage in early research and planning. Now give them plenty of time to raise and have questions answered. And with proper encouragement they *will* ask questions.

A FINAL WORD

Tight ships do sail better! And having a tight ship means that you have a sound structure, a well-charted course, and a commanding knowledge of the ship's direction. This tightness ensures a precollege counseling program that effectively spans many grade levels.

A well-charted course comes from a well-written college counseling curriculum. Such a document will help keep your ship from being inadvertently (or otherwise) blown off course by your publics.

Unfortunately, in some locales, the publics *are* trying to run the show. It's as if college planning were a free-for-all, where anyone takes the ball and runs with it.

Not so! *School counselors must do the quarterbacking*! The publics — especially the parents—should be more empowered, but *sensibly* so. You should give parents the same treatment that you give to students: continual support that emanates from *proper direction*.

SUGGESTED READINGS

ELKIND, DAVID. 1981. *The Hurried Child*. Reading, MA: Addison-Wesley. Takes a hard look at children and stress. The author examines the unusual pressures society has brought upon its children and offers insights as to how to deal effectively with them.

POWELL, A., E. FARRAR, AND D. COHEN. 1985. *The Shopping Mall High School*. Boston: Houghton-Mifflin. The report shows that by offering a wide array of subject matter possibilities, little attempt is made to engage students in serious learning; therefore, few opportunities are presented for high-quality education.

"Sex & Ethnic Differences in Middle School Mathematics, Science, and Computer Science: What Do We Know?" Contact: Elaine Guennel, 10 R, Educational Testing Service, Princeton, NJ. A 300-page report that reviews more than 400 studies concerning the participation and performance in these fields by girls and minority students in grades 4 through 8. Also described are several programs designed to help heighten middle schoolers' awareness and interest in technical fields and to develop their competence and self-confidence.

UTTERBACK, ANN, AND SHIRLEY LEVIN. 1985. *Summer on Campus*. Washington, DC: Transemantics, Inc., 1601 Connecticut Avenue N.W. A handy reference for working with those of your students who might be interested in summer academic programs on college campuses.

Chapter 8

Report Forms, Transcripts, and Profiles

They can come in salmon, aqua, chartreuse, or coffee. No, not men's spring sweaters—secondary school report forms, in single sheets, four-page openers, or fancy six-page fold-outs. It doesn't matter whether they are entitled "high school reports," "secondary school reports," or "school profile questionnaires," they are virtually the same: paper on which you must shade, blip, check, "x," and circle.

COPING WITH THE SECONDARY SCHOOL REPORT

So there you sit on Monday morning, picking up where you had left off on Friday afternoon. You draw a breath, reach for your pen, pencil, and crayons, and settle down to work. As you maneuver through the stack, you find yourself trying to figure out whether Tufts' "exceptional" is the same as Washington University's "enthusiastically" or Cornell's "poor" is as bad as Johns Hopkins' "below average."

But the real test of your mettle, memory, and maturity is in the general ratings section, where you are asked on a series of items to determine whether or not Suzie Smith is "one of the top few I have ever encountered in my career." My, oh my, what a challenge! No real problem for the practitioner who has only been in the business two years, but how about those of us who have been at this game for a long 24? Not even the best graduate course prepared us for such a formidable exercise. One counselor, who has worked in four different schools, keeps his 14 "top few" in front of him at all times. Yes, there they are, up on his bulletin board in flashing lights, for all the world to see and honor.

Not only do the colleges except you to cope with this rather bewildering and precise task, but they expect you to give it a great deal of serious thought. It's one thing to rate a counselee's academic promise numerically, but quite another to rate his sense of humor to the top 2 percent of the class, isn't it? Kudos to schools like Union College in New York, though, who now make the completion of this section optional: "Item 3 is optional, and you may wish to complete all, part, or none of it."

"The Information You Provide Is Confidential"

Is it? To what extent? Note well that there are differing interpretations of Public Law 93: The Family Educational Rights and Privacy Act of 1974 (Buckley Amendment). At almost all colleges and universities, your comments are held in strict confidence during the decision-making process. At least that's what the "warning labels" say on secondary school report forms. For example, Cornell University: "To the Secondary School College Adviser: The information you provide is confidential."

For sake of argument, let us assume that all collegiate institutions do indeed handle counselor comments in a most confidential manner. Now the question is: What happens to these comments once their classes have been formed:

At Cornell:

> After the selection process we will destroy all subjective evaluations of students who enroll in the university. We will keep only records of course marks, examinations, and standardized tests.

At Oberlin College:

> . . . your comments will be destroyed after the admission decision has been reached.

At American University:

> I understand that, under the provisions of the Family Education Rights and Privacy Act of 1974, a student has access to letters of reference and materials relating to admission to the American University when the student is admitted and enrolls, and the admission material become a part of the official university record. I also understand that this "Secondary School Report" will become part of the official university record.
>
> ____________________ ____________
> (Signature) (Date)

As you can see, American University not only warns you, but asks you to sign off as well. Dickinson College doesn't need your signature. It believes it has the Buckley Amendment "nailed down":

At Dickinson College:

> Under the terms of the Buckley Amendment, this report is *not* defined as a permanent record. Therefore it will not be transferred to the college registrar if the applicant is accepted and matriculates at Dickinson College.

At Bowdoin College (as with American University, your comments will be accessible to your matriculated counselees, but there is a most interesting twist in the Bowdoin statement):

> We feel you should be apprised of this so that you will understand your comments are essential not only to our selection process, but also as an aid to our Dean of Students in helping your advisee adjust to Bowdoin.

How about that? That should tell you something about the worth ascribed by Bowdoin to the school counselor recommendation. Does it mean that the more pertinent your piece is, the more valuable it is to Bowdoin?

What Does This All Mean to You?

It probably doesn't mean a great deal if you counsel in a school where students and/or parents have considerable input into the writing of the counselor recommendation—even better, where students and parents see the finished copy prior to mailing. But it *will* be meaningful if you write confidentially. Unfortunately, there are those counselors who "hide behind" the Buckley Amendment and consequently produce rather bland pieces of writing. If it is only *matriculated* students who have access to counselor comments—then, why all the fuss? Furthermore, informal studies of colleges and universities conducted by the authors and others indicate that very few, if any, collegians ever try to find out what was written about them.

Of course there is the never-ending question of what and how much a counselor should divulge about his or her counselee. At the same time, it's important to understand that a college would like to see a human being presented, complete with strengths and limitations. Certainly divulging something is far better than divulging nothing. This topic is further explored in Chapter 10.

Simmons Facilitates Communications

Department policy in some schools dictates that students submit *all* admission materials, including applications, checks, and teacher recommendations through the department. The reasons for this procedure include the feeling that applications should be checked for completeness and accuracy and the concern that materials might get lost if mailed separately. These departments believe that such a procedure better serves their senior applicants.

Other departments regard that kind of procedure in another way: they feel that it creates unnecessary paper pushing for both counselors and support staff, runs the risk of losing bank checks, and is yet another example of the excessive holding of young peoples' hands. In these schools, students are responsible for sending out their own applications and teacher recommendations. In other words, if there is *nothing* on the actual application that the counselor has to sign or complete, the student assumes the responsibility for submitting it.

Simmons College in Massachusetts is but one of the many institutions that don't mind if the applicant submits the application on his own. It asks a question that might appear to be inconsequential to some counselors: "Is the application being submitted by the school or by the candidate?" This is a question that more colleges should adopt. It can be a checkpoint for both sending and receiving parties: a method by which a college can be on the lookout for the application if being submitted separately by the student and a final check for the school counselor that all materials had been properly disposed of. Could the inclusion of the question by Simmons have anything to do with the college's perception that young people should become increasingly more self-directed?

Two thoughts:

- Colleges don't look kindly on counselors who give high marks on the objective assessment portion of the report form and then write lukewarm recommendations.
- The common application folk make the job a bit easier with their standardized form. But a pox on those counselors who shortcut by completing and then photocopying the entire form, thereby rating their counselee the same for Colby as for Colby-Sawyer, for Washington College as for Washington University.

TO ENDORSE OR NOT TO ENDORSE

The American School Counselor Association (ASCA) defines the endorsement section of college application materials as that portion of the application that asks a counselor to "recommend," "not recommend," or "recommend conditionally" a student to be accepted to a postsecondary institution. In its 1974 position statement (reaffirmed in 1980), *The School Counselor and the Endorsement Section of the College Application*, ASCA directs counselors *not* to complete endorsement sections. ASCA takes the position that secondary schools furnish a sufficient amount of objective data to postsecondary institutions to enable them to make an informed decision without having the secondary school counselor make a specific recommendation for admittance. A counselor is rarely—if ever—knowledgeable about the particulars of the pool of applicants with whom one of her counselees will compete. Neither is the counselor familiar with the explicit needs of a postsecondary institution to round out its student body.

Further, ASCA believes that forcing such a recommendation would work to the detriment of the counselor/counselee relationship. In some cases, a specific endorsement causes parents and students to credit the school counselor with more influence than she does indeed have in the whole admission process.

It is important to understand that the ASCA position statement is in no way intended to discourage or prohibit counselors from writing their usual letters of recommendation. There is considerable merit in ASCA's position on endorsement, however.

MAKING THE TRANSCRIPT MAKE SENSE

> Could counselors stress to their school districts the importance of *legible* transcripts? So many are difficult to read; and, consequently, application reviewers become frustrated. Also, it would be great if counselors could provide us with descriptions and/or titles of "generic" courses, i.e. Math II, so that we would not have to guess or telephone the high school.
>
> — An admission director

What do you think of this high school's listing of ninth-grade courses: FASH SERV 1, SCHOOL CIT, HIS IND ST, ORIENT HC, MTHSEQ 1A, and ERTHSCI AC?

We can readily guess that the last subject is EARTH SCIENCE (one wonders why the school couldn't have simply added an A). However, what the AC stands for is anybody's guess. The ORIENT HC is obviously HISTORY & CULTURE of the ORIENT . . . or is it ORIENTAL HORTICULTURE? Whatever—colleges *and* secondary schools do go "bonkers" in trying to decipher certain transcripts. A few admission offices have actually put together "survival" manuals which are kept close at hand to deal with this needless problem.

The fact that a high school would place gibberish on a student record is nothing more than gross insensitivity, not only toward colleges and others that receive such information, but also toward their own students—students who don't need the hassle of a college admission officer misinterpreting the submitted document or of a new secondary school placing them in the wrong course level.

High schools can still be seen listing their college preparatory mathematics courses as Math I, II, III, and IV. These schools should be calling their courses what they are: algebra, geometry, calculus, and so on. If this were uniformly done, perhaps a school like Penn State wouldn't have to ask whether or not an applicant had ever taken a semester of trigonometry. It is not being suggested that high schools utilize an official format, but a great deal more standardization is certainly in order.

Another area about which secondary schools might come to an agreement is in their placing on the transcript *all* the basic statistical information normally asked for on the school report form. The school report could then be abridged, avoiding duplication of effort.

Notice that virtually all these statistical data are neatly and clearly contained in the top portion of the transcript pictured in Figure 8-1.

EAST BRUNSWICK HIGH SCHOOL
Cranbury Road
East Brunswick, New Jersey 08816
(201) 257-8300

East Brunswick Board of Education
OFFICIAL TRANSCRIPT

SCHOOL INFORMATION	SCHOOL ACCREDITED BY 1. STATE OF NEW JERSEY 2. MIDDLE STATES ASSOC.	PASSING MARK D OR P	ENROLLMENT IN GRADES 9-12	PUBLIC SCHOOL	PERCENT OF GRADUATES ENTERING COLLEGE 4 Year College %	2 Yr. or Other College %

STUDENT INFORMATION

STUDENT NUMBER	STUDENT NAME	HOME ADDRESS	CITY	STATE	ZIP

PARENT OR GUARDIAN	DATE OF BIRTH	SEX	WITHDREW	WAS OR WILL BE GRADUATED	PREVIOUS SECONDARY SCHOOL ATTENDED (IF ANY)	DATE LEFT

RANK IN CLASS
BASED ON SEMESTER IS EXACTLY %ILE IN A RANKED CLASS OF
CUM GPA
ALL SUBJECTS GIVEN CREDIT, ALL STUDENTS RANKED, HON/AP COURSES WEIGHTED

TESTS

SAT TEST DATE	SAT VERBAL	SAT MATH	READ	SUB SCORES VOC.	TSWE	ACH. TEST DATE	ACH. 1	ACH. 2	ACH. 3	ACT TEST DATE	ENG	MATH	SOCS	NSCI	COMP

OUTSTANDING ACTIVITIES HONORS, AWARDS

CLASS RECORD

YEAR	SUBJECT	COM CODE	MID TERM	FINAL GRADE	CREDITS	YEAR	SUBJECT	COM CODE	MID TERM	FINAL GRADE	CREDITS

ATTENDANCE SUMMARY

GRADE	YEAR	TOTAL DAYS ABSENT	TOTAL CREDITS

COMMENT CODES

ACC: ACCELERATED
AP: ADVANCE PLACEMENT
AT: ACADEMICALLY TALENTED
HON: HONORS
LAB: LABORATORY SCIENCE
SS: SUMMER SCHOOL
*: SEMESTER COURSE

DATE

SIGNATURE

TITLE

Figure 8-1

TOWARD IMPROVED SCHOOL PROFILES

It is difficult to improve on something you don't have, and fully one-third of the nation's secondary schools have no profiles. This is an incredible percentage, considering that all a school has to do is to fill in and publish two sides of an 8½″ × 11″ piece of paper—yes, a one-page affair that could truly make a difference in the lives of college-bound students. (Colleges and universities report that a secondary school's failure to submit such a document can be disadvantageous to its applicants. It is also a reflection on the proactivity of the counseling departments of these schools, since it is usually the counseling departments that influence and control such projects.)

It is equally disconcerting to hear that at some schools, published profiles are sent out at the mercy of the individual counselor. A New England university reports that in more than a few secondary schools, where counselors do most or all of the transcript processing, some counselors will include the profile and some will not. With such inconsistency, you can't help but wonder wherein lies the supervision. This is, of course, but one more reason for having a sufficient number of transcript clerks or secretaries, who are the last to handle student records and can see to it that profiles are tucked into *all* envelopes.

The profile is to the secondary school what the nonacademic record is to the college applicant: both are indispensable documents that provide serviceable information to the user—provided, that is, that the contained material is presented in a concise, factual, and lucid manner.

Why a Profile?

There are many more arguments for having a profile than just the handing of one to a college representative so that he can bone up on the school prior to his next visit.

Profiles can be:

- A fine communication vehicle for keeping admission folk on base with such things as new courses, policies, and procedures. College representatives need to remember that secondary schools *do* change, and they should be alert for such change. Change can and should be reflected in a frequently updated profile.
- Of considerable assistance to *all* admission officials in correctly interpreting student transcripts. And they're of particular benefit to those admission committee readers who never visit schools, are unfamiliar with individual school academic programs and student bodies, and/or lack a sense of individual school and community settings.
- An excellent resource aid for the rookie admission counselor. The staffing of a college admission office is like a revolving door: there is constant turnover in personnel. Your "well-known" school may not always be that well

known to an unending number of new (mostly young and inexperienced) admission officials. Hence the continual need for your school to publish a quality profile piece.

- A means of giving admission officers a real feel for the academic rigor of a school through the examination of such statistical information as mean or distributed SAT/ACT scores, advanced placement testing results, and class rank and/or grade point average data.
- One of the best ways for admission counselors to observe the degree to which the applicant has used the available academic opportunities in her school commensurate with her ability.
- A valuable information device that can be sent from one secondary school to another when a student transfers schools.
- A real time-saver in the reciting of advanced placement courses to people contemplating moving into your community—just drop a copy into the mail to these would-be residents.
- Useful to school district personnel directors to orient potential employees to their schools and communities.

Helpful Guidelines from Two Organizations

While counselors might find difficulties in developing the transcript, they should have a much smaller problem with the school profile. This is due in part to the fact that a 1977 joint committee representing the National Association of College Admission Counselors and the National Association of Secondary School Principals worked for greater consistency, with the publication of their booklet entitled, *Guidelines for Designing a School Profile*. The publication addresses special problems encountered by both school counselors and college admission officials and makes specific recommendations for profile content and layout. The booklet was revised in 1984.

The committee urges secondary schools to make the text of a profile "concise, easy to read, and predictable in content." Additionally, the committee would like to see schools limit the text to the front and back of a single 8½" × 11" piece of paper. Colleges are not especially impressed with fancy foldouts or photos of white-columned buildings with charming cupolas. "Frequently, what is offered as a school profile reads more like a promotional piece from the chamber of commerce or real estate board, into which some school information has been added."

The committee *recommends* seven major headings to entitle the principal sections of your profile, but if you feel that this will prevent you from describing your school adequately, you can arrange headings and subtopics in any manner you wish. Frankly, if everyone were to adopt this seven-heading approach, it would certainly be easier for the profile user to find specific pieces of information.

Copies of this publication are available from the National Association of Secondary School Principals, 1904 Association Drive, Reston, VA 22091.

More Content and Design Considerations

- Black and white is better than nothing at all; a fancy piece in living color is unnecessary.
- Since other personnel in your district are potential users, it might be smart for you to solicit their ideas as to content and design.
- An annual review of contents is a must! A department chair can distribute copies to all counselors at one weekly meeting and ask for updating input at the next one.
- Read your profile with a jaundiced eye. Put yourself in the place of someone who is not at all familiar with your school. Would that person have a clear understanding of your curriculum?
- Listing all the colleges at which students were accepted is a questionable procedure. A few secondary schools even list all colleges to which their students apply. Wow! Many college officials view the inclusion of this extraneous material as pretentious and warn that this material could backfire on the secondary school.
- If your school has an unusual grading system—fine! Just make certain that the mechanism is clearly explicated on the profile.
- It can be most beneficial to colleges for you to describe the criteria your school uses to select its students for honors and advanced placement courses.

Chapter 9

Testing in College Admissions

Scores on tests continue to be a major factor in the admission decisions of some colleges. But you, as a counselor, must not lose sight of the fact that testing is but *one* of *several* input areas in these decisions. Besides, you know that for numerous other colleges, test results have little or no impact.

Researchers at the Carnegie Foundation for the Advancement of Teaching (who helped contribute to Ernest Boyer's *College*) estimate that there are "probably fewer than 50 colleges and universities in the United States today that can be considered highly selective, admitting less than half the students who apply." Most of those schools rely heavily on standardized testing. This is not a new statistic for you. If it is stretched a bit to include all the "most," "highly +," and "highly" selective institutions categorized in the *Comparative Guide to American Colleges*, you arrive at about 100 schools at which admission testing plays a significant role in the selection process. That leaves 2,900 others, one-third of which maintain open-door admission policies. Clearly, the overwhelming majority of collegiate institutions in America base their decisions on quality of coursework pursued, grades received, required essays, and an assortment of nonacademic factors. If testing *is* a factor, it comes in a poor last. So if you are going to lose your head over test scores, think about the number of times it will be an issue.

Of course, all this doesn't really address the problem: colleges *do* require test scores, and students *must* try to put their best foot forward. The effect of these scores on the admission process is beyond the realm of the secondary school.

TESTING UNDER FIRE

The controversy continues to boil as to whether or not admission tests are *fair* as they judge students' potential for collegiate success. The controversy appears to center on three problem areas: (1) the sexual, racial, cultural, and socioeconomic biases of test contents; (2) students who do not test well; and (3) private coaching courses that only affluent families can afford.

The first problem area raises questions that must be addressed by the testing companies themselves and the students and colleges whom they serve. If you or your counselees feel that they are being discriminated against, some action can be taken, through the courts if necessary.

Two questions come to mind with respect to the second area. First: Is "doesn't test well" a rationalization for "doesn't do as well as we want him/her to"? Second: Is *coaching* supposed to benefit those who experience problems with standardized testing?

The Scholastic Aptitude Test has especially come under attack. Defenders of this instrument are quick to state that today's students have more opportunities than ever to become better prepared to take the SAT: they cite growth in the number of tutoring programs and the easy availability of "how to score high" guides and computer software packages to improve test-taking skills.

And now we have area number three. The SAT defenders overlook the fact that as affluent 17-year-olds march off to take $500 weekend coaching courses, they leave their less affluent peers in the dust. And students *are* flocking by the tens of thousands to coaching courses. Why have these courses become increasingly popular? Because there has been an increased interest in the "most" and "highly" selectives (which might have something to do with Mom and Dad wanting to get the most for their very expensive tuition dollars), and students hope for high scores and acceptance into the "best" institutions.

Like other questions of equal opportunity, the "fairness" of coaching needs to be dealt with in each setting, but a bigger dilemma arises: What is testing and/or coaching doing to today's student? Among many other things, it could well be automatically biasing the SAT by providing a very specific group of youngsters a better opportunity to improve their scores—a group already in most instances receiving a challenging education.

Use and Abuse

In an article in the May 1987 NACAC *Bulletin* entitled, "SAT Scores: Use and Abuse," Eleanor Barron (director of college counseling at the Webb School, Knoxville, Tennessee) writes, "One counselor in a northeastern school reported that all of her students took two to three SAT preparation courses because the anxiety level for the whole school was so great. She told of the excessive crying, throwing up, and cheating that occur right around SAT test dates, and she noted the amount of counseling time she devotes to the testing process and fallout."

Can you believe that? You can't help but wonder how the educators in some schools have allowed things to get so out of hand. Have they been reminding their students, among other things, that the excessive taking of SAT prep courses and the SAT itself (more than three times) *can* backfire on an applicant because it can send a negative "personality" message to a college?

In the same article, Barron expresses concern that students will become so discouraged with continually rising testing medians that they will give up altogether on the very competitive colleges. It could happen, but if it does, *you* have a definite role to play:

1. Have a warm heart-to-heart with your counselee and *together* agree that, since the whole thing has the elements of a game of chance, they *must* be one of the players—they *should* apply.
2. Monitor your students closely to ensure that they have distributed their choices across *three* levels of selectivity: reach, target, and safety (that will be discussed in Chapter 16). If they don't stretch, they won't grow.

THE "OPTIONAL" SAT POLICY

Four selective colleges in the East (Bates and Bowdoin in Maine, Middlebury in Vermont, and Union in New York) have made the SAT an optional criterion for admission. These schools have done so for several reasons, including:

1. As an indicator of collegiate success, the SAT is no better than a series of achievement tests.
2. The SAT can't escape cultural, racial, sexual, and socioeconomic biases.
3. Entirely too much emotionalism is connected to the admission process by students and parents, especially to the testing aspect.
4. Testing hysteria has a negative impact on the school curriculum, as an escalating number of test preparation courses are added to high school curricula. (The SAT is particularly pernicious in its effects on secondary school education, because, in some schools, teachers are encouraged to teach toward the test.)

The Bates Letter

In a summer 1987 letter to secondary school counselors, William Hiss (dean of admissions at Bates College in Maine) states: "We continue to be very pleased with the results of our optional SAT policy. The freshmen entering in September will be the third class with optional SATs, and roughly 25% of these classes have chosen not to have their SATs considered. . . . We discovered when we opened the blind files of non-submitters' scores (intended enrollees are required to submit their SAT scores for research purposes) that they were lower than class averages by an average of about 40 points on both the verbal and the math, but we found that the GPAs earned by the students were not significantly different: both submitters and non-submitters earned a bell curve of GPAs that were within one-tenth of a point of each other."

Figure 9-1 compares the individual policy summaries of the four schools.

As you can see, with the exception of Bowdoin, the schools cited in Figure 9-1 have hardly abandoned admission testing. But what they have done is provide students with sensible options that enable them to present themselves in the best

Bowdoin College

Applicants are not required to submit SAT, Achievements, or ACT results. If submitted, these results will be considered by the Admissions and Student Aid Committee in reaching a decision, but will be treated as secondary importance.

Bates College

If Bates applicants elect not to have their SATs considered, they nevertheless must submit either ACT scores or the scores from three Achievement Tests. One of the Achievements must be English Composition or English Composition with Essay.

Union College

SAT results may be submitted but are not required except for candidates applying to accelerated programs. Three Achievement Tests are required, one of which must be in English Composition. Union will also accept ACT results.

Middlebury College

All applicants must take standardized tests and have scores submitted to the college. Applicants can submit any one of the following:

1. The SAT and three Achievement Tests, including one in English Composition
2. Five Achievement Tests in different subjects, including one in English Composition
3. ACT results

Figure 9-1

possible light. Here, scholastic *achievement*, as reflected in ACT and ACH results, appears to carry at least equal weight with scholastic *ability* in these schools' decision-making process.

Isn't it interesting that many colleges ask their applicants to select one of three essay topics, but do not allow them to select one of three testing possibilities?

Furthermore, what's amusing is that as the "highly selectives" make headlines with their "optional SATs," hundreds of other schools have been engaged in this practice for years. For example, according to the American College Testing Program, some 800 colleges and universities on the East Coast accept either SAT or ACT scores. Fifty other East Coast schools require the ACT.

Hiss continues: "The faculty gave three reasons in voting for optional SATs. First, since SATs and Achievements substantially overlapped each other in predictive capacity, Bates could continue to require Achievements (or ACTs) and make SATs optional without significant loss of ability to predict good academic performance. Second, the faculty wished to send a broad message to American high school students and their families to use their time in more constructive ways than spending 400 hours studying word analogies: to instead take AP Calculus, captain the soccer team, write and produce a play, or work in a soup kitchen downtown. Third, the faculty wanted to attract to Bates applications from rural, blue collar, minority, bilingual and other students generally not helped by standardized testing."

Edward Wall, former dean of admissions at Amherst College, a school that makes a sincere attempt to keep SAT scores in proper perspective, states the following in the pamphlet, "An Inside Look at the Selective Admission Process" (Octameron Associates):

> We have much higher expectations on test results for students who come from educated homes and so-called "advantaged" public schools as well as from some of the better private schools. Tests are always looked at in the light of a student's educational, linguistic, cultural, and socio-economic background. There is no reason to expect someone from an "uneducated" home, with few or no books or periodicals, from a bilingual home where English may be the applicant's second language, or from a home where no English is spoken at all, or from an inferior school with limited facilities or opportunities to do well on these *educationally, linguistically, culturally, and socio-economically biased examinations.*

In her concluding comments, Eleanor Barron asks, "When will the obsession with SATs end?" Some believe when the obsession with gaining admission to "name" schools ends. The authors doubt that this will ever happen. We've been obsessed for the past quarter century and will probably continue to be so. The situation may even further accelerate about the year 2000 when we begin to experience an increase in the college-bound population. But *some* of the nonsense could end if *all* the colleges and universities in the nation would offer testing options. *All college-bound students should be permitted to submit SAT, ACT, or ACH scores.*

An Uneven National Problem?

In the *sample* of states listed in Figure 9-2, note the number of collegiate institutions that accept ACT scores as well as the number that accept *both* ACT and SAT results. The table further reflects the extent of the acceptance problem nationally. It is interesting that most of the schools that honor ACT results also honor SAT data. The reverse is not true. (Information was obtained from the fifteenth edition of Barron's *Profiles of American Colleges.*)

Only those colleges and universities that reported test data to Barron's have been included in the state figures. For example, 78 of Pennsylvania's 90-some collegiate institutions reported test information to Barron's. Twenty-five of these institutions reported ACT data. It would appear that 25 Pennsylvania schools accept ACT results. Notice that 23 of the 25 accept scores from both testing programs.

A REVISED ACT ASSESSMENT

After nearly thirty years, the American College Testing Program (ACT) underwent a substantial facelifting. The enhancements introduced by the Iowa-based corporation in 1989 are the most comprehensive to date. In a brochure to secondary schools, the company notes that the revision is "responsive to changes that have occurred in the high school curriculum, is sensitive to current expectations about the skills and knowledge students need for success in college, and offers informa-

State	# Schools In State	# Report Test Data	Accept SAT	Accept ACT	Accept Both
California	91	62	59	29	27
Colorado	19	13	8	13	8
Georgia	39	29	28	10	9
Indiana	41	31	29	14	13
Maine	18	13	13	1	1
Massachusetts	65	55	53	6	5
New Jersey	40	30	30	2	2
North Carolina	46	40	40	6	6
Pennsylvania	98	78	76	25	23
Virginia	40	30	30	11	11
Washington	19	11	9	5	3

Figure 9-2

tion needed to address some of the many challenges now facing American education."

Figure 9-3, which compares features of the current SAT and the new ACT, can be a convenient guide for examining the differences between the two testing instruments. It can provide your counselees with the opportunity to make a comparison, and then to select the option that will best support their applications.

CONTENT COMPARISON OF THE ACT AND SAT

	ACT Assessment	**Scholastic Aptitude Test**
Purpose:	Measures classroom achievement in four broad content areas as well as the ability to reason and to apply problem solving skills.	Measures academic aptitude in terms of verbal and numerical reasoning and the ability to recognize standard written English.
Content:		Verbal Antonyms Analogies Sentence completion
	Reading test Arts/literature Social studies/sciences	Reading comprehension in social, political scientific, artistic, philosophical, and literary areas
	English test Usage/mechanics Rhetorical skills	Standard written English Punctuation Grammar Sentence structure Diction and style
	Mathematics test Pre-algebra Elementary algebra Intermediate algebra Coordinate geometry Plane geometry Trigonometry	Mathematics Arithmetic Algebra Geometry Other topics (logic and operations)
	Science reasoning test	

Figure 9-3

SOME AFTERTHOUGHTS

- A flagrant abuse of admission testing can be seen (contrary to the advice of testing corporations) when some colleges and universities, in order to "upgrade" enrollment, utilize strict cutoff scores to screen out applicants. And nothing is left to the imagination; these schools even publicize the fact that they have cutoffs, including higher levels for out-of-staters.
- Society tends to judge the quality of collegiate institutions by the test scores of entering freshmen. This, in turn, has led to an exaggerated view of testing in the selection process. Even though admission officials base their decisions on test results *and* rank in class, the lay public continues to place much heavier emphasis on test results. It erroneously equates test results with "brightness" and rank in class with "performance." Published anthologies with their selectivity indexes help to contribute to this craziness.
- How your counselees view their SAT or ACT scores depends not so much on how well they did as on how well they *think* they did. And how well they think they did is usually not related to the actual scores, but to how these scores stack up against the colleges and universities that interest them. For example, if a student has scores that are average or below for colleges that interest her, she will probably believe that she did not do well. Even if her scores position her in the top 10 percent nationally, yet are below the mean of enrolled freshmen at the schools she is considering, she can become discouraged. An organization that appears to be well tuned in to this pervasive discouragement is the National Organization for Women. NOW maintains that many young women, upset with their scores, settle for less challenging college and career experiences.

COLLEGE BOARD ACHIEVEMENT TESTS

ACH. An acronym for College Board Achievement Tests. It might better stand for A Chronic Headache, for that's what it can give counselors. The three letters rank high on many a counselor's list of potential "image destroyers." More precisely, advising on the ACHs has to be one of the most complex facets of the entire admission process. Here you are not just dealing with across-the-board verbal and mathematical testing. Not by a long shot! With the ACHs, you are expected to advise *properly* on 14 different subject areas, including the impact (scores *can* work against a candidate) the results of these examinations might have on your counselees, each one with his or her differing needs and aspirations. And you better have it all straight—or your image could suffer!

Do these questions and statements sound familiar? "Should I take the Biology test when I finish the course? I'm only a ninth grader and I plan on taking Chemistry and Physics." Or "I only have to take English Composition, but I need three achievements. What do I do?" Or "I don't want to take the French exam because I've only had three years of French." Or "I don't need Achievements, but I'd like to take some anyway to make my record look better. What do you think?"

A Handy Brochure

After years of continually fielding all kinds of questions concerning the College Board's Achievement Testing Program, one high school decided to publish a brochure on this issue. All department counselors had input into the question-type content material. This sort of publication keeps everyone on base on the topic. The brochure's most important pages appear in Figure 9-4.

OFTEN ASKED QUESTIONS

1. What are the Achievement Tests (ACH)?
   The Achievement Tests are part of the College Board's Admissions Testing Program (ATP). The series covers 14 different subject matter areas. All of the tests call for one hour of testing time except the English Composition with Essay, which consists of a twenty minute essay and forty minutes of multiple-choice questions. Approximately 140 of the nation's 3000 colleges and universities require one or more of these tests for admission or placement.
2. Do I need to take these tests?
   If you plan to apply to one of the more selective colleges in the country, the ACH may be required. As you can see in the above paragraph, most colleges and universities do not require them. While you might not have a definite college choice in mind, you probably have some idea as to the type and selectivity of the institutions to which you will ultimately apply.
3. How do I know if the colleges of my choice require these tests?
   The College Handbook, a publication of the College Board, gives a comprehensive description of college entrance test requirements. The brochures and catalogs of various institutions provide even better information about such testing requirements.
4. What are the subject areas the tests cover?
   The 14 different tests fall into five curricular areas: English (English Composition, Literature), Foreign Languages (French, German, Hebrew, Latin, Spanish), History and Social Studies (American History and European History), Mathematics (Math Level I, Math Level II), and Sciences (Biology, Chemistry, Physics).
5. When are the tests given?
   They are administered five times yearly: November, December, January, May, and June. Specific dates are listed in the Registration Bulletin for the SAT and Achievement Tests and in a special informative booklet, Taking the Achievement Tests. Both of these publica-

tions are official guides of the College Board and are available in the Guidance Office.

6. <u>When is the best time to take these tests?</u>
It is best to take an ACH as close to the end of study in a subject matter area as possible—while the material is still fresh in your mind. Please note that the English Composition with Essay, required by a few schools, is only administered in the month of December.

7. <u>How do I sign up?</u>
Use the same application as that for the SAT. The application is located in the center of the <u>Registration Bulletin for the SAT and Achievement Tests</u>. You <u>do not</u> need to indicate which test(s) you will be taking. You can make this decision at the time of testing.

8. <u>How do I know which tests to take?</u>
After you have determined that the college(s) of your choice require the ACH, it is good practice to consult the catalogs of those institutions. College catalogs will provide you with the most reliable information as to what is required. Your teachers, as well as your counselor, can advise you regarding the level of success you might expect to achieve.

9. <u>How will colleges and universities use my test results?</u>
College publications will generally provide this information in the section entitled, "Admissions Requirements." Usually if an institution will accept scores after January, the results are used for placement and/or credit, and not selection purposes.

10. <u>What happens to my scores after I take the ACH?</u>
Your scores are reported to those colleges and universities you designate on your test application. It is important to note, however, that as you request sets of scores, each computerized report lists all previous results, from the most current, back to the first test taken in the ATP program.

Figure 9-4

Some Words of Advice

Although students are urged to take an Achievement Test as close as possible to the completion of a course, they should consider the positives and negatives of such a move before they run off to take such an examination. Consequently, some of your counselees will need counseling on *each and every* test they intend to take. For example, the content of a specific course may not especially prepare students for the eventual taking of the related Achievement Test. Or you and John might be able to forecast that he would perform better on one science examination than another.

Incidentally, this is where achievement results can say something about the caliber of teaching in a given school. At least admission people think that they can. In contrast to their attitude about the Scholastic Aptitude Test, admission officials respect these one-hour examinations because they are able to (1) assess student mastery of specific subject matter, (2) acquire a feel for a school's general academic strength, and (3) gain a sense of a student's personality: extent of motivation, tenacity, industry, and the acceptance of new challenges.

MILEAGE FROM PSATs

Students *can* become discouraged as they face their SAT and ACT scores. The beauty of the Preliminary Scholastic Aptitude Test is that it is a "practice shot" and, for the most part, a private matter among students, parents, and counselors. Yet PSAT results can also act as a discouraging force, with the instrument continuing to be attacked for its development, use, and validity.

But PSATs can be a great encouraging force as well. In contrast to regular standardized testing, the examination is so tied to the college planning process, that when students who are "on the fence" about going to college see themselves as performing better than they thought they would, these students begin to visualize the college experience as more of a reality. This then, is a *big* and *sensible* argument for attempting to get as many students as possible to take the test. The PSAT *can* open doors—can raise levels of self-esteem. Convinced that this is so, some school districts have made the PSAT an integral part of their standardized testing program.

Of course, it would be great if in these districts, boards of education would "spring for" student testing fees. But, for the most part, that kind of happening remains light-years away. Student cost is no deterrent, however, to a school like Halstead High School in Kansas. Halstead believes so strongly in the worth of the PSAT that they even do a bit of arm twisting and bush beating to sign up as many students as possible for the examination.

The Halstead Program

The Halstead Public School District comprises 130 square miles in South-Central Kansas, 25 miles from Wichita, and is a small but powerful institution. It's small in an enrollment of approximately 750 students, K–12, and powerful in its proactivity in encouraging the students to engage in self-assessment activities and to "stretch" academically.

This district has a long, successful history of administering a comprehensive evaluation program that includes giving interest inventories and achievement, scholastic aptitude, and other individualized tests to students in grades K–12. The major thrust of the evaluation program is a positive effort to help students, parents, faculty, and administration understand each student's abilities more completely. This self-understanding then becomes the focal point for educational planning and career development for each youngster.

In a 1987 memorandum to the College Board, Halstead proudly states, "Since 1967, the district has produced: 4 National Merit Finalists, 12 Semi-finalists, and 9 Commended Scholars. A school that typically graduates some 60 seniors *should* be proud of its accomplishments, especially since there are schools larger than Halstead that have never produced a finalist, and surprisingly, schools that don't even administer the PSAT."

The PSAT/NMSQT is an integral part of Halstead's comprehensive program, and approximately 65 percent of sophomore and junior students sit for this examination annually. The procedures employed by the district to maximize the positive effects of the PSAT/NMSQT are as follows:

1. Prior to the opening of school and during the regular staff in-service workshop, past PSAT/NMSQT results are shared with the faculty. Counselors discuss how these results can be best utilized by individual students and faculty members.
2. In late August, the preliminary announcement booklet is mailed to *all* sophomore and junior parents along with a cover letter that highlights enrollment procedures and test-taking advantages.
3. Three weeks before the testing date, all sophomores and juniors who rank in the upper half of their classes and have not yet registered are contacted and further encouraged to do so.
4. One week before testing a group guidance meeting is conducted with all registered students to explore the rationale for taking the test, review test-taking techniques, and answer personal questions.
5. When the school receives the test results, copies of the results are mailed to parents along with a cover letter that contains individualized information relative to the results, a test booklet, a card that lists correct answers, and a personal invitation to meet with the counselor should the parents wish to explore the matter further. (See Figure 9-5. It is shown here with the permission of Dr. Allen D. McCune of Halstead High School.)

ADMISSION TESTING AND THE HANDICAPPED

In a long-standing effort to minimize the effects of handicaps on test performance, the College Board has provided special testing arrangements since 1939. Through a study of some 1,500 disabled students who applied to 121 colleges and universities in 1982–83, Educational Testing Service's research division found no evidence of any negative influences on the admission of handicapped students inadvertently caused by the fact that test scores were labeled "nonstandardized." The study concluded that when it came to the admission of the disabled, it was the applicant's full record that counted.

Halstead High School
520 West Sixth
Halstead, KS 67056
(316) 835-2682

Dear Parents:

Enclosed please find your youngster's PSAT/NMSQT results. Do discuss the results with your son or daughter and retain these materials for future reference.

Individual Score Record

STUDENT NAME	Year	Grade	Verbal	Verbal %ile	Math	Math %ile	Selection	Sel Ind %ile
Dan Smith	86	SO	53	87	64	93	170	92

As you can see, Dan did very well on the test. However, in order to be considered a National Merit Semi-finalist, he will have to score at least in the 97th percentile. I would recommend that he continue to work hard in his classes, and seek extra reading and mathematics experiences between now and next October.

We have found over the years that students improve their performance when they take the SAT or ACT provided they take the time to study their PSAT results, learn to appropriately pace themselves, and follow directions explicitly.

Accordingly, we are sending you a copy of the test, a card listing the correct answers, and an interpretive booklet.

I have scheduled each student who took the test for a personal conference to discuss his or her scores and what they mean. Likewise, I would be happy to meet with you to discuss individual planning for improvement of scores, and answer any questions you might have in regard to this particular program.

Sincerely,

Dr. Allen D. McCune
Counselor

Figure 9-5

Extended Testing Time

Formerly, ETS wanted the untimed testing of the learning disabled to take place on days other than the normal testing dates. ETS has since modified its position on this matter, and extended testing time service for students with learning disabilities is now available twice yearly, with the May and November testing dates. Students who require untimed testing must be accommodated if an established center is open on those dates.

SUGGESTED READINGS

OWEN, DAVID. 1985. *None of the Above*. Boston: Houghton-Mifflin.

WALL, EDWARD B. 1985. *Admission Procedures at the Nation's Most Competitive Colleges*. Alexandria, VA: Octameron Associates. A straightforward and informative pamphlet that covers a lot of territory. Interesting reading!

Chapter 10

Recommendation Writing

In the April 22, 1986, issue of *USA Today*, Boston University Vice President for Enrollment Services, Anthony Pallett remarks, "A well-written counselor recommendation is as rare as a well-written essay. The committee ignores most essays."

Note that Pallett doesn't say that the committee ignores most recommendations. Perhaps he has hope for better writing in the future. More probably, it was left unsaid because Pallett, like many other admission officials, knows full well that counselor recommendations—even poorly written ones—*do* play a potentially important role in determining the acceptance of applicants to colleges and universities, especially to the very selective.

And Pallett is by no means alone in his concern about this issue. Jack Davies, director of admissions at Glassboro State College in New Jersey, believes that one result of the Buckley Amendment is the reluctance of the counselor to give complete written evaluations. "A telephone call is often not enough," says Davies. "If counselors could again find a way to give 'the good and the bad' it would help tremendously in our evaluations. It may not be possible."

The hue and cry among admission officials is that many counselors are not even giving the "good" of it; that is, they don't write positive recommendations that are substantive and complete. As one college official put it, "A generic 'He's a good kid, who should do well in your college' is not enough. Strong anecdotal information is essential!" William Mason, director of admissions at Bowdoin College, Maine, states, "The quality and perceptiveness of your secondary school evaluation is critical at the highly competitive schools, and anything you can do to enhance the sharpness of your recommendations can really make a difference." Another official suggests that counselors *describe* rather than *recommend* an applicant.

There are institutions which, for varying reasons, pay little or no attention to teacher and counselor comments. A few even advertise the fact that such comments are not welcome. The frequent hearing and/or reading of such disinterest can act as a discouraging factor for counselors, resulting in their taking their writing responsibilities less seriously, because *no one* is out there listening.

Of course, nothing could be further from the truth, because you *can* make a difference in the lives of your counselees with any one of some 300 very selective colleges and universities who *are* listening. You can accomplish this by going significantly beyond students' "on paper" credentials.

Harvard-Radcliffe colleges certainly believe that you can do something. In a 1986 report to the nation's secondary schools, their admission office stated, "Counselor and teacher reports make a difference in admission decisions. They are usually the best means we have of judging the school's estimate of a candidate, since most applicants present good grades in a strong program."

The same report speaks to the written quality of some of these recommendations. "Most counselors are attuned to the complex and rather subjective nature of Harvard-Radcliffe admissions. On the other hand, every year after our letters are mailed, we receive calls from counselors and teachers puzzled about the decisions we have made. A quick check of the application may show that the teacher and counselor recommendations did not seem to the Committee to be either complete or supportive. In a competitive admission process, strong scores and records need to be supplemented by carefully evaluative counselor and teacher reports."

What can be read into this statement is the counselor's *underestimation* of the importance of the recommendation, with accompanying underestimation of counselor *power* in the admission process. The key phrase in the foregoing paragraph is "carefully evaluative," which would seem to include such criteria as completeness, accuracy, specificity, and honesty of rendered comments, as well as the extent of candidate support by the counselor.

Brandeis University, among others, states the following on its School Report form: "We welcome information that will help us to differentiate this student from others." They are looking for specificity. Now let's examine the comments (see Figure 10-1) that one counselor sent to Lafayette College.

Is this recommendation specific? Does it differentiate? When Lafayette distributed this particular piece to a seminar group of counselors, they naturally omitted all identifying information. Perhaps that's appropriate, since it appears that anybody's name could be inserted in the spaces.

Recommendation writing is a problem that needs to be taken seriously! Among the several hundred college admission counselors surveyed by the authors, the quality of counselor recommendations was the number one concern.

RE: ______________________________

______________ is an excellent academic student here at ______________ High School, enrolled in a rigorous course of study in which the competition is among the top 60 students in a class of more than 550.

______________ is always well prepared for class and has excellent teacher recommendations.

I am convinced that ______________ will excel in college based on his competitiveness and academic preparation and, therefore, recommend him for college with enthusiasm.

____
Guidance Counselor

Figure 10-1

THE ANATOMY OF A "COMPLETE" RECOMMENDATION

A *complete* recommendation might cover the following categories:

- Academic program
- Academic achievement
- Academic ability
- Personal qualities
- Extracurricular participation
  - In school
  - Out of school

A college's desire that the counselor touch on all or most of these categories is seldom a "do or die" proposition. Some counselors find it important to address all areas. And there is nothing wrong with this approach, provided that the recommendation doesn't become unnecessarily elongated and/or full of redundancies (material that can be found elsewhere in the folder). Other counselors like to focus on two or three categories, selecting those areas that will best support the counselee under discussion. Therefore, these suggested categories are only meant to serve as a rough guide.

Academic Program

Some would argue that describing aspects of a student's academic program, however briefly, is a waste of time. These same individuals probably believe that admission counselors are quite capable of analyzing a transcript and making inferences. On the contrary. There continues to be a considerable turnover in personnel within admission offices, as young and inexperienced counselors enter the field. These novices must deal with thousands of transcripts from thousands of different high schools. Therefore, most admission officials are only too happy to have you point out to them such factors as extraordinary course choice and unusual progression of coursework.

A more appropriate term than "describe" might be "highlight." For example, it is not difficult for an admission counselor, when noting that geometry was taken in the freshman year, to surmise that Algebra I had been carried in the eighth grade. But the same official might wonder why French I was being pursued in the senior year after the student had taken four years of Spanish, or why a student was taking a PSSC Physics course after having taken Project Physics in the previous year. In the one case, the school counselor could point up the fact that his counselee wanted to experience yet another modern language, since he was considering majoring in foreign language in college. In the other instance, the counselor might want to emphasize that because of her great success in Project Physics, this young woman was now contemplating becoming an engineer and therefore wanted to take PSSC as an important preengineering preparation course.

Yes, you can do much to highlight unusual aspects of your counselee's record. You can also provide the admission official with a sense of program quality and strength in relationship to the student's academic ability.

Furthermore, it is vital that you openly discuss any part of a record that could be detrimental to the total package. James Sumner, at Willamette University in Salem, Oregon, believes that when there is an obvious inconsistency in a student's academic record, it should be addressed. "We review transcripts carefully, and when a counselor ignores—or especially glosses over—obvious weaknesses in the record, it completely undermines the reliability of any other comments, including those that are positive."

Academic Achievement/Ability

Shelly Riecke, assistant director of admissions at Brandeis University in Massachusetts, echoes Sumner's feelings and makes two practical suggestions to the same point. The first refers to consistency *within* the student's record: "When writing a recommendation, take a 5-minute look at the student's academic record. Ask yourself, 'Is there anything here that is likely to raise questions?' (Example: A solid record of "A's" and "B's" in honors English courses with a "D" one semester in the junior year.) Do address such issues!" The second refers to a comparison of the record with your recommendation of the student: "When you have completed your work, make certain that there are no glaring inconsistencies between what you have written and what the record shows."

The number of academically capable people who do mediocre or poor work prior to their senior year is staggering. If your counselee falls into this category, take heart—it's not too late: many colleges love to see an "improved" student. Usually, the greater the academic ability, the greater the attraction. *Don't* think that such improvement is obvious to an admission committee. Take a moment to bring the "new" him or her to their attention, *briefly* citing the reason(s) for the past aberrations in the record.

Incidentally, in their evaluation of applicant pools, admission committees have to contend with all kinds of inconsistency, including the one that honors courses can vary in intensity from one school to the next. (Committee members cross their fingers in hopes that within the same school, such courses do not vary much from teacher to teacher.) This is but one of many reasons why colleges find it important to know the particular schools well.

If your school profile does not adequately describe grading policies and procedures or the arrangement of course levels, you might have to "fill in the gaps" in some of your individual commentaries. Considering that one-third of the nation's schools do not even publish profiles, there must be a lot of "gap filling" going on! The absence of such a document is certainly no picnic for admission counselors, who need as accurate a picture as possible of the quality of the coursework pursued.

Personal Qualities

It is with this category, more than with any other, that *the remarks you make need to be anecdoted*. A "B" grade in world history can be easily viewed; admission committees will accept 4-H involvement at face value; but nebulous statements like "strong character and personality" or "has an adventurous spirit" must be documented through exemplification. Without a doubt, this category is the most potentially revealing for admission officers.

The Harvard-Radcliffe report continued: "What is helpful is an explanation of special circumstances that might not be apparent in the credentials, and some estimate of subjective criteria like creativity, motivation, commitment, energy, enthusiasm, and potential for growth."

In short, one or two anecdotal comments about an applicant's personal characteristics can add considerable substance to a recommendation.

Figure 10-2 illustrates how one counselor supported her comments with anecdotal detail. This particular portion of the recommendation speaks to the student's sense of commitment and potential for growth.

The following two recommendations (see Figures 10-3 and 10-4) are from Blair Academy in New Jersey. The first (used with the permission of Richard C. Malley of Blair Academy, Blairstown, NJ) is an open, honest, and colorful piece that addresses the "special circumstances" issue. There is a lot of heart and soul to the work, and one can't help but get the feeling that this counselor knows his

"... This articulate young man was selected by Senator Walton to be a senate page in Washington, D.C. Unfortunately, the selection came on short notice and in October of this, his senior year. John carefully weighed the pluses and minuses of participating in this once-in-a-lifetime opportunity, or staying on here at Marshall and finishing out his final year. Quite frankly, John not only weighed his decision; he agonized over it. He has chosen to remain with us. I believe this fine young man has profited greatly from this decision-making experience, including strengthening his personality through the examination of priorities. John certainly has handled himself well these past few months, as critics have confronted him about his decision."

Figure 10-2

Harold is a square peg, and Blair is a round hole. For three years, we have been trying to get this square peg through our round hole. The result has always been fascinating, sometimes frustrating, but amazingly quite beneficial for both the hole and the peg.

The son of a hard driving and successful financial analyst, Harold moved in with his dad after his parents divorced. In his public school, Harold became extremely independent, disenchanted with the instruction, and quite convinced that he could be successful doing things his way. He didn't have to study to get by in school, so he didn't study. He could usually rally an A on a major test or exam; therefore, a perfectly horrid approach to his education was being reinforced by its obvious success ... Harold was accepted to Blair with the provision that he repeat his sophomore year.

At the end of the fall term, Harold had three grades in the low 60s and one failing grade. His teachers spoke of his tremendous talent and his awful work habits. We responded by placing him on scholastic probation. At the end of the fall term of his senior year, Harold ranked in the top decile of the most competitive class we have had in over a decade. Still his grades do not reflect what he and I know to be his true potential. However, there is simply no question that Harold has made it here, that the edges of his square peg are now slightly rounded, and that the hole is somewhat misshaped.

... At first the faculty and students did not know how to react to Harold.... How do you react to someone who buys and sells old comic books for profit; whose room is a disaster area; and who refuses to do anything by anyone else's schedule? In this respect Harold didn't bend. He founded his own literary magazine, Ground Zero, as an outlet for his own writing, and for generally offbeat writing that wasn't published in our more formal school magazine. His Wednesday evening cookouts to which he would invite a different assortment of students each week became infamous. His sense of humor came through in his dining room announcements, his writings, and his conversations with faculty and students. Through his participation in the Society of Skeptics, a history debate organization, Harold found another important outlet. . . . Harold has also taken an active role in the Model United Nations Conference and the Mock Trial competition for each of his three years at Blair. In sum, while students were at first turned off by Harold three years ago, he has now become one of the most popular and well-liked students on the campus. And he has done this by not being something other than what he is—he has done this by being Harold.

. . . Harold's recent academic success has been long in coming, yet it has not been without serious setback. For example, his failure to turn in a term paper on time last year for an AP American History course earned him a grade of 62 rather than an honor grade. His AP score is a much better measure of what he learned. The lesson was one that Harold needed to learn, and it has benefited him greatly this year. His papers now come in on time!

. . . I am convinced that we have been good for Harold and that he has been good for us. He will be successful in college, and the more intellectually stimulating the environment, the more he will gain and contribute. . . .

Figure 10-3

While it is true that Todd has never been on the honor roll, he has never received any notices of academic warning, either. He has never scored the winning touchdown, or even made the decisive play on our athletic field, but he also has never sat on the bench.

Todd is a genuine contributor who is never part of the problem, but always part of the solution; someone who can be counted on to back up his words with actions. This young man has a penchant for making the most distraught individual lighten up and laugh at himself. Todd's sense of optimism can find the avenue of resolution for what seems to be the most dismal of situations. . . .

Time after time, Todd's teachers indicate that they appreciate his genuinely serious approach: "Todd was a pleasure to teach this year. His sense of humor and positive attitude tend to rub off on those with whom he comes into contact." "Todd contributed a great deal and was a pleasure to have in class." "After his trip to Mexico, Todd returned with added enthusiasm to my Spanish class.". . .

Figure 10-4

counselee well. Furthermore, the counselor sees the use of errors as a way of growing, and the educative process as a developmental one. Note the unusual and attention-getting opening statement, with the author returning to this idea midway through the writing. Note as well the rather extensive use of anecdotal material, including the manner in which the counselor highlights his counselee's performance in AP American History—a description bound to be helpful to any admission counselor.

In examining the first two paragraphs of the next recommendation (used with the permission of Henry Milton of Blair Academy, Blairstown, NJ), note the counselor's worthwhile and judicious use of teacher comments for purposes of illuminating his counselee's personality and adding substance to the piece. The rather dramatic opening statement forecasts what is to come with respect to this young man's level of assertiveness and positive thinking.

Although you might think it is a plus to comment on a candidate's physical appearance, telling what she looks like doesn't say a thing about what she does. Again, James Sumner at Willamette: "Please do away with physical descriptions such as 'handsome,' 'blonde,' 'attractive,' and 'cute.' Since these descriptions occur most often in recommendations for female applicants, they become not only irrelevant, but also sexist."

Extracurricular Participation

Don't sacrifice your recommendation by "laundry listing" a counselee's extracurricular activities, for example, "Harold has been a member of our Literary Society, Math Team, and Computer Club. He has also been on varsity Cross-Country and Winter Track teams."

While listing is not the way to go, there is nothing wrong with *expanding* on a student's extracurricular involvement, especially if it can emphasize "presence" or certain personality traits. In the following example, see how the personal and extracurricular participation categories can be interwoven:

> Biking through Europe and the Canadian Rockies for weeks on end; leaving one's bike and traveling by horseback for four days; snow skiing since the age of 3. All of these activities attest to Adam's adventurous spirit, general determination, and wholesomeness of character.

At times students will underestimate the importance of out-of-school extracurricular participation; they will even overlook significant activity. When you suspect that this is happening, or you simply want to describe an aspect of such involvement, go to it! You are also ensuring that such participation is not overlooked by an admission committee. Here again are two more illustrations of the interweaving of the personal and extracurricular participation categories. In the first example, notice how creatively the counselor opens his recommendation.

> "The game is still not finished," said Aaron. "There are six of us in the tournament, and we're still playing." This persistent young man has been

playing postal chess for years. It is a rather unusual endeavor. But then so is his periodic participation in mini triathalons, where he swims, bikes, and runs.

There he stood, under the lights in a high school gymnasium, doing a benefit performance in karate for the area's handicapped association. He also instructs preschoolers and elementary children in this sport, in cooperation with our local Y.M.C.A. This kind of voluntary participation is understandable in Tom's case, because he is such a giving sort of person.

OTHER USEFUL APPROACHES TO WRITING RECOMMENDATIONS

The following are short excerpts that demonstrate how different counselors have approached and described particular aspects of their counselees' records:

- The issue of achievement versus SAT score

  Christine puts a great deal of effort into her academic work. It is interesting to see that she has consistently done excellent work in English (note the honors program during the sophomore year) in spite of a rather mediocre SAT verbal score.

- Achievement, ability, and the work setting

  Melissa has not only displayed considerable prowess in mathematics here at Towson, but has also utilized this skill outside of the school setting. She has been assisting her father, an associate publisher of a medical magazine, in certain business operations.

- Leadership and ingenuity

  If anyone will "make it" in public relations, Matthew will. He has acquired a certain amount of practical experience in this field. For example, when our local board of education abolished the school's 20-year-old ski club and racing team, Matthew and his father reorganized the club on a nonprofit basis through the auspices of the local public library.

- Support for the learning disabled

  If Emmys were awarded for industry, courage, and dedication in the academics, Steven would win hands down. The going got rough last year, but this very fine, mildly disabled young man held his own quite well. He richly deserves a shot at collegiate study. A proud youngster, he has had to live in the shadow of two academically talented sisters.

- Tying academic program to career choice

. . . a delightful young lady who has pursued a most demanding program of studies, and at one time managed to incorporate three years of engineering drawing into the picture. She thoroughly enjoys drafting, knowing as well that such exposure should be personally beneficial in her search to become an architect.

- Clarifying ranking procedures and scholastic achievement

With Louis, there has been a certain amount of underachievement present. At the same time, this reserved young man doesn't run from challenges. He usually elects the more difficult courses of study, and had we weighted our rank for seniors, as we now do for sophomores, Louis would have ranked higher.

- Anecdoting character and leadership

He may not be an Ansel Adams, but Steven's interest in photography is probably just as intense. It all began when his Dad bought him a camera to take along on a California bicycle trip. Everyone thought his photos were quite good; hence, a continued fascination with this particular art. This year Steve was selected to be the school newspaper's photography editor. Incidentally, this is the same young man who, after accepting the congratulations of our school board for his National Merit Semifinalist achievement, gestured to a large gathering of teachers and stated, "These are the people we should be thanking; these protesting teachers, still without a contract, deserve our considerable support."

- Pulling together the past of a counselee

We are lucky to have David—even if it is for just one year. Was David lucky to have had Louisville for three? How important was it that in Louisville he had had the National Teacher of the Year as his United States history teacher? That he had scored a perfect "5" on his AP American history examination without ever having taken the course? That he and his celebrated history teacher had met with President Reagan in D.C.? That he had developed, and still maintains, a strong Kentuckian identity, and will probably return to live in the blue grass state? For David, very important!

- Highlighting an inconsistency on the transcript

This past academic year, Sandy was thinking of changing from our most difficult Algebra II program to a slower-moving one. But he "hung in." He did so knowing that he would receive a more thorough background in this vital subject. I give this young man a lot of credit for his perseverance, because he doesn't like to receive C grades. But then this is Sandy: willing to go that extra mile, willing to write rough draft after rough draft.

- Supporting an early decision candidate

> Karen is destined to distinguish herself in the field of special education. . . . I encouraged her to submit the enclosed newspaper clippings to you. Karen's transcript, record of involvement in musical and theatrical ventures, wholesome family experiences, and well-shaped career intentions, all attest to the considerable breadth and depth of her personality and character. No sitting in the dormitory for this one: Karen would be out there on the University of Virginia campus doing her share to improve the quality of collegiate life.

WHEN YOU'RE NOT TOO KNOWLEDGEABLE

Even where departments maintain a proactive philosophy, if the counseling load is excessive (more than 200 to 1), odds are that counselors will not know all their counselees well.

There are several approaches you can take in those cases where, for a variety of reasons, you are not too knowledgeable about your counselee. One method is to get together with other people who are involved with the student (teachers, coaches, advisors, etc.) to create what is known as a *composite recommendation*. Ask two or three of the people to give you their impressions in writing. (See Figure 10-5.) Now *you* work it up, using about 50 words from each party.

Everyone involved in this unusual approach must understand that it's the responsibility of the counselor to organize a meaningful final copy and that the material other persons write will not just be copied into the worked-up composite.

Another approach in working with those elusive counselees is to enlist *their* assistance in writing your recommendation. You can encourage—or require—them to submit an autobiography or resume to you. (See Figure 10-6.) One high

TO: Teacher

FROM: Jack Stafford, Counselor

RE: College Recommendation

<u>Anne Strickland</u> is working on her applications for college and gave
(student name)
your name as a resource person for my recommendation. Any comments about her that you feel are appropriate (about 50 words) would be most helpful to me in completing the task.

Thank you!

Figure 10-5

AUTOBIOGRAPHICAL SKETCH

____
(Student Name)

Dear Counselee:

The responsibility of your counselor in preparing the "Secondary School Report" for colleges and universities is to provide a summary of your academic and extracurricular achievement. The counselor also presents some sense of your promise for further personal and intellectual growth. Conveying your "unique" qualities is not an easy task. Therefore, we would appreciate your giving us an honest estimation of yourself, what you have done, and what you have left to do.

Please take the time to think about who you are, and where you're headed. Don't limit your discussion only to what has happened to you in school. Include experiences drawn from any part of your life.

Thank you,

The Counseling Department

1. What are your academic interests?
2. Which courses have you enjoyed the most?
3. Which courses have given you the most difficulty?
4. Which specific courses might you like to study in college?
5. What do you choose to learn, when you can learn on your own? What do your choices show about your interests and the way you like to learn?
6. List the books you have read on your own in the past 12 months.
7. Describe an instance in which an article, book, play, or film has caused you to change your way of thinking.
8. What has been your most stimulating intellectual experience in recent years?

9. Is your high school academic record an accurate measure of your ability and potential? If not, what do you consider the best measure of your potential for success in college work?

10. What circumstances, if any, have interfered with your academic performance?

11. Has any summer experience, work, or study been of significant importance to you? Please describe.

12. Have you traveled or lived in different localities? Where? Comment on any significant travel experience(s).

13. What do you consider your greatest strengths?

14. What do you consider your greatest weaknesses?

15. Is there any other information you would like to share with your counselor so that he or she can make an accurate appraisal of you to colleges and universities?

Figure 10-6

school requires all its college-bound students to do that at the end of the junior year.

ADDITIONAL TIPS IN WRITING YOUR COMMENTS

1. Many professionals, in an attempt to avoid the "fine personality" and "splendid character" cliches, endeavor to compose a thoughtful and purposeful piece. One problem, however, is that some counselors don't realize that quality is better than quantity. There probably isn't an admission person around who wouldn't prefer 200 well-written words—anecdoted, specific, and illuminating—to 400 that are general, flowery, and cliched. Natalie Aharonian, director of admissions at Wellesley College, Massachusetts, remarks, " 'Enlightening' does not have to mean lengthy." Reverend Harry Erdlen, dean of admissions, Villanova University, adds, "A brief, forthright recommendation is much preferred to an exercise in high-flown prose that, when stripped of superlatives, really says little." Remember, a recommendation is not read in a vacuum. It should not carry the entire application.

2. Be alert to the fact that some colleges handle their applicant folders in batches according to secondary schools. Some of these colleges report seeing the same phrases popping up again and again. In other words, they are noticing counselors repeatedly using the same phraseology in describing their counselees.
3. It is helpful if you can write well, but what is more important is that your work is not scribbled, riddled with typo's and spelling errors, written in pencil, or photocopied from your pen copy.
4. Many counselors find it convenient to write one recommendation and then photocopy it for each school to which the student is applying. However, where a college has supplied an official form, you should attach your recommendation to this form, at the same time making certain that you have checked all boxes on the official document. Your checked responses assist colleges and universities to place the applicant in perspective with other students in your school in the given year and in past years.
5. When the recommendation has been typed and photocopied, some counselors will often write a personal note at the bottom in an attempt to "tie" their counselee to the college, or they will write a few extra words on the Secondary School Report form. A good idea! Always mention the college by name, and use *blue* ink, not "Xerox black."
6. Remember that a good statement simply *presents*. Beware of becoming too subjective.
7. Some counselors continue to waste time and effort repeating academic material that can be found elsewhere in the application packet, for example, "Barbara Sue entered our school in her junior year. She had been enrolled in Italian I, Algebra II, World History, English, and Chemistry. Her grade point average for that year was 3.2."
8. Encourage your chairperson to set up an in-service workshop. Sit down for a couple of hours to discuss the whole recommendation process, including a review of departmental policy and procedures. It is most helpful for the group to share each other's recommendations—or peruse samples—and critique these writings for such things as substance, meaningfulness, creativity, and length. Another way to improve skills is to create a hypothetical case, with each counselor writing a recommendation, and then sharing and critiquing all writings. The development of an in-service workshop can indeed pay big dividends both in common understandings and in battery recharging.

THE CHALLENGE

There is no denying that your responsibility for writing a complete and substantive recommendation is in itself a substantial one, considering that institutions like Harvard actually *rate* what you say about your counselee. To quote again from the

Harvard-Radcliffe report: "As each application is read by members of the Committee, the counselor report and the two teachers reports are evaluated and rated on a number scale. The more detailed the reports, the easier it is for admission officers to evaluate the candidate and rate the reports accurately."

SUGGESTED READINGS

BAKER, SHERIDAN. 1972. *The Practical Stylist.* New York: Thomas Crowell Company, eighth printing.

HAYDEN, THOMAS. 1983. *Writing Effective College Recommendations: A Guide for Teachers.* Princeton, NJ: Peterson's Guides, Inc. A fine pamphlet that can be used with teachers in a workshop setting.

STRUNK, WILLIAM, AND E. B. WHITE. 1979. *The Elements of Style.* New York: Macmillan.

Chapter 11

It Can Take More Than You

It certainly can. Effective precollege planning is a team effort—and you should be the captain. You do have a special role in "tying together" the education of your counselees, and postsecondary planning is a critical aspect of a youngster's total educational experience. In your counselor capacity, you are sometimes "caught in the middle," of course, but because you are a promoter of cohesion, the role of coordinator should be a natural one.

THE SCHOOL PRINCIPAL

In Chapter 7, we spoke of the crucial part played by the department chairperson in the design and development of a college counseling curriculum. But for the success of the *total* college counseling effort, it is the school principal or headmaster who is the pivotal figure. It is he or she who sets the tone and molds the environment for such a program—an environment that is favorable to program growth or is at least essentially free from serious impediments to goal attainment.

Ideally, the school principal sees the advancement of a college counseling program as a forward edge in the advancement of the total school program. In this kind of setting you see a "leader" at work, not just an "administrator." So, whether your program is "full speed ahead" or temporarily becalmed, remember that the fate of any college counseling program can be tied to the feelings, attitudes, and bent of the principal.

Knowing this, then, you see how important it is that the building principal play a role in the initial design and development, and subsequent modifications, of any college counseling curriculum.

- Inviting your principal to attend selected department meetings can be a wise maneuver; he or she gains knowledge and appreciation of your special problems and can join in the attempt to solve them.
- A principal needs to sense that you are using your special skills to make her job easier, as she plugs away at running a smooth and efficient operation in the face of monetary restraints and all kinds of public reaction.
- A principal will respect, even admire, you for sensibly promoting your cause. He knows full well that any improvement on your deck will improve the whole ship.

Next to counselors, administrators are probably the most maligned group of educators. ("Coping" has become a popular word with administrators as it has with counselors.) A little empathy on your part for your principal's position and special problems will probably go a long way.

YOUR SECOND MOST IMPORTANT PUBLIC

The "school" people most directly concerned with the welfare of your students are the teachers. Next to your students, then, teachers are your most important public. A teacher with positive feelings about counselors can share these "vibes" with 130 or more students.

Teachers need to be involved in the admission process, too—and it should include more than just recommendation writing. Teachers can (1) talk up the importance of postsecondary education, (2) serve as role models of successful participation in the college experience, (3) set and *maintain* academic standards that are consonant with the beginning levels of higher education, and, where suitable, (4) advise students on options available at particular collegiate institutions.

If you take the initiative to involve teachers further in the admission process, you once again will make a difference in your students' postsecondary futures.

TOWARD BETTER TEACHER RECOMMENDATIONS

One big area of teacher participation is the recommendation process, of course. For those colleges that require them, teacher comments become an integral part of an applicant's folder. Colleges that solicit such information are looking for additional objective assessment material, in order to view the candidate from yet another perspective.

Usually, the same teachers get "hit hard" each year with recommendation requests. (A good English teacher gets no rest!) No different from anyone else, teachers need periodic reinforcement: they would appreciate a message from the counselor or the college that their contributions are indeed important. To help in this matter, a few colleges send thank-you notes to teachers. So should counselors!

Misuse and Abuse

But the opportunity can be misused—or abused. For example, a teacher might devote an inordinate amount of space to discussing a student's extracurricular involvement, which is something normally found elsewhere in the folder. Or an audience of New Jersey counselors was stunned when Brad Quinn, admissions director at Lafayette College, PA, read recommendations written by a science chairman on two different applicants. The two recommendations were identical—only the names had been changed. (Lafayette is one college that handles applicant folders in batches from each high school.)

The following recommendations (see Figures 11-1, 11-2, and 11-3) are examples of "misuse" and "use." There are two problems with Figure 11-1: the introductory paragraph is vague—it could be about anybody—and the second paragraph needlessly "litanizes" the student's extracurricular activities.

In the more specific piece of writing of Figure 11-2, note how the student is aptly shown from two different perspectives.

> This letter is a personal recommendation for a student who is now a senior at Town High School, William Johnson. I have personally known him for the past three years and can speak of his character and academic achievement as excellent. In his sophomore year at the high school, William was a student in my algebra class. He obtained an "A" average for the year and was constantly involved in the classroom situation.
>
> William has also been involved in many different activities outside of the classroom. He is a member of the National Honor Society. As a member he participated in the volleyball marathon for the Lung Association. He is also a member of the ski team and the soccer team. During his sophomore year he earned a varsity letter in soccer. During his junior year he tutored geometry. He also taught science to third and fourth graders in an after-school program. His community activities include ...

Figure 11-1

> ... Scott was a student in my composition class last year. He worked diligently and showed marked improvement throughout the school year. Scott was one of the most self-motivated students in the class. His assignments were always on time and he utilized class time efficiently and productively....
>
> Scott ... works very hard for the student body in his capacity as treasurer to the Student Council. Since I am adviser of the Council this year, I can give a firsthand report of his dedication. He never gripes about meetings, offers solid advice on issues being considered, and thoroughly enjoys the challenges....

Figure 11-2

> Peter was my student last year in the Institute for Political and Legal Education, a class in which we simulate congressional committees and students research, write, and debate contemporary issues.... Peter was a very good student: his written work was thoroughly researched, well-documented, and clearly and logically organized. His oral presentations were also rationally and succinctly stated. For our Model Congress, held annually and attended by over 400 students from New Jersey, Peter wrote an original bill on revamping our income tax structure that was excellent. The bill was simple and to the point, and he backed up his arguments in support of the bill with a most comprehensive and well-written essay....

Figure 11-3

Figure 11-3 is quite explicit about the academic work of the student. Note how the teacher suitably encapsules her course.

Staff Retraining

Is retraining ever in order? Absolutely. One high school felt that the time had come to work with the teaching staff to help them improve the quality of their writing. A workshop was designed and conducted by two of the school's counselors. Another school invited a nearby college admission director to speak to the faculty about recommendation writing. Yet another school developed and distributed guidelines to its entire staff. (See Figure 11-4.)

COUNSELING DEPARTMENT

TO: All Staff

FROM: Robert Evans, Chairperson

RE: Guidelines for Letter of Recommendation

It's that time of year, again, when students may be asking you to write a letter of recommendation. Some of you have asked us for guidelines. Here is one suggested procedure for writing such a student evaluation.

Paragraph 1: Introduce yourself and explain your relationship to the student. The information about yourself should be pertinent to the student's activities with you.

Example: I have had the pleasure of knowing Mary Jones as a student in two different English courses, ________________ and ________________.

Paragraph 2: You should highlight the student's accomplishments in your classroom and the skills she has developed. Limit your involvement to a teacher's insights, and do not mention the importance of the course; rather focus on the student's development. Where possible, cite specific incidents in which he or she has shown evidence of the skills and growth to which you refer.

Example: As a leader in class discussions, Mary has made provocative and insightful comments that have enabled other students to understand the subject matter. In "footnoting," for example, she once questioned the importance of notation when few references are used, and allowed the discussion to turn from a technical discussion to a more intellectual one, in which ethics and honesty became the critical issues.

Paragraph 3: If you can discuss the student in the larger context of the school or local community because you've had firsthand knowledge through observation, this is the place to do it.

Example: Although I've never been the advisor for one of Mary's activities, I've had the occasion to witness her enthusiasm during school events sponsored by her group. I am impressed with her vitality and willingness to participate in extracurricular projects.

Note: Honesty in your assessment of the youngster's ability, achievement, and character is all-important. Honesty can be couched in words that indicate growth and development: "Although she makes careless errors, Mary develops formulas with considerable logical reasoning."

Figure 11-4

The Hayden Pamphlet

For a more detailed treatment of teacher recommendation writing, you might want to turn to a pamphlet by Thomas Hayden, director of college placement, Phillips Exeter Academy, NH, entitled, *Writing Effective College Recommendations: A Guide for Teachers*. The publication, designed especially for secondary school faculty members, instructs on how to deal effectively with the arduous task of writing college recommendations and includes interesting representative letters that provide insight into admission officers' probable interpretation of various statements. The pamphlet can be distributed to your teaching staff—or, better yet, how about a workshop utilizing the Hayden material to assist teachers to write more effectively?

The pamphlet is available through Peterson's Guides, Inc., Princeton, NJ 08540.

Better than Plain Paper

A student will sometimes ask a teacher for a recommendation, but will have no specific form to hand to him. Wanting to be of service, and tiring of hearing teachers ask, "Should I just put it on a plain piece of white paper?" one department designed its own form for teacher use. (See Figure 11-5.)

ADVISING STUDENTS ON SECURING RECOMMENDATIONS

When we speak about recommendations we are talking about support systems. We're trying to show the college that *other people*—besides the applicant himself—think that this person is worthy of admittance to the institution. We do it by weaving together the academic and personal material from different points of view, showing the student in different lights. Most colleges ask for supporting materials. Others simply suggest that they are open to the receipt of such data. Some let it be known that such material is not welcome.

In Search of the Master Writer

Authors who advise young people to seek out teachers who know them well from both inside and outside of the classroom (clubrooms, halls, athletic fields, and streets) might be naively missing a point. Naturally it's great if John's sociology teacher is also his golf coach. But, for better or for worse, the days of the teacher taking in a late afternoon baseball practice, or returning on a Friday evening to watch his top biology student in "Our Town," are all but gone. At least they are in many union-oriented suburban and inner-city schools, where, for a variety of reasons, teachers live by the bell. It's in at 7:30 and out at 2:30.

Therefore, in their effort to get the most appropriate teachers to write their recommendations, students would do well to just concentrate on selecting

STUDENT RECOMMENDATION

To Be Completed by Student:

STUDENT NAME ______________________ GRADUATION YR ________

PROSPECTIVE COLLEGE OR EMPLOYER ______________________

ADDRESS ______________________

To Be Completed by Person Making Recommendation:

COMPLETED BY ______________________

TITLE ______________________ DATE ______________

Please give your candid estimate of the above student's academic or job performance, intellectual promise, and personal qualities. Please provide specific examples where possible.

Figure 11-5

teachers who can write fully and *substantively* from a classroom performance viewpoint. Besides, if a teacher knows a student well, it's quite possible to weave nonacademic factors into the recommendation.

In their request for such information, a few colleges slip in a sentence or two that encourages an instructor to comment on a student's extracurricular participation. Other admission officials disapprove of this tactic. They are only too happy to have a well-written piece that focuses exclusively on life in the classroom and feel that the quality and extent of extracurricular participation can be found elsewhere in the applicant packet. Besides, there is the added danger of a piece of writing becoming too broadly focused. Just as counselors should avoid "litanizing" extracurricular participation in their recommendations, so should teachers.

Tips for Your Counselees:

1. Where possible, your counselees should select teachers who know them well, normally from grades 10 or 11, so that current academic achievement and potential for growth can be discussed intelligently. It is mystifying to

see colleges encouraging recommendations from senior teachers. Students should have their senior teachers for at least a semester before approaching them for a recommendation. Lucky are those students who have had a teacher more than once.

2. Teachers should be afforded ample time to compose a thoughtful piece.
3. Even where a college does not require teacher recommendations, your counselees should consider sending some—especially to their "reach" schools. *Two* is sufficient. If a school makes it known that it does not want to receive this type of document, however, then the applicant should not press the issue!
4. Advise your counselees to seek a balance of recommendations, where possible, from teachers that represent a variety of academic disciplines. Colleges like to view their applicants from different perspectives.
5. Some schools will specify that not all recommendations need be from educators. For a varying viewpoint, it might make sense to request a recommendation from someone outside of the school system, such as an employer. However, unless these "outsiders" are most familiar with the applicant, he or she should look elsewhere. Letters from superintendents of schools, mayors, governors, and congressmen should be avoided like the plague. Note the pathetic job done by the mayor in Figure 11-6, including the impersonal phrase, "I understand that . . .".

From the desk of
Mayor Samuel R. Augenrode
Suite 450, City Hall

I am writing this letter of recommendation on behalf of Robert Watkins who is applying to your institution for admission in September 19xx. There is no question that Robert is a model citizen. I understand that he is not only an excellent student, but a fine athlete as well. As young people go, he certainly has been civic minded. His work as an umpire with our township recreational committee has been most commendable.

Recommended with enthusiasm!

Sincerely,

Samuel R. Augenrode

Figure 11-6

6. It *is* important for students to try to uncover good writers. Perhaps what is more important than writing ability, though, is that the selected individual take the time to compose a caring, individualized, substantive, and anecdotal piece.
7. You might want to "teach" your counselees how to approach individuals about writing recommendations.

THE INDEPENDENT COUNSELOR

When asked why his parents had engaged the services of an independent counselor for the college admission process, a young man stated that his school counselor was overworked and had too many other obligations. This young man could have been from any state in the union.

Although there is truth to the argument that school counselors can provide qualified college admission assistance, large caseloads with limited time to discuss college and career options eliminate the opportunity—so parents employ a private consultant. (Cynics cite the private consultant trend as just another example of a faulty basis for our society: it's better because it costs money.) Even when their own school system has an excellent reputation for college counseling, some parents employ private consultants for "another opinion." An additional reason for the boom in the private college counseling business is that parents are pulling out all stops in an effort to get their offspring into the most prestigious colleges. As one mom aptly put it, "There may be fewer kids these days, but they all want to go to the same schools."

Here to Stay

Since the number of private practitioners increases yearly, you will probably have to decide how much cooperation you're going to give this new breed of specialist. Suppose an "independent" asks you for a profile of the school and you throw the letter in the trash. Will that earn you a reputation for being uncooperative and defensive? Or suppose that an independent team wants to meet with the department, and you cooperate. Will that make you look cooperative and healthy? If you don't cooperate with an independent counselor, is there a chance that the two of you could end up working at cross purposes? School counselors need to realize that the independents are here to stay. Therefore, it is in everyone's best interest that the two professions cooperate as much as possible.

But what should be your role when you have a strong feeling that that consultant down the block is minimally qualified? Many states don't require licensure: anyone can hang out a shingle. Some independents are "regular counselors" in public or private schools. Some aren't. Are the latter any less qualified? Prior to the hiring of an independent counselor, families would do well to check his or her credentials carefully.

The Primary Counselor: Now and Forevermore

What students need to have pointed out to them, however, is the fact that you, the school counselor, are the one who will be completing the secondary school report form and writing the recommendation. (With regard to this issue, perhaps we need to communicate fully to students the idea that strengthening the bond between counselor and counselee is essential and a *mutual* responsibility.)

Anyway, there *is* some question as to the appropriateness of independents submitting recommendations on their clients. In an interview with Earl Gottschalk, Jr., of *The Wall Street Journal,* William Fitzsimmons, dean of admissions at Harvard College, states: "We have to view any recommendation by a private counselor as that of a paid relationship. It's not the same as getting a recommendation from a counselor from the school itself." Mr. Fitzsimmons goes on to say that a recommendation from a private counselor may even cause a "backlash" at some colleges.

There are a lot of unanswered questions here, and the whole issue can't help but affect your image in some way.

HAIL THE RETURNING GRADUATE

Feedback from Graduates: The Lawrenceville Project

Students at The Lawrenceville School in New Jersey get to browse through a looseleaf binder of comments from former schoolmates about the colleges and universities they now attend. "Page two" of an annual follow-up survey of graduates, supervised by William Dickey, former director of college counseling, provides for direct feedback from previous Lawrenceville students on their collegiate experiences. Surveys (see Figure 11-7) are mailed to the students at their respective colleges. The response sheets, placed in a binder and organized by name of college, become available to juniors and seniors in kind of a coffee table arrangement in the counseling department's outer office. (Other secondary schools request similar feedback from their graduates and then log it into a computer.)

Alison Stewart, a counselor at the school, reports that the comments are most helpful to (1) juniors as part of their early planning activity; (2) accepted seniors, who prior to their making final decisions want to see what grads have had to say; and (3) professional staff looking to update themselves on particular institutions.

Stewart and colleagues naturally encourage students to use the material, but caution them to read "with a grain of salt thrown in." (It might be said, though, that the personal biases of former Lawrenceville students probably don't differ appreciably from the views expressed in such "tell it like it is" publications as the *Insider's Guide to the Colleges.*)

There is a constant stream of traffic through the Lawrenceville counseling office. With such relevant material so readily accessible to its students, Lawrenceville Prep may have developed one of the world's most usable and useful coffee table books.

THE LAWRENCEVILLE SCHOOL
Lawrenceville, New Jersey

I. Which college are you attending? ______________________
(If not in college, please describe your present activity.)

II. How do you rate the academic program at your college?

	Excellent	Adequate	Insufficient
Interesting?	______	______	______
Diversified?	______	______	______
Challenging?	______	______	______
Faculty accessibility?	______	______	______
Facilities?	______	______	______
Advising?	______	______	______
Class size?	______	______	______

III. How do you rate the nonacademic aspects of your college?

	Excellent	Adequate	Insufficient
Clubs/extracurricular?	______	______	______
Athletics?	______	______	______
Recreation?	______	______	______
Social life?	______	______	______
Friendliness?	______	______	______
Housing?	______	______	______
School spirit?	______	______	______

IV. What do you like most about your college?

V. What do you like least about your college?

Figure 11-7

PARENTAL INPUT

It is imperative that communication with parents be open and honest—with special attention paid to parental expectations. Most parents don't have the experience or objectivity to have a *realistic* assessment of their youngster's chances in the competitive world of college admissions. They look at their offspring through colored glasses—sometimes rosy, but frequently shadowed gray.

Students often find it difficult to select "target" schools. Some pick "reaches" predominantly; others stick with "safeties." Are the former overly-confident? Do the latter underestimate themselves? Or are the youngsters reflecting parental attitudes? Conferring with students *and* parents should bring things more into focus.

You, the counselor, have the experience and objectivity to help your counselee and his parents get to his "targets." And there's no reason at all why your communication can't be both realistic and warm at the same time. It is not only what you say and how you say it that matters, but also the whole aura of professionalism that you present to them. Parents need to see that *you* are the professional.

Homework for Parents?

An effective means of dealing with a student's self-assessment is to ask his parents to share with you *in writing* their expectations of his future career and college endeavors. (Schools that utilize this approach find that the fall of the junior year is the ideal time to do so.)

This worthwhile-but-seldom-employed technique is especially popular with people from private secondary schools as it can broaden lines of communication between home and school. It can also enable you to receive early warnings of unrealistic expectations and/or special problems.

Westfield High School in Westfield, NJ, uses a concise and revealing piece solely to obtain parental input into the youngster's achievements and potential, which can then be employed in the development of a quality recommendation. (See Figure 11-8. It is shown here with the permission of Cas Jakubik, director of guidance at Westfield High School.)

Written parental input can expand your knowledge of a student, including his or her family situation. It is a technique that you might want to consider adopting.

DEPARTMENT OF GUIDANCE SERVICES
WESTFIELD HIGH SCHOOL
Westfield, NJ

Parent "Brag Sheet"
College Recommendation

Name of Student: ______________________________

1. What do you consider to be the outstanding accomplishments of your child during the past three or four years? Why did you select these as most important?

2. In what areas has your child shown the most development and growth during the past three or four years?

3. What do you consider to be his/her outstanding personality traits?

4. If you had to describe your son/daughter in five adjectives, what would they be?

5. Are there any unusual or personal circumstances which have affected your child's educational experiences or personal experiences?

Please feel free to use a second sheet of paper if your comments do not fit into the space provided.

______________________ ______________________
Name of Counselor Parent Signature

Figure 11-8

WHO ELSE?

Humanity is social. Two hundred years ago our forefathers held barn raisings and quilting bees; then came volunteer fire fighters and the pony express. Some of us still know potluck suppers or making the dinner rounds, going from appetizers to soups to main course to dessert.

It seems that the more populated we become, the more competitive we get, and the less willing we are to cooperate. And that's unfortunate, because the broader our vision, the more friends-colleagues-compatriots we will have, and the richer will be our experience. The same holds true for young people. If they see that *we* can *co*operate—work with—others, then maybe they will learn that it is not good for a person to be alone, that there is depth in society.

Some of your potential co-workers will give more grief than others, but you'll get a surprising amount of help and cooperation from most folks. Keep trying.

SUGGESTED READINGS

BOOTHROYD, R., D. CHAPMAN, AND J. KAUFMAN. 1987. "Proprietary College Counseling." *The Journal of College Admissions* (NACAC, 1800 Diagonal Road, Alexandria, VA), no. 117.

HAYDEN, THOMAS. 1983. *Writing Effective College Recommendations: A Guide for Teachers.* Princeton, NJ: Peterson's Guides, Inc. A fine pamphlet that can be used with teachers in a workshop setting.

Chapter 12

Athletic Recruitment and Eligibility

As athletically talented youngsters move onto high school varsity teams, some of them dream of not only "making it" in intercollegiate competition, but also in the world of professional sports. Hence, an issue that needs to be addressed by all concerned with the individual athlete is the *extent* of any talent. How talented is talented? Even if youngsters win NCAA Division I scholarships, many later learn that they don't have what it takes for the pros. The hard statistics reveal that only 1 of every 100 college football players, and 2 of every 100 college basketball players, ever see the print of a professional contract.

Whether in high school or college, the student-athlete needs to learn how to cope effectively with the dual, and often severe, pressures of classroom and playing field competition. Since life in athletics can be a short-lived affair, the sooner this lesson is learned, the better. And there is no time like high school for the athlete to comprehend the importance of doing well academically. Unfortunately, with certain of them, study can get sidetracked in favor of the roar of the crowd. Athletes must bring to the classroom the same amount of discipline, concentration, and industry that they bring to their athletic endeavors. Even the "stars" need to develop their intellect fully and ready themselves for life outside of the world of sports.

You can do much to "show the way." Most of the disappointments can be avoided, if prospective student-athletes are properly prepared for the unique problems that will confront them. Perhaps an in-depth exploration of life after the locker room, or some awareness exercises that relate to the penalties of academic neglect, might be appropriate. Scholastic/athletic issues are fine topics for group counseling activity.

Figure 12-1 gives terms frequently used with student-athletes.

INCREASED STANDARDS

In an attempt to strengthen academic requirements for prospective athletes moving from high school to college, the National Collegiate Athletic Association (NCAA), one of several national organizations that governs collegiate athletic participation, adopted new eligibility requirements in 1983. The new regulations came

TERMS FREQUENTLY EMPLOYED

Prospective Student-Athlete	A student who, because of special athletic prowess, is recruited to play on an intercollegiate team.
Full Ride	A comprehensive (tuition, fees, texts, room, and board) athletic scholarship that can be renewed annually.
Blue-Chip Prospect	A "star" athlete that most major institutions would like to have as a player.
Letter of Intent	A statement that the prospective student-athlete signs, whereby he or she indicates his or her desire to attend the institution and receive an athletically based scholarship.
Signed Student-Athlete	A prospective student-athlete who has signed a valid letter of intent, and/or an institutional agreement.
Red Shirt	An athlete on scholarship who is held out of competition for a season, so that he remains eligible for a fifth year. This happens when athletes are injured, when they need to develop more physically, or when there is a "crowd" at a given position.

Figure 12-1

in response to frequent reports that some college athletes were students in name only, attending college simply to engage in sports with the hopes of winning a professional contract. Cases were even cited where players graduated from college without being able to read or write properly.

Despite the fact that the rules were approved well in advance of the effective date of August 1, 1986, many secondary schools and colleges were caught off guard. Hundreds of high school athletes, scheduled to receive Division I athletic scholarships in 1986, failed to meet the new minimum standards and therefore became ineligible to compete.

Since the 1983 regulations can be complex as they apply to particular students, no published guidebook should be relied upon exclusively. You might want to contact the NCAA national office in Mission, KS, for proper interpretations in specific cases. If you would like an in-depth treatment of high school academic requirements for initial athletics eligibility and information relative to athletic related financial aid at Division I member institutions, send for "Guide to the New College Freshman Eligibility Requirements for NCAA Division I Institutions." All details aside, Figure 12-2 shows the academic eligibility requirements for all students entering a Division I NCAA member institution as of August 1, 1988, and thereafter.

NCAA "AT LEASTS" IN A NUTSHELL

Prospective student-athletes must have completed a high school curriculum of 11 "core" courses, including at least 3 in English and 2 each in mathematics, social science, and natural or physical science (including at least one laboratory course, if offered by the high school). The 11 courses must reflect a minimum grade point average of 2.0 on a scale of 4.0. Students must also present a combined SAT score of at least 700 or a composite score of at least 15 on the ACT.

NCAA defines a core course as a recognized "academic" course designed to prepare a student for college work. Courses that are taught at a level below a secondary school's regular academic instructional level are not considered core courses, regardless of course content.

At least 75 percent of the instructional content of any core course must be in one or more of the following NCAA specified subject areas to qualify:

English—must include instructional elements in the following areas: grammar, vocabulary development, composition, literature, and analytical reading or oral communication.

Mathematics—must include instructional elements in algebra, geometry, trigonometry, statistics, or calculus. Statistics must be advanced, that is, algebra based.

Social Science—must include instructional elements in history, social studies, economics, geography, psychology, sociology, government, political science, or anthropology.

Natural or Physical Science—must include instructional elements in biology, chemistry, physics, environmental science, physical science, or earth science.

Additional Core Courses: foreign language, computer science, philosophy, or nondoctrinal religion (e.g. comparative religion).

Figure 12-2

Note that NCAA core requirements for eligibility, and institutional requirements for admission, are *not* always the same. A student could be admissible at a certain institution, but not meet the core requirements, and vice versa.

SENIOR YEAR PRESSURE

Things can get hot and heavy for top athletes in the senior year, as these students become virtually hounded by recruiters from various colleges and universities—who will do almost anything to make their institutions look attractive to a prospect. Yes, recruiting college athletes is a very earnest and competitive game. In *The Athlete's Game Plan for College & Career*, Stephen and Howard Figler remark, "As games go, it is a strange one because those who at first believe they have won may find out later that they really were losers. And those who thought they had lost may turn out in the long run to have won after all." Your students *must* delve into some of the critical issues.

Figure 12-3 lists several questions that the student-athletes should consider before signing a valid letter of intent.

GETTING THE WORD TO THE STUDENT-ATHLETE

In all of this, it is *imperative* that you work *with* the athletic department. The guidance and athletic departments of some secondary schools, such as West Windsor-Plainsboro High School, Princeton Junction, NJ, jointly publish booklets for student-athletes and their parents. The National Association of College Admission Counselors has this type of publication available for distribution to families, as well. (See Suggested Readings.) NCAA publishes an amazing amount of useful literature. You might want to order its attractive publications catalog entitled, "NCAA Sports Library."

BEFORE SIGNING ON THE DOTTED LINE

1. What will be my total cost per year over the scholarship?
2. What are the prevailing campus attitudes toward various minorities, ethnic groups, and religious affiliations?
3. Are special programs in academic counseling and/or tutoring available?
4. Do I get a comfortable feeling when I visit the campus?
5. How does the school stand academically?
6. What are the course requirements of the academic department in which I am interested? What time demands will be placed on me?
7. How and where will I fit into the athletic program: starter? specialist?
8. Do they have plans to "red shirt" me?
9. I might want to play both fall and spring sports. If I am primarily being considered for a fall sport, will there be spring ball? What is the athletic department's attitude toward two-sport athletes?
10. How stable is the coaching staff in terms of employment?
11. Am I really being offered a scholarship, or are we just at the talking stage?
12. How are the players generally treated?
13. Can I meet the coaching staff?

Figure 12-3

Another piece worth employing as you counsel your students to handle stress appropriately is "Your Rights and Responsibilities as a Student Athlete in Higher Education." Created by the National Association of Student Personnel Administrators, this pamphlet focuses on what the student-athlete can expect once enrolled in college. Copies can be ordered from NASPA, P. O. Box 21265, Columbus, OH 43221.

RELIEVING ATHLETIC STRESS

Student athletes are under a great deal of stress. They are visible people, under public scrutiny and pressures from colleges, coaches, and alumni. They often put themselves under considerable pressure to excel both athletically and academically: some are scholar-athletes; others must work hard just to remain eligible.

They're placed under pressure by peers and family, as well: they have to live up to expectations. There is a disruption of normal family routine, for example, planning meals around practices, and unique monetary considerations on college choice must be dealt with. You can sensitize yourself to the special problems faced by the student-athlete, and counsel accordingly. In doing so, you will find yourself cooperating more closely than ever with your athletic department.

You probably have already discovered that your obligation toward athletes has intensified as (1) local boards of education institute minimal grade point average requirements for participation in all extracurricular activities, (2) state departments of education announce their own minimum GPA requirements for athletic participation, and (3) the NCAA and NAIA raise the standards that govern the issuance of athletic scholarships by universities.

All this monitoring has provided you with additional important duties:

- Advising athletes each year on selecting the proper courses of study.
- Stressing the importance of sitting for an SAT or ACT more than once, with one of the examinations taken *prior* to the senior year.
- Counseling athletes to keep their special talents in perspective (athletics should be secondary to academic work).
- Communicating closely with coaches on college selection to avoid working at cross purposes. College coaches need to know who can be successful both as a student and as a player. But with Division I, the bottom line is: can the student play? Remember: counselors and high school coaches should not *choose* the college, it can backfire.

SUGGESTED READINGS

FIGLER, STEPHEN, AND HOWARD FIGLER. 1984. *The Athlete's Game Plan for College & Career*. Princeton, NJ: Peterson's Guides, Inc. A most comprehensive guide that deals with the commitments of the student-athlete—academic achievement, athletic responsibilities, and career choice—and shows him or her how to keep them in balance.

High School Planning for College-Bound Athletes. National Association of College Admission Counselors, 1800 Diagonal Road, Alexandria, VA. A concise brochure, well worth distributing to student athletes. Also includes an introduction by Joseph Paterno.

The National Directory of College Athletics. Amarillo, TX: Ray Frank Publishing Ranch, Box 7068. Great for locating the names and telephone numbers of athletic directors and coaches and for information on conferences and associations. Available in both men's and women's paperback editions.

NCAA Guide for the College-Bound Student-Athlete. National Collegiate Athletic Association, P. O. Box 1906, Mission, KS. An informative, easy-to-read publication that provides a general summary of NCAA regulations to prospective student-athletes and high school officials. Guidelines relate primarily to the recruiting and eligibility of prospective student-athletes as well as to the financial aid they are permitted to receive.

SECTION III

COUNSELEE, FAMILY, AND YOU

Today's high school students are capable of developing a good college and career choice strategy, provided that conscientious counselors are afforded the time to show them the way. The development of a sound strategy can become even more of a reality where an *appropriate* amount of concern and support from parents is evident.

For students to present themselves well, they must know themselves well. The role of the counselor in student self-assessment and presentation is treated. Section III also discusses ways in which counselors can sensitize youngsters to the wide variety of common and unique career possibilities, and it studies the involvement of the professional in three critical areas of the admission program: application completion, personal interview, and essay writing.

At no time in our history has sound family financial planning been of more significance than today. Both financial aid and financial planning are examined. Who is responsible for assisting students to make the high school–to–college transition as smooth as possible? This issue is addressed, as we take a look at stress factors and at the methods several schools are using to help students "go with it."

Chapter 13

Parents as Partners

> Help parents to become an active force in the admission process, and get them to state their own goals and aspirations *early on*. If a student applies to a number of colleges far from home, and then discovers that her parents disapprove of the distance, it *is* a problem for *everyone*.
>
> — An admission director

In the college planning process of the 1950s and early 1960s, the parents ran the show, and son or daughter usually fell in line. The Vietnam era of the late 1960s and early 1970s witnessed a reversal of roles: young people became the directors, and their parents became the actors. But this is the late 1980s and early 1990s, and words such as wealth, career, and conservative are respectable once again as youngsters rush to emulate Mom and Dad. Parents, upstaged for more than a decade, are now playing center stage. This time around, though, the picture shows more co-direction: a kind of joint responsibility on the part of both parties.

College admission people have quickly learned wherein lies the action. One has only to drop by an admission office to see parents' literature very much in evidence in the waiting room. Special travel guides have been designed and published for parental consumption, and mail recruitment has caused a certain amount of back strain, as parents try to remove large quantities of viewbooks from mailboxes during Johnny's junior and senior years. Ah, yes, parents are definitely sharing the driving.

All this concern at the collegiate level, however, does not seem to have filtered down to the secondary school level. While studies indicate that parents continue to desire a greater participatory role in the public school education of their children, parents still feel locked out of the school setting. But with college planning, it would seem that the entire process would be more efficient and meaningful if parents were more locked *in*. (Besides, wouldn't greater parental involvement improve counselor image? Certainly the behind-the-scenes influence of parents is strong and pervasive.) Research conducted at Southern Methodist University in Texas uncovered, among other things, that parents, through their perceptions of individual colleges, have a great influence on where their offspring ultimately matriculate.

You will want to be especially sympathetic and helpful to "first-timers" (parents going through the admission process for the first time). Like other parents, they look to you for professional *direction*. Much of the 1980s admission scene is cloaked in a mystique of competition and prestige. So let's counsel! Frankly, school counselors are doing too much dispensing of information and not enough *advising*.

Parents' perceptions can differ markedly from those of counselors as to the amount of influence they (counselors) have in the college admission process, particularly the admittance decision aspect. At times parents credit counselors with having much more influence than they really do have.

You *must* know what are, and are not, your responsibilities within the counseling process. Do you help the student write his essay? Fill out financial aid forms? Guarantee that you can get him into a particular institution? This is an issue that mandates departmental policy that clearly delineates counselor role and function. And, just as important, your publics must understand your position. What you don't need is to have an absentee parent telephoning you with an irate, "Why did you let my son apply to all those expensive schools?"

As you work with parents, you need to be sensitive to the confusion and resentment they feel about spending $50,000 on something over which they have little or no control. Consequently, the prime thrust of your *professional* advisement should be to help these bewildered people realize that they do indeed have some control over their youngster's college admission, to empower parents to act on their own—and to show them how to go about doing it.

FACE TO FACE WITH MOM AND DAD

Of course, you can't empower parents if they don't come to your office to be empowered. One department, after wrestling with caseloads of 410 to 1 in the early 1970s and 310 to 1 in the late 1970s, managed to reduce ratios further to 220 to 1. Aware that their publics would now be focusing on them to see if there would indeed be increased student/counselor contact, the department "upped them one": it designed a project whereby counselors met in private 40-minute sessions with all juniors *and their parents* to do some career and postsecondary educational planning. (See Figure 13-1.) No matter how brief the session time, such a program does provide the beginnings of solid communication between home, school, and youngster—a triangle of communication that is absolutely essential to proper and efficient planning. Counselors find that even telephone communication is facilitated once there has been face-to-face contact.

WHOSE LIFE IS IT ANYWAY?

Some kids become lions or tigers or bears because their grandfathers and fathers were, and tradition must go on! (A small college in Pennsylvania prides itself on having enrolled four generations of Harringtons.) Other youngsters are told by their parents that they're heading for State U. and that's that! Or the reverse happens—the "unfulfilled" parent says, "You're not going to State U. the way I did. You're going to Yale!" And then there are those who refuse to believe that colleges can change and 25 years later continue to think that this one's a rich man's school or that one's awash in alcohol.

Still others won't let their offspring totally "leave home," as evidenced by one set of parents who followed their son to a New Jersey engineering school, dining with him once a week in the school's cafeteria. And you know about Douglas MacArthur: his mother moved her residence to a state from which MacArthur

Dear Parent(s):

We cordially invite you and your child to meet with __Mr. Brown__ in a precollege counseling session to be held here in the Counseling Office.

This will be an excellent opportunity for you and the counselor to discuss areas of mutual concern regarding the college admission process.

The session will last approximately 40 minutes. Your appointment has been set for __Wednesday, April 15__ at __9:00 AM.__

We look forward to having you with us.

Sincerely,

Kenneth Rodgers
Chairperson

Figure 13-1

could get an appointment to West Point; she then followed him there, and lived in a hotel from which she could watch his dormitory.

Whose life is it anyway? It's the student's—or it's *almost* the student's. The essential role of parents is to help their youngster become a wonderfully functioning adult. That means that as the youngster grows, he does more and more decision making about his life, and parents do less and less—but they haven't finished quite yet! Their involvement is twofold: (1) they've lived with their children for a long time and still want the best for them—which their years of experience might help—and (2) somebody still has to pay the bills. Besides—where could your counselees find nicer people to help them present themselves to colleges properly? So, when it comes to college admission, most parents want to be in on the action, *and they should be*. The problem is the *extent* of the involvement, which can range from overanxious/overprotective, to completely laissez-faire.

COMMUNICATION

A superintendent once asked ten National Merit Scholarship semifinalists if they would like to invite a teacher, one who had especially helped them, to attend a board of education meeting where they were to be commended. Nine of the students invited staff members; the tenth invited her parents.

Such an unusual move on the part of this semifinalist signals the existence of a warm and close family relationship. Unfortunately, strong relationships among family members don't exist in many homes. It is not at all uncommon for counselors to hear parents say: "I can't talk to him." "She never tells us anything." "Most of our conversations end up in shouting matches."

In their own way, and for the perfectly proper process of growing up, young people contribute to this distancing problem. Therefore, it is more than wise for your counselees to tap their parents on the shoulder and reintroduce themselves, because college planning is the time for *solid* communication among family members. You will do a great deal if you encourage your counselee to sit down with Mom and Dad and do a little quiet communicating.

If, however, some of your counselees find that this is next to impossible, they should be encouraged to look to you for help. You can be an excellent third-party facilitator. Even if the discussions were to go swimmingly at home, three-way communication with parents, student, and counselor can be extremely beneficial in college planning.

Parents and students usually welcome the opportunity of sitting with a counselor. Parents get the opportunity to voice their concerns; young people get the chance to talk. After one rather productive session, a young man told his counselor, "I'm really glad you were there. I could finish a sentence." Later, over the telephone, the mother of the boy told the counselor, "It was nice to be able to talk without my son running out of the room."

Expense is a perfect example of where open and honest communication between parents and youngster is a *must*. To avoid bitter disappointment and the "I knew I'd never get to go to that private school" syndrome, parents need to be straightforward with their children about their financial support capability as early as possible.

And the parents' interest is more than just paying bills: it's their wanting to participate in getting the very best for their child, yet not knowing how to *best* proceed. Again, most parents welcome professional *direction.*

THE OVERBEARING TYPES

There are numerous parents who continue to satisfy their own selfish needs through their children, and parental involvement becomes excessive. Examples of excessiveness can be seen in parents who:

- Think they can buy their youngster a college.
- Set unrealistic limits on the number of applications to be submitted.
- Extend carte blanche privileges to their youngster—the "let's see how many *we* can get into" approach.
- Have their youngster apply to only "reach" schools.
- Are hell-bent on having their offspring go to an alma mater—even to his own fraternity.

But you can work to break through some or all of this as you advocate for your affected students. You should attempt to take control in order to return more control to them.

Don't hesitate to assume a take-charge attitude in your counseling sessions with overly dominant parents. The meeting should be well structured, with little or no time wasted on your being defensive. Once Mom and Dad have had their say, you should periodically use such expressions as, "In my professional (a word counselors should use more often) opinion, this is the direction I think we should take," or "This department believes that if the student has done her homework well, then six is an appropriate number of schools to which to apply."

Sometimes your third-party role seems more like that of a referee at a sporting event. One counselor, when a parent keeps answering for his child, states warmly but pointedly, "I want *him* to talk!" The parent usually backs off with, "Oh, okay."

In cases of incessant parental interruption or vocalization, an effective technique is to raise your hand to the parent signaling silence, while you continue to listen to, and focus on, your counselee.

EXTENDING A HAND VIA SPECIAL PROGRAMS

To augment the annual junior "information giving" night, a few secondary schools now conduct various parent programs, a goodly number of which are centered on special topics. One northern New Jersey school presents six single-topic programs yearly.

A Two-Night Seminar

Typically, schools present the basics of college admission to parents during the youngster's junior year—but they try to cram it all into one night. One department developed a two-session seminar (see Figure 13-2) that obviously enabled them to explore each topic in greater depth. Notice that the program was conducted in the fall, providing parents with the opportunity to receive some early-planning advice on such things as achievement testing and campus visitation. (If you distribute a printed program to your audience, it's nice to leave space between topics to facilitate note taking.)

SENIOR YEAR CRAZINESS

The senior year is a particularly crazy time for everyone concerned with college admissions. Suddenly students are being asked to be unusual and different, when for the past 17 years they've been trying to go with the crowd. Applying to college comes at a time when many of them are wrestling with other significant teenage problems, which can influence their emotional behavior and their family relationships. Parents lose track of the fact that their offspring really *do* care about what they, the parents, think. And the same parents who have cared for John from day 1

PARENTAL SURVIVAL OF THE COLLEGE ADMISSION PROCESS

SEMINAR I: 7:30 P.M. Wednesday, October 19

- INTRODUCTION
- THE IMPORTANCE OF SELF-ASSESSMENT
- EXAMINING THE MARKET
- SELECTING YOUR TARGET AREA
- THE CAMPUS VISIT AND THE INTERVIEW

SEMINAR II: 7:30 P.M. Wednesday, October 26

- COMPLETING THE APPLICATION
- THE PERSONAL ESSAY
- COUNSELOR/TEACHER INVOLVEMENT
- FINANCING THE VENTURE
- THE THRILL OF VICTORY/THE AGONY OF DEFEAT

Figure 13-2

are now telling him to be more independent—yet they're still paying his bills and doing his laundry. A student can get excited about going off to college, but there is still that fear of the unknown—not the least of which is living on his own, with an unknown roommate.

To minimize the pressure of the senior year, parents can start procedural matters early in the junior year. Since parents often miss timelines tucked away in planning guides, one department distributes theirs as a single flier and asks its parents to tape it onto their refrigerators. (See Figure 13-3.)

PARENTS' TIMELINE FOR COLLEGE ADMISSIONS

11th year: FALL	Begin Research on Colleges and Universities
October	Take PSAT
11th year: SPRING	Conduct Intensive Research
	First College Visitation Period
May–June	Take First SAT
	Appropriate Time for Certain Achievement Tests
11–12 SUMMER	Send for Applications
	Second College Visitation Period
12th year: FALL	Complete and Mail Applications
	Third College Visitation Period
November	Take Second SAT
12th year: WINTER	
December–January	Appropriate Time for Remaining Achievements
January–February	Complete and Mail Financial Aid Forms
12th year: SPRING	
March–April	Make Final Decisions

Figure 13-3

ADDITIONAL WAYS IN WHICH PARENTS CAN HELP

Because they are adults with a unique role in the lives of these young people, parents can also:

- Do a great deal to relieve stress within the family structure by being supportive and open-minded. They, like your counselees, must understand that final decisions are to be made in the *spring* of the senior year, not the fall. They must understand that the admission process is a "keeping options open" process. They must also be ready to experience—and appropriately handle—both April happiness and April disappointment.
- Assist their youngster in selecting appropriate schools. The entire family can travel together and stand together as a unit at college visitations.
- Proofread applications and essays.
- Suggest adult friends who might be willing to act as resource people.

Yes, parents can and *should* be partners in the college planning process. The real challenge to everyone is *to make the most of the partnership*. At a recent Bucknell graduation, you could sense that at least one young woman and her family had done just that. After taking the stage and receiving her diploma, the perky coed turned to reveal to the audience the warm words of tribute she had so carefully pasted to the back of her graduation gown: "Thanks, Mom and Dad."

SUGGESTED READINGS

HAYDEN, THOMAS C. 1986. *Handbook for College Admissions: A Family Guide*. Princeton, NJ: Peterson's Guides, Inc. Read Chapter 8, "For Parents Only: The Myth of College and Success."

SHIELDS, CHARLES J. 1986. *The College Guide for Parents*. Chicago: Surrey Books. This interesting and informative paperback might well be the only comprehensive guide written expressly for parents.

Chapter 14

Self-Assessment and College Choice

Each year, thousands of freshmen suddenly wake up to realize that they have matriculated at a school that is either too pastoral or too citified, too conservative or too liberal, too big or too small, too tough or too easy. It is a legitimate dilemma, which is often resolved by transferring schools—or dropping out. The question is: What caused the mismatch? Chance? Or insufficient consideration of the institution *and oneself*?

High school students *must* come to grips with the fact that selecting a place at which to spend their next four years is a *decision* that calls for a great deal of self-analysis. Deep inside, they know that the less they know about themselves, the more difficult this task is going to be. No matter what, it is important for young people to know who they are, and college choice can precipitate the awareness. Students can use the admission process as a great way to learn about themselves. Therefore, *before* they touch a computerized college search program or plow through any number of guidebooks, *they should know themselves well*!

And they can take heart. With your assistance, it's not too late for them to do a little soul searching: What is my life-style? What do I like? What can I handle? What kind of career should I pursue? Why do I want to go to college in the first place?

SELF-IMAGE AND SELF-ASSESSMENT

> An individual's self-concept is the core of his personality. It affects every aspect of human behavior: the ability to learn, the capacity to grow and change, the choice of friends, mates, and careers. It's no exaggeration to say that a strong positive self-image is the best possible preparation for success in life.
>
> — Dr. Joyce Brothers
> (quoted by Skip Ross in
> *Say Yes to Your Potential*)

Terminology here is a bit tricky. "Self-concept" refers to those ideas and attitudes one has about oneself at any given moment. And while "self-concept" is cognitive, "self-esteem" is affective; it refers to the extent to which one values oneself. "Self-image," then, might be considered to be the sum *total* of the attitudes, facts, and feelings a person has accumulated about himself.

The self-image of most students is a vague, nebulous feeling about their status, but if some attention is paid to the concept, quality growth can occur. As Don Hamachek states in his book *Encounters with the Self*, "Acquiring a self-concept involves a slow process of differentiation as a person gradually emerges into focus out of his total world of awareness and defines progressively more clearly just what and who he is." Figuring out what one *is* and *has* (self-assessment) is a vital tool for helping young people find out what they want to *be* and *do*.

Actually, the process of self-assessment has always been one aspect of the entire educational endeavor. At this point in a student's life, however, it is important to make that analysis more specific: *self-assessment is the acknowledgment of one's abilities, interests, aspirations, and values—as they are now.* Youngsters should not be discouraged by faults or lack of growth. At their stage of life, it is *good* to be "unfinished"!

HOW SHOULD THEY DO IT?

Your counselees should start taking *serious* stock of themselves early in the junior year. They should find some time to sit down under a tree with a big yellow legal pad and a pencil and reflect on who they are and what they want. And, as they work, two principles should be kept in mind: their notations should be *specific*, and all thoughts should be *written down* so that each person can begin to see what he or she looks like.

Since the way someone sees herself is not always consonant with the manner in which others see her, it might be beneficial for your counselees to talk with you, their parents, their siblings, and their classmates. Sometimes an "outsider" can recognize characteristics of which one is unaware.

Your students should not try to list everything in one sitting; they won't be able to pull it all together. Self-assessment is an ongoing process that will form a more perfect picture as pieces are added to it, little by little. It's like a good piece of writing—it keeps getting better as you return to it and refine it.

ABILITIES

Getting a "handle" on one's abilities, especially the academic, should be a relatively easy task. Heaven knows, students have been tested to death since kindergarten.

What is imperative is that they *see* the figures—that they examine with you their *actual* achievement and aptitude scores, so that they can fully assess specific strengths and weaknesses and can comprehend national and local positioning. You know better than most that young people tend to underestimate their potential, both verbal and mathematical. And one can't capitalize on what one doesn't understand. A thorough knowledge of where an individual presently stands is crucial to sound future planning.

Some abilities are less easily documented, however. Does your student like to draw, paint, and design? have a natural aptitude for creative expression? If the answer is even a hesitant "yes," then it is important to seriously evaluate the range and depth of the artistic ability. The same is true of the performing arts, or athletics, or woodworking, or using sign language. Your counselee should note—on paper—*every* ability she has, its strength, and any means by which it can be affirmed. For the visual arts, affirmation might be a portfolio; for performing arts, an audition; for governmental skills, being a senator in a statewide model congress. Or an award, or a newspaper article, or a recommendation from a teacher. The abilities can be prioritized later: the strong can be retained and the weak eliminated. The student won't necessarily use all of them, but seeing them *in writing* will give her a better appreciation of her own worth. The beginning of her list might look like Figure 14-1.

Developing several abilities is essential to becoming a whole person. But the fact that these are secondary school *students* signifies that a significant portion of their involvement should be in the academics. *Academics are relevant.* For, after all, the more one knows, the better he or she will be at creating something new.

ABILITY	HOW GOOD?	EVIDENCE?
Math	Very good	SAT = 740
Verbal	Not so good	SAT = 420, but took reading course this semester
Tennis	Pretty good	Varsity team two years
Work with kids	Good	Tutored fourth graders in math

Figure 14-1

INTERESTS

"Interest" is defined in *Webster's New Collegiate Dictionary* as "the quality in a thing that arouses a person's concern." The term thus defined is exceedingly broad and can be applied to almost every aspect of living. Therefore, your counselee must examine his or her whole life. And, since activities are motivated by interests, the first question to ask is: "What am I involved in?" Then from the activity, the interest can be deduced: "*Why* am I in the Key Club? Because I like serving humanity." "*Why* am I on the fencing team? Because of my interest in one-on-one competition."

Young people tend to overlook and/or minimize the importance of their engagement in out-of-school activities. They think that everything that's important happens to them in school. Not so! The real "you" is the 24-hour "you." (Most students spend but a third of their day in school.) Counsel them to avoid shortchanging themselves by including valuable out-of-school activities.

Step 1: As your counselees continue to take pencil to pad, they should list *all* their interests, large and small. The listings should be categorized into two distinct groups: *school* and *out of school*. An important distinction should be made here. Extracurricular involvement *in school* is usually restricted to grades 9–12, but students can reach farther back in time with *out-of-school* activities, in an attempt to show mastery and followthrough. What they will want to do is demonstrate good old perseverance and dedication! For example, the fact that someone has been playing the French horn since age 8, and now as a high school junior finds himself All State first chair, is certainly noteworthy. He has been evidencing PDM: perseverance, dedication, and mastery.

Step 2: At this point, students should prioritize their listed activities from the most important (as *they* see it) at the top to the least important at the bottom. And as they position these items, they should *consolidate* the two lists. In doing so, they need to *identify commonalities*, bringing together related or similar activities.

For example, Megan, a talented writer, had had several sports articles printed in her local newspaper (out of school). In high school she had been writing for the school paper since her freshman year (in school). During her junior year, Megan was elevated to the position of sports editor (which showed leadership). In addition, she won a National Council of Teachers of English achievement award for an essay she had written. Since Megan was a capable writer, was enthusiastic about her work, and wanted to major in journalism, she wisely brought all her writing contributions together (in school plus out of school), placing them at the *top* of her list. Any admission counselor perusing the list would easily see PDM and the "real" Megan.

(As admission officials examine compilations, they are trying to become acquainted with the real *you*. They often take for granted that he or she has placed his or her most personal and worthwhile accomplishments toward the top of the list.)

Step 3: "I can't prioritize my activities because I haven't got any," states Anthony, who has been working to help support his disabled mother. In Anthony's case, colleges would overlook his limited extracurricular participation because of the severity of the family's financial obligations. But colleges won't overlook some things—such as working for a better pair of snow skis or supporting an unnecessary car at the expense of both curricular and extracurricular learning.

Your counselees *can* make their work experience work for them, however. Displaying a little financial independence is good. Continual employment in one job can demonstrate maturity and extraordinary discipline. (For some students, it can have a salutary effect on school grades, provided the work schedule isn't too heavy.) Students should *tie their work experience into their activities profile*. If Megan had been employed at a local print shop part time, she could have included this work experience with her other writing activities. That would have strengthened her profile even more.

Incidentally, the best paying job is not necessarily the most respected. Babysitting is one of the most underrated (and underpaid) jobs in the world, yet the responsibility, creativity, and human relations skills utilized can all be related to such interests as elementary education, social work, business management, and so on. As students search for jobs, they might be encouraged to make their final selection a meaningful one.

Step 4: Examine for the "unusual." Colleges, especially the "highly" selective ones, love the unusual! That's how they get their "well-rounded" classes. Take someone who enjoys group biking, and who leads expeditions through the Canadian Rockies—now *that* is an unusual activity. A student would place such an activity near the top of a list. (If a student can't find something that is unusual, he should not force the issue; he should go with what he has.)

Step 5: Keep any final list brief. *Quality*, not quantity, is the name of the game. Laundry lists of superficial activities are now passé. Quality of participation is evidenced by perseverance, dedication, and mastery.

ASPIRATIONS

Now we come to the question, "What do I want out of college?" Or "How does college fit into what I want out of life? And what do I really want?"

Since 1967, Alexander Astin has directed an annual survey, conducted by the Cooperative Institutional Research Program of UCLA and the American Council on Education, to determine the college students' lifetime goals. The 1987 report, "American Freshman: National Norms for Fall 1987," seems to indicate that college freshmen are creating a "national trend to materialism." A record number, 75.6 percent, identified "being very well off financially" as an essential or very important life goal (double the level in 1970). In addition, 71.3 percent indicated that a key reason for attending college is "to make more money" (up from 49.9 percent in 1971). Contrast that with a commitment to "developing a meaningful philosophy of life," cited by 39.4 percent, down from 82.9 percent 20 years previously. Goals seem to be changing. What trends will you see this year, as you work with your students?

One of the "aspirations" most closely linked with college choice is that of potential career selection, the treatment of which is an opus in itself. Work is one of the things that gives purpose to life, and, through it, identity, status, and security are gained. It's no wonder, then, that high school students start to panic when they don't know what career they want to pursue.

They shouldn't worry. Two-thirds of all collegians change their career plans at least once; most people will hold more than one type of job and work for more than one employer. Commentators have even suggested that individuals might want to modify their careers every ten years, to prevent burnout. Students should not tie their career plans *too* closely to their educational plans!

The object here is to get an idea of how planing for college relates to long-term goals. The desire to become a nuclear physicist, for instance, will necessitate the selection of a certain kind of school, certain courses, and so on. If there is no tentative career decision, then plans should be made to seek a broad educational background.

Other aspirations are important, too: studying in a large city, moving to another part of the nation, being in "ski country," graduating from a "name" college, getting married, becoming fluent in Italian.

On their yellow pads, your counselees should list all the aspirations they have that relate to college life; then they should compare and prioritize them. Under each long-term goal they should list the short-term goals necessary for its achievement. For each of these they should note the preparation necessary to reach the goal, the obstacles to be overcome, and the dates by which the goals will be reached.

This is a very difficult assignment, but if it can result in the simplification of one college-choice judgment (even if it is in the negative), then it is worth the effort. "If I really want to be a nuclear physicist, then I shouldn't go to a small humanities-oriented college." Or "If I have to choose between ski country and minoring in music, I'll choose ski country."

VALUES

"Why am I going to college, anyway?" Now this is a question that is seldom fully addressed by parents, students, or counselors. For many people, college just seems to be the thing to do, and it is vital that your counselees think about more reasons than providing great economic security for themselves. Money and protection can be found elsewhere. In a newspaper advertisement, St. John's University of New York has some suggestions: "Learn to use your mind; acquire greater appreciation for the world of culture; receive training in self-discipline; prepare for living a fuller, more useful life; attain greater perspective into the world around you; cultivate a greater awareness of social problems; and become better equipped to handle your obligations to society."

Great goals—but who thought of them? Where do the *students'* aspirations come from? Some seem to be assimilated from parents (We want you to have an education) or from society (You'll be happy if you are rich), and others seem to come from deep inside the person (I really want to discover a cure). The source of all these "wants" is someone's value system—the question is, *Whose*?

Richard L. Morrill, in his book, *Teaching Values in College* (Jossey-Bass, 1980), defines values as "standards and patterns of choice that guide persons and groups toward satisfaction, fulfillment, and meaning." Parents, educators, religious leaders, politicians, all think that their role, at least in part, is to transmit *their* standards and patterns to "their" young people. That might be true, but for those youngsters to *have* values, to act according to values, *they must develop their values themselves*.

Morrill agrees with Louis Raths and other prominent theorists that valuing involves an active process of *choosing* one's beliefs and behavior, *prizing* the same, and *acting* on one's beliefs. What could be more characteristic of young people? It is important that you convey to your adult publics that, for all people, valuing is a very important part of life, and to your young public that valuing, like any other educational proceeding, involves listening to those who have studied the matter to greater depths! As your students personalize their values, they will learn what it means to hold values as truly one's own.

So how can your students figure out what their values are, and what they want their values to be? Values can only be located by means of specific things, actions, or experiences (a nice house, a loving act, feelings of contentment, reading a good book) that indicate value. Your counselees have thought about—and listed—their interests and aspirations; they have collated and prioritized them. Now they should ask, "Why?" *Why* do I run for two miles before I go to school? Because I value physical fitness—it's important to me. Why do I want to go to a "different" college? Because I don't want to be like everybody else—I want to be me. Why do I like to join groups with lots of people, such as service clubs or dance committees? Because it's important for me to share my day with others.

By this time, the legal pad should have brackets and arrows and equal signs. Your counselees won't have assessed themselves perfectly, but at least they will have a much better idea of who they are and what they want. Most young people spend less time contemplating their values than they do their interests and abilities. But such contemplation may well be their *most* important under-the-tree activity.

MORE INTENSIVE CARE

Because counselor-student time is so limited, the self-assessment project discussed thus far has been relegated to a "do-it-yourself" project: you have asked the *student* to analyze abilities, interests, aspirations, and values. Obviously, the essence of the search depends on the student himself or herself, but school systems can—and probably should—provide greater resources to aid in their youngsters' self-awareness and self-acceptance.

How can this be accomplished? Workshops, offered during the school year or in the summer, elective or mandated courses available on a semester or quarter basis for all students or for those of a specific grade level. There is a wealth of information and a host of skills that you could transmit to your counselees.

IS ANYTHING ELSE IMPORTANT?

You have been asking each of your counselees to look honestly at himself. The question now is: What conclusions can they draw? You can help them prioritize and amalgamate their values, interests, abilities, and aspirations; but they will need something more:

1. They will have to make choices in their prioritizing.
2. They can see their personalities as guides from which they work.
3. Above all, they must be able to *appreciate* themselves.

This is all part of a normal growth process; it is often extremely important to *help* such growth rather than to just let it happen.

Decision Making

The transition from high school to college calls for many personal, educational, and vocational choices, and the ability to make well-considered, well-informed decisions is a skill that young people sorely need.

In 1972, the College Entrance Examination Board published *Deciding*, a decision-making curriculum for middle school students, integrating three major components of the process: examination and recognition of personal *values*, knowledge and use of relevant *information*, and knowledge and use of an effective *strategy* for converting information into action. Part of the positive response to the program was a request for a curriculum geared to senior high school students, college students, and adults. This was accomplished by the publication of *Decisions and Outcomes* in 1973.

Each curriculum can be covered in a minimum of 15 class periods; if additional recommendations are followed, the course can be extended to about 45 days, or leaders can spend a semester working once a week with their groups.

Personality

"That's the kind of person I am!" Everyone knows what that means: it means that certain characteristics make their opposites difficult to experience (being an introvert makes it difficult to speak to a large group, for instance). These characteristics are common enough so that one can speak of a certain "type."

Knowledge of their personalities—that is, their basic tendencies, the attitudes they feel at ease with, and types of behavior they find difficult—can help young people deal more readily with their choices, their studies, their lives. Different personalities react differently to testing, studying, planning, time management, perception, memory. If your counselees can rely on their strong points, then they can more easily manage their weaknesses.

Several personality indicators are available, but perhaps the most promising for use in the educational process is the *Myers-Briggs Type Indicator*. It is widely used for a variety of applications: for counseling in the areas of career choice, marital situations, and personal growth and for the building of a team or community.

Some counselors have combined its use with the *Strong-Campbell Interest Inventory* to help counselees see areas in which they would be comfortable—and *why* they would be comfortable. Careful leadership in the process can assist in the determination of strong and weak preferences, which can help students both in the *selection* of college and/or career and in *living* with them when they happen.

Administering the inventories and discussing the proclivities of the types could be done in a short workshop, but individual consultations are essential and would take more time.

Self-esteem

"One's self-esteem" refers quite literally to the extent to which one admires and values the self. For each young person, this is indeed a sticky wicket. Each is on the verge of being independent. Each sees some characteristics in himself that he likes and that others have approved; he sees some that *he* values, but parents or teachers don't; he sees some with which he is quite *dis*pleased. Consequently, he approves or disapproves of himself—and it is dawning on him that that "defendent" will be the ruler of his life.

Gary G. Peer, in his article in *The Humanist Educator* (October 1982), "The Antecedents of Self-esteem (One of Education's Best Kept Secrets)," holds the notion that "educators can influence pupil self-concept positively or negatively, provided that they are sensitive to the dynamics involved . . . key elements [of which] may have been largely overlooked by educators."

The "best kept secret" is enunciated by Hamachek in *Encounters with the Self*:

> Research is rather clear in showing that adult qualities most clearly associated with high self-esteem in children include warmth and caring, encouragement, freedom for exploration, *high expectations, and firm discipline*. (emphasis added)

Peer's point is that there is a false dichotomy between the traditionally humanistic qualities and "high expectations and firm discipline"; *both* aspects, taken together, provide balance in working toward greater self-esteem. You, the counselor, are in an excellent position to use these qualities with your students as you help them walk through the admission process: you can show them that what they *want* is important, but they must adhere to the regulations, timelines, and procedures needed to attain it.

Additional Programs

Many courses are being developed that might be used at various levels of the educational process to enhance the general capabilities and the self-image of the students.

"Project 'Self' (Self-Esteem and Learning Through Feelings)" is a classroom program consisting of 12 45- and 60-minute sessions, designed to heighten awareness about self-confidence, sensitivity to others, communication skills, and decision-making skills. It is adaptable for use in grades 6–12. Contact Jeri R. Sardella, 12 Christopher Street, Ramsey, NJ 07446.

"Choices: A Course in Personal Decision Making" (by Joan Kosuth and Sandy Minnesang, The Wright Group, San Diego, CA 92126) deals with communication, personality, career exploration, interviewing, values, behavior modification, and several other topics. Eight two-week segments can form a semester course, a year's program would utilize all units, or individual units could be used in other courses (English or social studies, for example).

"Affective Skill Development for Adolescents" is a highly structured curriculum designed to help students develop their self-esteem and interpersonal skills. The topics—self-knowledge/self-esteem, responsibility, communication, assertiveness, and problem solving/decision making—are covered in a program held one period a day for a semester. A novel and extremely interesting approach is the parent program that is held simultaneously, for eight sessions during the semester. While this course can be used from grades 6 through 12, the positive response has induced the authors to develop a "part two" to be offered for the higher grades. Contact Constance H. Dembrowski, Affective Skills Development, P.O. Box 5700, Lincoln, NE 68505.

IN THE END

Values—interests—abilities—aspirations. Your students have been spending hours, days—even weeks—in objective assessment. As they worked their way through it all, chances are they've already shifted some priorities. Yes, there's nothing like a little quiet self-analysis. And once your counselees understand themselves better, they will be able to make those worthwhile decisions.

It doesn't hurt for you to remind a counselee occasionally that he or she is indeed *unique*, biologically and experientially. There is *nobody* in the world just like him or her.

SUGGESTED READINGS

HAMACHEK, DON E. 1978. *Encounters with the Self*. New York: Holt, Rinehart and Winston.

MORRILL, RICHARD L. 1980. *Teaching Values in College*. San Francisco: Jossey-Bass.

ROSS, SKIP, with CAROLE C. CARLSON. 1983. *Say Yes to Your Potential*. Waco, TX: Word Books.

Chapter 15

Counselor Role in the Selection Process

Language. Common Basic Language. Everyone—students, parents, and counselors—should be speaking the same basic language and, where appropriate, using the same terminology.

Practices. Common Basic Practices. Everyone in a department must be willing to utilize certain common basic practices and, in turn, recommend such use to their publics, especially to students and parents. (See Figure 15-1.)

All this is vital for the running of a highly effective and efficient college counseling program. It *should* make a big difference in departmental image and morale.

Visualize yourself in the hallway trying to answer a "quick" question from someone else's counselee or emergency pinch hitting in your office for an absentee colleague. How much easier it is when everyone speaks the same language and uses and recommends the same basic practices. Adopting such a policy can't help but send a "tight ship" message to your publics.

ROLE OF THE DEPARTMENT HEAD

Of course, the key figure in all of this is the department chairperson whose responsibility it is to see that counselors work toward the proper end. Those departments

COMMON LANGUAGE

Example 1: Facilitate communication by having everyone use the same selectivity level terminology: RTS (reach-target-safety), for example. If the College Board can do it with ACH, you can do it with RTS.

Example 2: Agree to spread the word as to the importance of students pursuing as substantive and demanding a senior year program of studies as possible. Then practice what you preach in your counseling.

Example 3: Speak a similar language with regard to the College Board Achievement Testing Program: "It is best to take an ACH as close to the end of study in a subject matter area as possible–while the material is still fresh in your mind."

COMMON PRACTICE

Example 1: When more than one counselor is involved with a small-group guidance program (or even when you are doing it yourself), the presentation should be scripted or done in outline form. Here you become the teacher; your outline is essentially a lesson plan. The most successful group guidance sessions are not disjointed, off-the-cuff presentations. They are creative, well-orchestrated affairs, the contents of which are substantive in nature.

Example 2: All counselors should be making the same basic recommendations to parents sitting with them in private conferences. Nothing sends a college counseling program down the tubes faster than a counselor in one office recommending something quite different from his colleague next door. For example, one might advise his counselees to take the SATs as often as they wish; the other would recommend that the test be taken but twice.

Figure 15-1

that have staffs that are communicative as to overall departmental policies and procedures and that publish a yearly updated manual are generally the ones with well-structured and accomplished college counseling programs.

Common basic language and common practices are foundation stones of a college counseling program! The information in this chapter and that contained in Chapter 16 builds on this foundation.

EXPANDING HORIZONS: HOW FAR IS FAR?

Very few colleges work harder than Grinnell, in Iowa, to ensure that its campus reflects a diversity of students in race, ethnicity, and geographics. Grinnell, a widely respected liberal arts and science college, places a high priority on providing a rich cultural and social environment for its students. The school even has an admission counselor who spends a considerable amount of time and energy recruiting international students.

There are numerous other Grinnells that work enthusiastically to build the same kinds of freshman classes. All one has to do is pick up the *Comparative Guide to American Colleges* to read the words of appeal from both public and private institutions: "diverse student body of major importance," "university welcomes students from out of state."

To accomplish this task, these institutions rely heavily on secondary school counselors.

The Argument Advanced

The argument goes something like this: since many colleges and universities make a concerted effort to attract all kinds of candidates from the four corners of America, shouldn't you make the same concerted effort to expose your counselees to the widest possible range of higher educational opportunities?

Stirling Huntley, director of admissions, California Institute of Technology, certainly thinks so. "The greatest help that counselors can give is by being *thoroughly* acquainted with as many colleges and universities as possible, and at the same time, by being actively involved with students rather than turning their college counseling work over to a 'career technician.' I recognize that counselors are overworked with other burdens, but somehow the old relationship between students, counselors, and colleges has been lost over the years past."

Mr. Huntley is not alone in urging that school counselors be well versed on a large number of institutions. One of the six questions in the authors' survey of some 300 colleges and universities read, "Would you please provide us with two or three ways in which *you* believe that secondary school counselors, especially those in public schools, can make a *greater difference* in the college admission process?" About every third response contained some reference to counselors expanding their knowledge of institutions, including awareness of student bodies, programs, and facilities.

The World Ends at Pittsburgh?

You and your families work jointly to arrive at the "best possible matches," but because *you* are the experienced professional, leadership responsibility for "expanding horizons" naturally lies with you. One energetic and open-minded New Jersey counselor finds that he has to chip away continually at the provincial attitudes of some of his counselees who believe that the world ends at Pittsburgh.

An admission counselor from a midwestern college, who resides in the East, was overhead lamenting the fact that the local guidance department was hardly expanding its students' horizons. In a planning effort with juniors, the department distributed a worksheet that contained 20 sample colleges and universities for these students to use in making profile comparisons. Not one of the colleges on the worksheet was located south of Virginia or west of Pennsylvania. The failure to include a few southern, midwestern, or western schools could have been conscious, unconscious, or subconscious. It does, however, point up the fact that *if an important educational objective is to encourage students to be more global in their thinking, then we as counselors cannot afford to be regional thinkers.*

On the other hand, counselors report that "our students don't want to leave the state." Counselors themselves adopt an attitude of "Why go elsewhere? We have it all here." And such an attitude wouldn't be too difficult to adopt in a state like Virginia, with its two powerhouse public institutions: the College of William and Mary and the University of Virginia—and its private rising star, the University of Richmond. The same thinking could easily take place in other states loaded with excellent schools.

It's also true that in some states counselors have to deal with pressure (real or imagined, subtle or overt) from their departments of higher education to "keep the kids in state." New Jersey is a prime example of a state that has been spending hundreds of thousands of dollars on "We've got it all" advertising, to keep the college-bound from crossing the border. Financial support of public institutions can be tied to the numbers: numbers of students enrolled, as well as numbers of credit hours in progress. Some educators become nervous because they believe that going out of state will result in the permanent loss of their talented young people. Yet, if resources are poor, the talented will probably leave anyway, and if resources are good, others will move in and take their places, and the state will be richer for it!

Nevertheless, counselors should not restrict collegiate knowledge to the boundaries of one state—or even to a small cluster of states. Why not? The world is getting smaller—our *country* is getting smaller—and cooperation is becoming even more imperative. But how can you work with other people if you only know your own? How can a senator from New York work with a senator from Kansas if neither has "learned to learn" (probably by experiencing other states) to be open to the concerns and life-styles of other people?

Counselors are aware of the negatives of remaining in too narrow an environment: provincialism, cultural inbreeding, restricted thinking—and prejudice. You can't accept what you don't know. Most students haven't experienced the similarities and differences of people in other states or other types of community. And some counselors haven't, either.

Counselors are also aware of the difficulties involved when a youngster moves to a "different" place: a city instead of the country, a large college instead of a small school, a private rather than a public institution, a single sex setting rather than a coed one. The known is comfortable; yet in this world of ours, there is a tremendous amount of good to be found in "other" places. Something new can be problematic, but in discomfort there can be growth.

Should *all* youngsters leave their locale or state or region? Of course not! But "expanding horizons" means that you can give your students good reasons to *think* about going farther from home.

The Argument in Writing

Those counseling departments that do place a high priority on exposing students toward opportunities west of Pittsburgh and east of Las Vegas, often incorporate their beliefs in a written philosophy-and-objectives statement. They find that by reducing such beliefs to writing, *all* department counselors are encouraged to internalize and, subsequently, to practice the department's direction concerning this issue. Nevertheless, departments that embrace a philosophy of wide-ranging options find that they have to work with it continually, as they urge families to remove blinders and consider other colleges and universities besides the "names" and the regionals.

Geographical Desirability

If it's important to New York parents that their medical school–bound daughter attend one of the "highly selectives," then (aware of the tremendous numbers of multiple applications to "prestige" schools) you can suggest to the young woman that while considering Cornell, she could think about Washington University in Missouri or Vanderbilt in Tennessee, two spots where she *might* have a geographical "edge."

Besides: Any effort on your part to expand the family's vision to factors beyond "name" can't help but temper society's continuing overemphasis on having the "right" decal on the back of the family station wagon. You are in a great position to influence the development of the decision-making and mind expansion processes of your counselees. *But this means educating both students and parents.* Lay parents need to be shown the possibilities!

INSTITUTIONS LOOK ALIKE

In spite of what some believe, there are no "look-alike" schools, just as there are no "look-alike" students. You shouldn't have a problem with that statement if you accept one of the great counseling tenets: the individuality of human beings. Ah, yes, there *is* a certain beauty in being one of a kind, and most colleges and universities like to think of themselves as such.

The truth is that all colleges are different—similar, maybe, but really different. David Behrs, coordinator of admissions, Penn State at Harrisburg, urges counselors to "become more acquainted with what makes each institution *unique* and more *valuable*."

Grammarians cringe at the overuse of the word "unique." Traditionalists are uncompromising in their insistence that the word is an "absolute" term—either something is one of a kind or it isn't. Behrs is not saying that a college is unique in its "schoolness"; it is unique as a total entity, an amalgam of its own particular aspects. Different students should go to different schools. To find the "differences," *students, counselors, and parents* should join forces to uncover the unusual and valuable aspects of colleges and universities. With this in mind, it should make real sense for you and your counselee to try to arrive at a candidate/college match as nearly perfect as possible.

A good match provides good feedback. In the College Board's 1985 *Admissions Strategist*, Washington independent counselor Joan Dorman Davis quotes from two of her former clients' letters: " 'Thank you for showing me there's life outside of Washington,' wrote a freshman at Pomona; and, 'I'd never heard of Carleton College until you told me about it. I love it here!' " (Those individuals who feel that the matching effort is not especially necessary are often the very ones who find it difficult to explain away the 25 percent of unhappy collegians who annually transfer from one senior college to another.)

As you diligently work, convincing students and parents that they should *not* self-limit themselves and that they *should* arrive at "best possible matches," does not the expended effort cause your services to be more valued? Could it be that the more knowledgeable you are about a wide-ranging number of institutions, the *greater the difference* you will make in the college planning lives of your students and their parents?

ROADBLOCK IN THE SELECTION PROCESS: COUNSELOR BIAS

As important as it is to be well informed, it is equally important for you to get a handle on your own biases as they relate to *all* aspects of the college selection/refinement process. This is an *absolute necessity* if you want to be optimally effective as a counselor. Face it: *everyone* is biased to some degree. If you went to a large university and loved it, you might be biased to size; if you were unhappy about a $200 trip home, you might favor regional schools. That's human nature. But counselors have to try to reach a bit farther.

Richard Davis, director of admissions, University of Wyoming, summed up the feelings of many of his cohorts: "As for 'making a greater difference,' completely unbiased sharing of college information would be the best method I could suggest. From my background in counseling and guidance, I believe counselors should work *one on one* with all seniors to discuss their various college or career interests. Steering them to particular schools (as often happens) should be a strict no-no."

GROUND ZERO AND COUNTING

"Here, catch . . . go read this," says the counselor, as he rather callously tosses a *Lovejoy's* or a *Barron's* guide to a confused counselee looking for some initial direction on selecting colleges. Or a popular step-by-step paperback suggests to a young reader that her first move is to come up with a list of "right" schools she thinks she might like to attend.

Quite frankly, plowing through college guides or creating lists of schools can be a bit perplexing when students are at ground zero in their thinking and planning. (Of course *your* counselees will not be at ground zero. You will take Chapter 14 seriously and will have spent a fair amount of time working closely with each of them.)

So often you hear students and/or parents ask, "Where do I/we begin?" The "homework" begins with the usual basic selection criteria, and although you've seen and heard it all before, read on! The presentation is a bit different here: geographic and locale considerations become all important. And, above all else, keep reassuring your counselees that their initial decisions are *tentative*.

IMPORTANT SELECTION CRITERIA

"Knowledge is power." The selection and refinement aspects of the admission process certainly illustrate this adage. Once your counselees are ready to examine the market, the *very first* consideration in their search for appropriate colleges could be:

Distance and Travel Time

Separation anxiety is one of the top stress factors that affect the college bound. "Leaving the nest" can be a traumatic experience for some individuals, certainly a troublesome one for others. Consequently, this topic should receive the *highest* priority in your counselees' selection effort; the distance of a college from home must be carefully considered! Striking out on one's own is nice and all that, but youngsters *have* to be true to themselves and their feelings, and these feelings are often ambivalent. Just as it is totally acceptable to want to "go away," there is absolutely nothing wrong with wanting to attend school close to home. Naturally, there will be those who for varying and legitimate reasons will prefer to commute for a year or two. If a student lives on campus, and doesn't go home too often, she can be just as independent around the corner as she can 300 miles away.

Most students locate themselves on campuses within a four-hour radius from their homes. This makes an occasional weekend with parents and friends feasible.

Yet there are those who want greater distance: people from the west go east, and vice versa. When a Louisville, KY, boy went home and announced to his parents that he was "working it out" with his counselor to attend college in California, all hell broke loose.

But Kenneth, a New York City student, was just as happy to be turned down by Cornell so that he could attend the University of Colorado at Boulder, even though his mother predicted that he'd be home in a week. You see, Kenneth was an avid skier, and he knew what he wanted. Kenneth went on to graduate after he had skied his heart out. It didn't matter that he was ready to give up the Midwest in his senior year—the first three had been heaven.

If close communication is ever needed between students and parents, it's now, at this "looking for" stage. This means that all parties must agree on distance and travel time. Your counselee's conception of what is close to home may not be his parents'. If he is from Delaware, attending St. Lawrence University near the Canadian border might seem wonderful to him, but it may not be his parents' idea of "reasonable" distance.

Students also need to understand that sometimes an intended major, such as sports medicine, can substantially influence locale and geographical choice.

A State-by-State Approach

It is not enough to break the geographics down distancewise. Your counselee's homework needs to be done on a *state-by-state* basis. If he is from Maryland, how far north will he go? Will it be Maine? There are those who will include Rhode Island, Connecticut, and Massachusetts in their planning, but not Vermont, New Hampshire, and Maine (too far and/or too cold). If they are from southern California, would they be willing to go to the state of Washington?

As you work with your counselees on distance and travel time, it will quickly become apparent why many educators believe that geography is not a particularly strong suit for American students. Interestingly, you can ask someone from the Philadelphia area if she'd consider the University of Pittsburgh, and she'd say yes. But then ask her about Boston University and she'd say that it's too far. Boston is but 1 mile farther from Philadelphia than is Pittsburgh. Or this young lady might go to Pittsburgh and Boston, but not to the southern part of New Hampshire, yet the "bottom" is only 50 miles from Boston.

Perhaps you can convince your counselee to do some real stretching. If she is from the East, what about the Midwest? Perhaps she'd like to check it out. Ohio, for example, has some fine schools, like Antioch, Oberlin, Baldwin-Wallace, Denison, Miami of Ohio, and Case Western Reserve.

If you're from the North, go south young man! There are plenty of Yankees at Emory at Atlanta, Tulane pulls them in from all over the country, and Washington & Lee has gone coed. There are those northerners who will draw the line at Virginia. Why? As a counselor and a third-party communicator, you can be most instrumental in getting counselee and parents to address this most important issue of distance and travel time. How far is far is *up to them*.

Again, some schools take geographic distribution into consideration when selecting their freshman classes. Yes, geographic diversity *can* work for an applicant. For example, if your counselee is from New Jersey, which sends forth literally tens of thousands of students each year, he can increase his chances of admission by selecting schools in other regions of the country. Eastern students become geographically desirable at such excellent institutions as Reed in Oregon, Grinnell in Iowa, Earlham in Indiana, Rice in Texas, Carleton in Minnesota, and Harvey Mudd in California—that's right, Harvey Mudd. A Westerner with an eye on Stanford might find Columbia, Swarthmore, Williams, Amherst, or Wellesley more receptive. Besides, living in another part of the nation can prove to be a most valuable experience.

So, have your counselees sharpen their pencils and list all those states of the nation to which they *will* go. (See Figure 15-2.) So what if American students are notoriously bad at geography! This is their moment to do something practical, and Rand McNally can be fun and enlightening at the same time.

The Physical Location

For some, the charm of remote Lewisburg, Pennsylvania (home of Bucknell University), Gambier, Ohio (home of Kenyon College), or Hanover, New Hampshire (home of Dartmouth College) can wear a bit thin by the junior year—if they made a mistake and should have opted for the vibrant life of the big city. On the other hand, Washington Square benches can get rather hard, and the New York University campus atmosphere can become too hectic and impersonal for yet other students, who might have opted for cleaner air and a more subdued environment.

Now that your counselees have their states in order, it's time for them to think about *critical* environmental factors. It is not only a question of adjusting to regional life-styles; it is also one of adapting to new and specific locales. Not everyone wants to be within walking distance of downtown Boston. Not everyone needs to roam around on 600 acres. Some don't want to live in high-rises. Others would go stir-crazy in too pastoral a setting.

A very practical way to attack this problem is to understand that college locales can be classified into four basic categories:

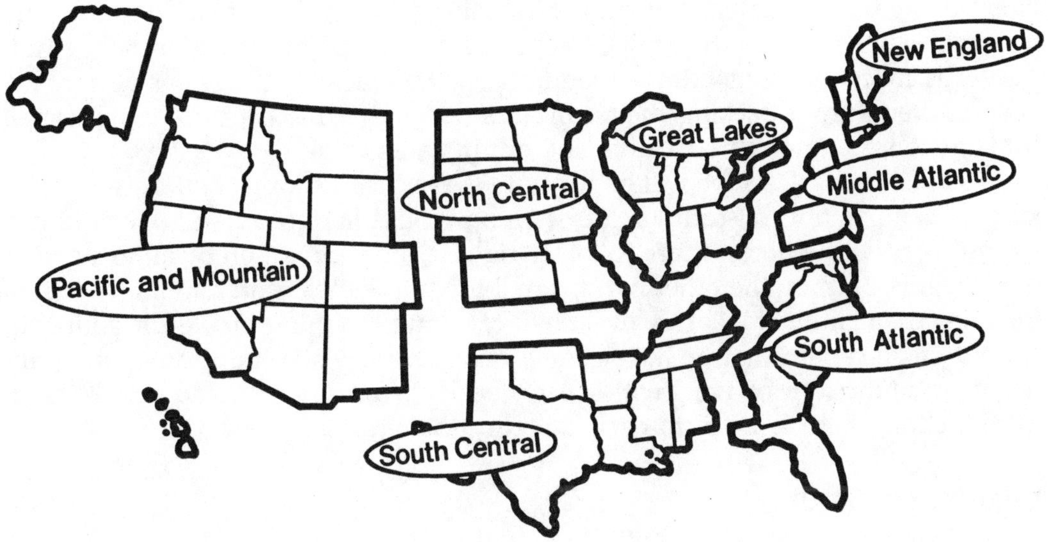

Figure 15-2

1. Institutions right within a city
2. Institutions in a residential part of a city
3. Institutions relatively near a medium or large city
4. Institutions in or near a small town or village

Drexel, Columbia, and Boston and George Washington universities are all in category 1. Here the city becomes an extension of the university campus, with students having ready access to intellectual and cultural activities and sporting events. Certain curricular majors, for example, art, government, and politics, lend themselves to being "where the action is"—and there's plenty of action in a city—sometimes too much. Noise, traffic, and congestion are big drawbacks.

There is still traffic and lots of hustle and bustle in category 2, but considerably less than in category 1. The student is in a residential area, perhaps a mile or two from center city. The setting is quieter and the streets are tree lined. One has a greater feeling of openness. The prime advantage for the student is a more subdued atmosphere while being very close to the "action." Examples of schools in this category are Rice, Syracuse, DePaul in Chicago, and Washington University in St. Louis.

Villanova, Haverford College, Boston College, and Davidson College, found in category 3, have beautiful and spacious campuses. The atmosphere at these schools is definitely more serene. On a Friday night, students can find themselves downtown in Philadelphia, Boston, or Charlotte within 30 minutes or less.

"Secluded" or "isolated" are terms frequently employed by writers to describe institutions in category 4. These are rather severe terms, and the extent of the seclusion can be exaggerated and/or misleading. It's all a matter of degree; certain schools are more remotely located than are others. Some of our most prestigious colleges are situated near or in rural villages or small towns. There may not be much action in "them thar hills," but there is often plenty of action on the campuses, as college administrations spend big bucks on activity programs designed to keep students from packing their suitcases on weekends. Dartmouth, Bucknell, Juniata College, and Alfred University are in category 4.

Your counselee's job will be to study these classifications and decide on the kind of campus and off-campus life-style he would like to pursue over the next several years. If he doesn't care to locate right in a big city, then by all means rule out category 1. If, on the other hand, small-town quietness and familiarity are not for him, then eliminate 4. However, before ruling anything out, each youngster should make certain that he has *carefully* and *accurately* studied the positives and negatives of the style of living within each locale. What has been said here is but an introduction; there is more to each category that needs to be explored.

Large Versus Small

Three hundred students on 300 acres—meet tiny but courageous Wilson College in Pennsylvania. Thirty thousand strong on 3,000 acres—here we have Ohio State University. Most everyone else falls somewhere in between.

Enrollment size is yet another distinctive characteristic of a college or university. When your counselees research for size, they normally have but one school experience upon which to base their future decisions. How *can* a student who has attended a high school with a senior class of 700 know what it's like to attend a college that is fully enrolled at 700? Students need to understand that the size of the student body can be a critical factor in a successful personal adjustment. There *is* a considerable difference between being 1 of 2,000 and 1 of 20,000.

"Small" is usually defined as enrollment under 3,000, and "large" begins at 15,000. Care should be taken that the word "small" is not equated with college and "large" with university. They are not synonymous: Susquehanna University in Pennsylvania may well be the smallest university in America with 1,500 students. Montclair State College in New Jersey has 10,000 students.

You should not believe *all* the cliches you hear about the size of the school. Although it might take a bit of effort, it is possible to maintain one's privacy at small schools. And, contrary to public opinion, close faculty relationships and small classes can be enjoyed at some large schools, especially as students move into their major subject areas. Yale, for example, offers small-school warmth in a midsized university: students can live in 1 of 12 small (about 400 students) residential colleges. Each living and learning community has its own library and dining facilities, and the colleges compete against each other in intramural sports.

Small schools tend to have some characteristics that a student might find *either* positive or negative. Your counselees might find that:

- Students feel a sense of belonging—a sense of community.
- More individualized instruction is possible; one can become better acquainted with the professors. (You could find advanced seminars meeting around a professor's dining room table. Even its president teaches a few courses at Bard College in Annandale-on-Hudson, NY.)
- Greater interaction among students takes place, with the consequent development of closer relationships.
- There is more opportunity to demonstrate leadership and to belong to athletic teams.
- Some small schools have plenty of money to support activities and athletic programs. This is especially true with the more isolated schools.
- It's tougher to "do your own thing" and to be a nonconformist—everyone is witness to much of what you say and do. The small school can be a mirror of the small town.
- The variety of campus activities may be limited because there are fewer individuals available to participate in them, or college support money may be minimal.
- The course offerings may not be as extensive as one would like. Know, however, that the more selective small schools have a vast array of courses: some even have full accounting majors and/or management science majors.
- Three professors teach all the courses in one major, or the catalog requires

the acquisition of 32 major credits, but gives only 32 credits of courses from which to select. That can constitute a problem.

Therefore, it is important that you check to see that the small school indeed has what your counselee is looking for. Assume nothing!

Large schools also have potentially positive or negative characteristics:

- A large school is alive, vibrant, and always surprising. There are endless new social contact possibilities.
- The curriculum is one big smorgasbord of course offerings.
- There is usually an extensive cultural affairs program, and every intercollegiate sport imaginable can be found. If you can't make a team, a big intramural sports program is undoubtedly available.
- It is easier to "do your own thing" in a large setting. It's possible to get lost in the crowd, and there will be plenty of other students who will tolerate eccentricities.
- In many large schools, one can meet a great cross section of students who arrive on campus each year from all parts of the country—from all parts of the world.
- Heading to Sociology 105, you've passed 249 people and haven't seen a familiar face. How does it feel?
- Sitting with 949 others in Western Civilization 222, you're getting neck cramps watching a TV monitor hanging on the side wall of a colossal lecture hall. The "instructor" is there, but he's a microscopic fly down front. How does it feel?
- Survivors of large institutions are often those from large high schools where they had plenty of practice in hallway congestion.
- Forty-five students vie for one position on the tennis team. This can be discouraging, but real glory to the one who makes it!
- A graduate assistant teaches and grades the papers. The assistant *may* be stimulating, but this isn't exactly what was paid for. Regular faculty members are often busy publishing so they don't "perish." On the other hand, some large schools pride themselves on the attention they pay to freshmen and to the teaching quality these newcomers receive.
- Certain large schools can be an extension of the large city outside—purposeful but cold.

As a counselor, with your counselees, you can further and more deeply explore the virtues and shortcomings of large versus small. Your counselees can also communicate with the college reps who periodically visit the high school, or with college admission officials, with whom they might interview on campus.

Coed, Single Sex, and Coordinate

Only a handful left, now—all-male schools, that is. Places like The Citadel, VMI, and Wabash College in Indiana are still "hanging in," while others have been rushing to coeducation. It has been a strange phenomenon these past years, this meeting of the sexes over scrambled eggs and coffee at colleges that were formerly for him or for her. It has also been an Excedrin headache for high school counselors to keep track of who's on what campus. The women are doing better than the men, though: at last count there were 80-some women's colleges in the country.

Of course, practically everyone is attending coeducational institutions, which again come in all sizes and shapes, both public and private. For some individuals, coeducation just seems to be a more real situation. Exchanging pleasantries or engaging in an intellectual debate with him or her in the classroom can be a productive and broadening experience. Most of the schools that have "gone coed," such as Vassar, Skidmore, Haverford, and Williams, have done so quite successfully.

Then there is "across-the-street" coeducation, otherwise known as coordinate schooling. Here a student can have the best of both worlds—togetherness and separateness. Men and women have the coeducational experience of socializing and attending class together, but each college has its own student government association and separate admission offices, and students can retire at night to their own respective dormitories. You can count on fewer than five fingers the purely coordinate situations that still exist today. Harvard/Radcliffe and Hobart/William Smith are examples of this type of organizational structure.

Private Versus State

Convince your counselees not to shortchange themselves! *Don't* let them close doors too early! Urge them to apply to *both* state and private schools and make their final decisions on May 1—*not* October 1—of the senior year. A most difficult task it is, indeed, to convince young people to keep their options open.

Another difficult task is to convince parents not to "second-guess" private schools as to financial aid. Even though private schools often cost twice as much as their state school counterparts, students and parents should give the private school a chance! Many private institutions are well endowed and have extensive financial aid resources. The spring of the year may bring disappointment, but it can be full of surprises as well. (More about this in Chapter 23.)

The quality of education and the prestige of certain state schools, such as the universities of Virginia, Illinois, Michigan, and California, are very much in evidence, but with many state schools, the prestige is somewhat less than that of their private counterparts.

Families must eventually weigh prestige against cost. Again, they should do their weighing in May, not October. Your counselee should never have to regret that he didn't apply to Muhlenberg, Tulane, or Wake Forest.

IN CONCLUSION

As students consider the ramifications of distance, geographics, locale, size, and composition of student body, they should be able to see more clearly than ever the need for real self-knowledge. They will have to look into *themselves* before they look into their schools. All this will make the selection process that much easier and more accurate for them—and for you, too!

Chapter 16

Counselor Role in the Refinement of Options

Your counselee has now come to the moment when a *Lovejoy's* or a *Barron's* guide can be sensibly tossed to her. Either guide can provide the reader with all the basic admission information necessary to *begin* to make informed decisions. Another extremely useful publication is *The Comparative Guide to American Colleges*, by Cass and Birnbaum.

THE HANDY YELLOW LEGAL PAD

Since your counselee has been doing her homework, and has made tentative decisions on geographics, locale, size, student body composition, and so on, she should now place *Lovejoy* or *Barron's* on her left, Cass and Birnbaum on her right, and a yellow legal pad in the center. It's time to begin scanning all colleges and universities located *within the states* that she has agreed to consider. If she gave an absolute "no" to small colleges and/or very large universities, then obviously she'll just "breeze on by." Remember the advice on keeping options open, however. She should eliminate with caution!

On her pad, your counselee should list all schools that appear interesting, and, of course, meet the considerations previously decided upon. Let's take an example:

The young lady lives in Maryland and is uncertain of her intended major. (Knowing one's major can obviously shorten this process.) New York State is one of a dozen states on her list. A medium or large school (preferably under 20,000) would suit her just fine. She would like the school to be near a large city or in a residential section of a city, and it must be coed. Ready? One possibility is Syracuse. Another possibility—the State University of New York at Binghamton.

In the scanning process, it is hoped that students will uncover a dozen or more schools to which they will want to write for additional information. It is imperative that students understand college selection as a refining process. They may initially uncover as many as 30 institutions, which they will eventually narrow to 6.

THE MEAT AND POTATOES OF SELECTION

Counselors will invariably hear parental utterances such as, "She'll never get in anywhere with grades like that," or "Stanford will never take her with those SATs." Deep-breathing counselors constantly find themselves reminding parents that, "Yes, she'll get in somewhere with her grades as they are" or "Stanford might not take her, but someone else will." Regrettably, reassuring words are sometimes lost on some parents. This highlights the need for the *entire* family to be active participants in the *structured process of options refinement*.

It is *most* important that your families understand that they will be utilizing *only* rank in class and/or GPA and admission testing scores in this *initial* refinement activity. The fact that Leslie is strong in other areas is not a consideration here. Adjustment for additional academic and nonacademic factors is to be made at a later time.

Now your counselee will engage in one of the most critical activities of the entire selection process: making tentative choices and then comparing her academic profile (SAT and ACT scores and class rank/GPA) to that of each listed institution. Your counselee will begin to refine her choices to those colleges and universities *whose academic expectations reasonably correspond to her academic abilities and achievements*.

At the *top* of her legal pad she should write down her *best* SAT or ACT scores. She can even split them, if she wishes to do so. For example, her best Verbal might have been in May, her best Math in November. If she is a junior, she probably took the test only once. No problem: she can work with those scores. For this *early rough* research activity, students can even work with their PSAT scores to project their first set of SATs. This is accomplished by multiplying their PSATs by 10, then adding an additional 100 total points, split according to how well they performed on each of the two sections. (Scores of 45 Verbal and 62 Math would become 450 and 620, plus 100: 490 Verbal, 680 Math.)

The young lady might be able to get the class size and her GPA/rank figure from your office. (In many high schools, students can obtain such data from their guidance offices at the end of each year.) Now your counselee needs to determine in what fifth of the class she falls. She should enter this information at the top of the pad as well.

Next to each of her listed schools she should place two pieces of statistical information: (1) the college or university's mean freshman SAT or ACT scores and (2) the percentage of freshmen who graduated in the top fifth or two-fifths of their high school class. (The Cass & Birnbaum guide is a perfect place to find these data. Most, but not all, of the included institutions have reported this information to the authors.)

Making the Actual Comparison

Now the young lady is in a position to compare her own academic profile to that of each of her listed schools. As she makes these comparisons, she is to determine into which of three levels of selectivity each school falls: reach, target, or safety. (It is vital that students and parents (1) understand the meaning of these three terms, (2) accept this maneuver as an *important basic procedure* in the college selection process, and (3) become involved in the procedure.)

Before your families can determine a "reach" or a "safety," they need to know what a "target" is. A target college or university is one for which the student's academic profile (SAT or ACT, and GPA/class rank) is similar to that of the typical freshman. If the student's profile is significantly stronger, the school would be considered a safety. If the profile is significantly weaker, it would be considered a reach. The "+" sign is utilized for shades of "in between." A student who applies to a reach school would have roughly a 3 out of 10 chance of gaining admission, target would be 6 out of 10, safety, 9 out of 10.

How do you judge the level? Look at Leslie's legal pad in Figure 16-1. In the case of Back Woods U., while Leslie's SAT math was below its mean, her verbal score and class rank were very much in line with those the school was accepting. She correctly judged Back Woods U. to be a target school.

My best SAT's: Math, 475 Verbal, 510
My class rank: 145/480, 69th percentile, top 2/5

COLLEGE	SAT'S (M)	(V)	RANKING	SELECTIVITY
Back Woods U.	520	515	70% top 2/5	Target
Coast College	445	470	72% top 2/5	Safety
Upstanding U.	575	550	79% top 2/5	Reach
Old City U.	590	575	68% top 1/5	Reach +
East State College	480	510	80% top 2/5	Target

Figure 16-1

Now compare Leslie's record to that of Coast College. Leslie felt she had a very good shot at Coast. Consequently, she regarded this school as a safety, although she knew she wasn't a shoo-in. (While it is rare, students have been rejected by their safeties.)

Half the students at Upstanding U. are running around with considerably higher SAT scores than Leslie. (Hers is 140 points below their combined mean.) Additionally, only 21 percent of the freshmen graduated below the top two-fifths. Obviously this is a reach.

Now look at Old City U.—it's even harder to get in to, but this was Leslie's first choice. Sixty-eight percent of the freshmen were in the top *one*-fifth, and the SATs were considerably higher. Old City is a *real* reach for Leslie—what might be termed a reach +.

Leslie regarded East State as a target.

Has your counselee figured out her selectivity levels? There should be a spread: several reaches, some targets, and a few safeties. If not, she might have to adjust her priorities. (For example, she might have to expand her geographics and not restrict herself to one or two states, or she might have to face the difficulty of finding intercollegiate volleyball at small colleges.)

Problems with the System

Arriving at reasonable reaches, or even reasonable reach pluses, can be problematic. Although you don't ever want the words "never get in" to leave your lips, you nonetheless have the responsibility of alerting your counselees to their admission chances. Sometimes the suggestion that they might not have "sufficient aptitude and/or achievement to guarantee success in a very intensive academic environment" can be the way to go with it.

Uncovering a sufficient number of target schools can also be a problem for students who tend to either overestimate or underestimate themselves. Some counselors consider target selection as a "realistic-stretching" maneuver: there is a 60 percent chance of acceptance, yet a 40 percent chance of rejection.

Note: The chief objective for the family's engagement in Academic Profile Comparison is *empowerment*. It is *vital* that you, the counselor, help families feel more and more in control of the choices they make. Go with APC!

The information that has been placed on the legal pad can now be transferred to a more formal college selection worksheet. (See Figure 16-2.) The student has the opportunity of listing any ACH scores and indicating, as well, those colleges that require these examinations. As you can see, ACH results were not used in the initial profile comparison activity, but remember that certain institutions do eyeball these results in their candidate selection process.

Blair Academy in Blairstown, New Jersey, has a profile comparison program similar to the one shown in Figure 16-2. A worksheet with the novel title "Running the Numbers" is completed by students on *each* researched college or university. Figure 16-3 is a slight adaptation of the Blair form, shown here with the permission of Henry Milton of Blair Academy.

COLLEGE SELECTION WORKSHEET

STUDENT DATA

Name:	Jr. SAT V ______ M ______
	Sr. SAT V ______ M ______
Address:	ACHs ______________________
	Class Rank ______________________
Telephone:	GPA ______________________

RECOMMENDED SCHOOLS	SELECTIVITY *	PUB/PRV	ACH

NOTES:

* CODE:
R = Reach
T = Target
S = Safety
\+ = More difficult

Figure 16-2

MAKING SELECTIVITY LEVEL ADJUSTMENTS

Not all admission decisions are rendered solely on the basis of class rank and SAT or ACT scores—not by a long shot! But families have to start somewhere, and "roughing-in" selectivity levels by making academic profile comparisons is an excellent *beginning point*. Although you will want to suggest some schools, and indeed work out an APC on a few of them, your counselees and their parents should do most of the work.

"RUNNING THE NUMBERS"
or
Your Standing in the Applicant Pool

Name of College: ____
Location: ______________________________ Enrollment #: __________
Percentage of Applicants Accepted: __________

SAT Scores of Incoming Freshmen

Verbal		Math
________	Above 700	________
________	600–699	________
________	500–599	________
________	400–499	________
________	300–399	________
________	Below 300	________

Rank of Incoming Freshmen:

______ % upper 1/5,
______ % upper 2/5

ACHs required: ______; ______;
______ ; ______
______ ; ______

Minimum GPA necessary for acceptance (if any): ______

....

My GPA at the end of the __________ term: __________
My class rank at the end of the __________ term: __________
My best SAT: V __________ M __________
My ACHs (Subject/Score): ______/______; ______/______
______/______; ______/______

Based upon "numbers" alone, I stand in the (circle one)
top 1/3 middle 1/3 bottom 1/3
of this particular college's applicant pool.

Figure 16-3

It is at this point where you can really earn your stripes: advising families on selectivity-level adjustments. As a knowledgeable professional you (1) comprehend and appreciate a good many of the strengths and weaknesses of your students, (2) are familiar with the little subtleties of the admission process, and (3) can articulate the differences among institutions. *You can use these capabilities to help your families feel even more in control of the choices they are making.*

Adjusting for Quality of Coursework

The first thing an admission committee examines in an applicant's folder is usually the quality of coursework pursued. And "quality" does not always mean honors or advanced placement work. (Some schools offer little—or none—of this type of study.) It can mean "stretching" within a normal college preparatory program of studies.

Where two applicants have similar academic aptitudes, but one extends himself to take what his high school has to offer while the other chooses not to, an admission committee might just give the nod to the one who sought the challenge. Because there is a potential "edge" with quality of coursework (and many other advantages as well), you should urge your counselees to stretch where possible. Colleges are especially wary of those candidates who want to "rest" in their senior year. All this underscores the fact that placing students in *appropriate* courses, according to abilities, interests, values, and career aspirations, is one of the most *serious and vital responsibilities of the school counselor.*

You can advise your counselees, then, as to what extent, if any, they can adjust their selectivity levels.

Adjusting for Achievement (ACH) Scores

If your students plan to apply to "achievement" schools, then (naturally) they will have to follow through and take the ACHs. For those colleges and universities that utilize ACH results as additional selectivity criteria, scoring well (defined by many to mean 550 and higher) *can* provide an admission edge. For example, there are students who score in the low 500s on the verbal portion of the SAT, yet go on to do exceedingly well on the English Composition Achievement Test. Similarly, students with middle 500 math scores, whose beginning algebra and geometry courses date back to eighth and ninth grades, can score in the high 600s on Level II Mathematics.

Therefore, performing well on two or three of these one-hour tests (particularly if taken in the general subject areas of English, mathematics, and science) can enhance students' academic profiles and can indeed adjust the selectivity levels of certain colleges in their favor. Your counselees *should* take advantage of your expertise for this "fine-tuning."

Achievement results can also work to a student's detriment, where scores are low. That is why it is more than wise for a student to consult with his teachers and counselor before he "runs off" and sits for these examinations. Such conferring is especially important where testing is not required (only 145 schools require ACHs), but a youngster nevertheless wants to submit scores in hopes of bolstering his record.

Adjusting for Nonacademic Factors

> Admission decisions at almost any selective college involve much more than going by the numbers. . . . The goal of the selection process is a *class*, not a *profile*. Of course, the class will have certain measurable characteristics, but ideally it will also possess an immeasurable and undefinable "mix" that will mesh well with the college and, in fact, shape the future of that college in positive ways. . . .
>
> Everyone knows that colleges admit some students with "special consider-

> ation." . . . At Lafayette about one student in five was admitted in a "special consideration" category, as defined by the "Lafayette College Statement of Admissions Guidelines." Most of them belong to one of three groups: students with special talents, minorities, and alumni children.
>
> The more cynical among you may believe that the "special talents" category exists only to accommodate those who can throw a neat spiral sixty yards through a swinging automobile tire, or those who measure 6'10" and move well to the left. But it also includes some who can throw a neat couplet to the back row of the theatre and some who measure 5'1" and move sensible motions through the student government.
>
> — Richard W. Haines,
> former director of admissions,
> Lafayette College
> (*College Digest*, April 1986)

As they work to create their classes, admission counselors do try to take into account that being on the AV squad is a more prestigious achievement in some high schools than in others. The status of being an All State flutist or an All Shore soccer forward can sometimes turn a reach into a target, or a target into a safety, or something in between—especially if Old City is looking for a flutist or East State needs a soccer star. The significance of nonacademic factors in the admission process should not be underestimated, therefore—especially if your counselee is headed toward any of the colleges and universities that place "major" importance on such factors. (This term is used in the *Comparative Guide to American Colleges*.)

Incidentally, the term "nonacademic" needs to be broadly defined. Examination of the material under the subheading "nonacademic factors" in the Cass and Birnbaum work will give you a good "feel" for the kinds of things that colleges and universities are seeking. Many want a "diverse" student body. "Extracurricular activities" is but *one* of many nonacademic factors on which certain selective colleges place a premium in their search for such diversity. In addition to the basic selection criteria, and like Lafayette, Reed in Oregon seeks students with special talents, while Hamilton in New York emphasizes geographical distribution. William and Mary in Virginia stresses leadership, creativity, tenacity, and character. Other predominate phrases from the Cass and Birnbaum Guide include alumni children, religious affiliation, promising disadvantaged minorities, extracurricular leadership, and community activities. And with extracurricular involvement, Massachusetts Institute of Technology sees "more value in active participation in and commitment to a few activities than somewhat passive membership in a large number of clubs, teams, and organizations."

How Nonacademic Factors Can Work for Your Counselees

One young woman had average SATs and a "B" average in a normal college preparatory program, but she was also a champion equestrian and had studied French intensively at a private language school. She and her counselor had initially determined a very (+) selective college of liberal arts and sciences in New York

State to be a definite reach. The college had an equestrian team, however. Taking into consideration her prowess in riding, and the unswerving pursuit of the French language, she and her counselor adjusted the selectivity level to "target +." After reading her two well-written essays that gave testimony to the *quality* and *extent* of involvement in these two unusual activities, the counselor suggested that the selectivity level be further adjusted down to "target." She was accepted.

If a student takes an ordinary talent, like writing, does a better job than most in developing it in high school and in the local community, and then *presents* it well on her college application, she will thereby improve her chances of getting into her target and reach schools. Note how Sandra Burns has nicely "grouped" her participation in writing, government, and art in Figure 16-4.

Colleges rather openly give special preference to minorities, the exceptionally talented, and children of alumni (legacies). The talented provide their own gift, minorities add an easily recognizable difference, legacies provide tradition. If a student finds himself a member of any of these three classification groups, his reach could become a target, etc. So if your counselee is Korean, or plays golf in the seventies, or has a mom who graduated from Prestige U., he will have an "edge" on being admitted to Prestige. If he is all of the above, he'll probably walk right through the door.

IT ONLY TAKES A POSTCARD

Your counselees will want to send for additional information on their listed schools. Guides are helpful, but students need to see applications, catalogs, viewbooks, and financial aid materials. (Good luck on getting a catalog out of most admission offices because of printing and distribution costs. But your counselees will at least receive a viewbook.) Besides, they can always locate catalogs in your office.

Gone are the days when admission folk determined their applicants' admissibility by scrutinizing the request letters for errors in spelling and grammar. Therefore, students should feel free to submit a *plain* postcard in making their requests. (Believe it or not, some students have never heard of a plain postcard. One young man thought the counselor meant picture postcards, so that's what he sent—shots of his hometown.) Care should be taken to complete the cards neatly, because these handy little wonders *have* ended up in admission folders. Students should mention their prospective major, if they know it, since schools often publish special departmental brochures. Students should be upfront about their need for financial assistance as well.

An institutional response can take anywhere from two to six weeks, but if your counselees have not heard within 30 days, they should send a second request and mark it as such at the top of the postcard. A sample message is provided in Figure 16-5. Note that it is stated simply—we need to encourage students continually to "write lean."

EAST BRUNSWICK HIGH SCHOOL
SCHOOL/COMMUNITY ACTIVITIES SUMMARY

NAME: Sandra Burns YEAR OF GRADUATION: ______
ADDRESS: ______

ACTIVITIES & AWARDS	GRADE 9	10	11	12
Nat'l Council of Teachers of English Writing Award			x	
Editor-in-Chief, Clarion (school newspaper)				x
Folio (literary magazine) staff		x	x	
Asbury Park Press Newspaper Seminar, school delegate			x	
1987–88 student liaison to the Board of Education			x	x
East Brunswick delegate to New Jersey Girls State			x	
School Representative to Congressman Jim Courter's political seminar for H.S. students			x	
Nat'l H.S. Model United Nations—Award of Excellence			x	
N.J. State Model Congress Leadership Day			x	
Vice President of Student Council				x
Sophomore Class Secretary		x		
Graphic Arts Editor, Clarion		x		
Art Layout Editor, Yearbook	x			
Private Art Instruction	(1982–1988)			
National Honor Society			x	x
Spanish Honor Society			x	x
EMPLOYMENT:				
Camp waitress		x		
Party-Planning/Decoration Service Assistant			x	x

Figure 16-4

Dear Sir:

I am interested in applying to your school for admission in September 1990. Please send me an application, catalog, financial aid form, and any additional information that I might need. I am tentatively interested in majoring in ______________.

Sincerely,

Robert Lincoln
119 Probasko Road
West Windsor, NJ 09999

Figure 16-5

GOOD OLD IN-DEPTH RESEARCH

This is where the "house of cards" can collapse: the important additional in-depth research is just not done. Susan didn't realize that tradition and gothic architecture were what she really wanted after all. Workout-freak Jonathan didn't remember that he would have preferred a sports complex outfitted with Nautilus equipment. Cynthia forgot to research department size; consequently, she was disappointed when she discovered that there were only two professors on the German faculty.

As stated in Chapter 14, thousands of freshmen suddenly wake up to find that they have matriculated at the wrong school—and for a variety of reasons. With Susan, Jonathan, and Cynthia, it was not that they had avoided self-analysis. It was that they had not done a sufficient amount of *additional research*—they had failed to *explore thoroughly* each of their schools.

Can I Speak with the President?

Of course, it's much more than Nautilus equipment or gothic architecture, or even the size of an academic department. Student/institutional compatibility implies wide-ranging considerations that have far-reaching implications. Is asking an admission rep about meeting the president outlandish? Absolutely not! A student-oriented college or university is very likely to have open doors to that office.

Peter Freyberg, dean of admissions at Emory & Henry College in Virginia, believes that counselors should "counsel about learning styles, not majors. Everyone offers English—how it is taught (how one learns it) makes the difference."

Similarly, Admission Director Sarabelle Hitchner, of Sterling College in

Vermont, suggests that students be encouraged to ask questions on issues that *really* make a difference to the student once he or she arrives on campus. "They need the guidance and confidence to raise questions about such things as program quality, and pose questions that can truly distinguish colleges on the basis of educational philosophy, teaching styles, and learning styles." She finds, for example, that the following issues are rarely researched by students and parents:

1. Is there a special approach to learning that permeates much of the coursework at this particular institution?
2. How do the goals of this institution relate to my development as a student? In what ways does this school expect me to be different by the time I complete my education?
3. How will my progress be measured toward those goals? How often will I receive an evaluation of my progress? What role, if any, will I have in the evaluation process?
4. Does the location of the institution influence the curriculum? If so, how?
5. Does the size of the institution influence the curriculum? If so, how?
6. If I start to lose direction (cutting class, poor performance, etc.), will anyone notice, *and* will they let me know that they have noticed?
7. When will I have a chance to sit and talk with the president?

This kind of questioning presupposes that the student has some knowledge of himself and that he sees the collegiate experience as an educational process in which he is involved. Unfortunately, many of our students are simply "going to college." And, quite honestly, we counselors don't spend nearly enough time helping our families explore selection characteristics that are more substantive in nature. Questions must be asked about topics ranging from the sublime to the inconsequential, but without proper advisement, students and parents can focus too intently on superficial considerations. To get a better sense of the process, it might help to group the questions a bit.

The general "feel" of the college, for example:

1. What is the history of the college or university? Is its history important to the college's general philosophy and objectives?
2. How old is the school? Is it liberal, conservative, or middle-of-the-road in its political and social thinking? What is the mix of the student body in regard to this same question?
3. Where does the student body come from? To what extent, if any, is there racial, ethnic, and geographic diversity?
4. What is the general campus atmosphere? Heavily intellectual? Normally intellectual? Collegiate? Nonconformist? Pseudointellectual? Socially concerned? Experimental?

5. What are the weaknesses that the college admits to?

Life on campus:

6. What are the facilities for worship on campus? Off campus? What are the campus religious organizations?
7. Fraternities? Sororities? What percentage of the student body joins? How does this percentage relate to my social adjustment on the campus? What are living arrangements like? Are meals served in the houses?
8. What are the health facilities on campus? Is there an infirmary? If so, who comprises the permanent medical staff? Is there a medical and/or dental plan for students?
9. If I do not qualify for financial aid, are there still jobs available on campus or in the community? What is the pay scale?
10. Are there any hidden costs?

"Educational" questions:

11. What are the honorary and professional societies?
12. What percentage of the seniors directly enter graduate school? Does the school have a job placement office? How and where are graduates employed? What is the placement record of the graduates of the school's various departments?
13. Can an entering student change from one department or school to another without a lot of hassle? If not, what *does* it take to do so?
14. Is it relatively easy to get into the courses I want? If the school is a consortium member, is intercampus transportation available so that I can take coursework on other campuses?

Questions that are more "physical":

15. How about the library? What is it like? How many books? What are the hours? What do the physical arrangements for quiet study look like?
16. What is the physical condition of the dormitories? What percentage of the students live in them? What are my housing options, single-room, single-sex, coed, and so on? Must all freshmen live in a dormitory? Is housing guaranteed for all four years? Dorm regulations?
17. What are the dining facilities like? Quality of food? Are there eating clubs? Is there more than one dining plan? Accommodation for special diets, such as kosher or vegetarian?
18. Do the facilities live up to the pictures in the viewbook?

But loading families with questions and then leaving them stranded, failing to assist them to interpret possible answers, should be avoided. Sarabelle Hitchner: "More importantly, I don't feel assured that students know how to interpret the answers they get to the questions they are told to consider asking. They need help to *understand the implications of the different kinds of responses they receive;* responses, once properly interpreted, can go a long way toward informing them about the commitment, character, and culture of an institution."

Helping your students to interpret responses will demand a large commitment of time and energy on your part, especially since you will have to deal with each individual counselee. But much of the discussion—and the actual demonstration of how answers can be interpreted in various ways—can be accomplished in group activity.

Additional Approaches

Another way in which your counselees can conduct in-depth research is to question people who have attended, or are presently attending, schools on their lists: graduates of their high school, relatives, teachers, friends, their parents' associates, or professionals in their field of interest. They should ask these people to tell them everything they can about the colleges they attended.

It is possible that the representatives from some of those colleges and universities will be visiting the high school. This is a fine opportunity to really "dig." Your students won't have to worry about asking basic questions, because they will already have done some initial research. The one thing students should *not* do in these meetings is sit on their hands. Even "sticky" issues should be probed.

Careful examination of catalogs and viewbooks can reveal much, including the range and relative strength of certain academic departments, distribution requirements, degree requirements, special programs, and financial aid opportunities.

If graduate school attendance is "in the cards," your students might want to examine for what schools the graduates of their listed colleges typically attend. Places like Lafayette College in Pennsylvania carefully track their graduates and even publish informative brochures on graduate school attendance in such fields as engineering, law, and medicine.

Of course the best way to "in-depth" a school is to visit it! Campus visitation is not always a simple or convenient task, but students should force themselves to do it. Furthermore, they should convince their parents that this would be a real eye-opener—a *must* activity. (More about this in Chapter 21.)

Warning! It would be wonderful if your counselees could visit all their schools before settling on their final six, but that can rarely be done. Even if they can't get to all they would like to, they should still narrow their choices by October 1 of the senior year *at the latest*. It can't wait.

By utilizing one-to-one and group session approaches, you can assist your counselees to delve more deeply into their schools and reach more deeply into themselves.

PLACEMENT INFORMATION AS A REFINEMENT TOOL

David Seifert, a counselor at Valley City Multi-District Vocational Center, Valley City, ND, is a long-time advocate for the publication by higher education of some type of comprehensive standardized placement information. Needless to say, much of Seifert's pleading has fallen on deaf ears, as many colleges hesitate to publish anything that might detract from their salability to prospective students. But times *are* changing. The Higher Education Reauthorization Act of 1986 states that colleges who process Guaranteed Student Loans and advertise a positive placement of their graduates must publish such information.

In an article in the College Board's *Admissions Strategist*, entitled "Job Placement Information Completes the Recruitment Puzzle for Students," Seifert pulls no punches as he ponders why colleges spend large sums of money in other areas but not in the recruitment and marketing of their most precious commodity, the students themselves. The author, with his Vocational Center, has a natural concern for the eventual job placement of students. It is noteworthy that the center sends 30 percent of its graduates to four-year colleges.

As for the recruitment of the college bound, Seifert is more concerned about what is *not* being told than what *is* being told:

> By omitting what I consider to be very important information, recruiters are tacitly giving students inflated ideas about the specific occupational utility of a particular major. I believe that this lack of information is actually a misrepresentation of the truth. . . . In my counseling experience, it seems that little or no communication exists between some admission people and their college placement office's personnel. By not mentioning placement information and figures during their presentations, recruiters appear to be passively relying on the old belief that a college degree guarantees employment and are using this as a selling point.
>
> As a high school counselor, I do not think that one of my counseling activities should be to dissuade a student from majoring in a particular field of interest because little or no job openings currently exist in that area. I do, however, think it is imperative that I show students and parents alike specific information about the potential employability of that particular major, and then help them decide whether or not to pursue that option. Factual specific information (both good and bad) also needs to be liberally dosed with other information about the intrinsic, social, personal, and professional advantages of obtaining a college degree.

In your counseling, you have undoubtedly seen where positive placement information can at times be the determining factor by which some of your counselees select one college over another.

For many reasons, including the fact that its consumerwise families are more than ever concerned about what should be the return on their educational dollar investment, East Brunswick High School, East Brunswick, NJ, has begun to collect placement information and make it available to its publics. The school's College & Career Center maintains an open file of such data. The counselors ask to have this type of material as they meet with visiting representatives. If the reps do not have it in their possession, the interviewer asks them to send it along at their earliest convenience.

WHAT TO DO WHEN YOU DON'T KNOW WHAT TO DO

As a counselor you cannot help but see the concern and confusion on the faces of some high school students as they feel societal pressure to select a major *before* they enter college. There are legions of perplexed high school seniors out there, totally "in the dark" about what to do.

Your students probably changed a great deal during high school, and the chances are that the same thing will happen in college. Therefore, they should find a school that will *let* them change. One of the most important qualities to look for in a "marketplace" is *flexibility*. For example, switching one's major should not become a test of courage or endurance. Possibilities should exist for double majoring, creating one's own major, or pursuing a strong minor. A college should stand ready to respond positively to any early indecision and/or confusion on your counselees' part. The freshman year in particular should be a year of exploration.

When in doubt, students should be encouraged to go with liberal arts and sciences. Today's executives realize that the best route into business and industry may not necessarily be an undergraduate degree in business management. These professionals are worried that our youth are being narrowly educated with too great a focus on technical business courses—that communication skills are lacking.

The boast of a liberal arts and sciences education is that it teaches young people how to better express themselves on all levels. It broadens the mind and prepares a person to learn and to adapt. Advocates of the liberal arts and sciences argue that students can vastly improve their understanding and enjoyment of the world around them: they will become people who will always have something to do, something to think about, something to enjoy. The products of colleges with strong liberal arts and sciences approaches are never bored.

Furthermore, there appears to be no incompatibility between studying the liberal arts and sciences and earning a living. Indeed many argue that there is, in fact, a synergistic relationship between the two. So don't rule out the liberal arts and sciences college. A major in English at Dartmouth, Dickinson, or Douglass just might be the edge needed to land a trainee position at Citibank.

Note: Your counselees need continual reassurance that there is absolutely nothing wrong with "x-ing" the "intended major" box on an application "undecided" or "undeclared."

Put "Sciences" Back into Liberal Arts

College guide editors call them "liberal arts colleges," but most would like to be known for what they really are—liberal arts *and sciences* colleges. Many small colleges have powerhouse science departments and are naturally proud of them. Middlebury in Vermont is a case in point: with a national reputation for the strength of its foreign language department, Middlebury would also like to be known for the caliber of its science department. So as secondary school counselors, let's help spread the word that many of these erroneously labeled schools do indeed support strong science programs.

Figure 16-6 is a *sample* of small colleges across the country that have unusually strong science departments. Information was obtained from the thirteenth edition of the *Comparative Guide to American Colleges*, James Cass and Max Birnbaum (Harper & Row, New York, 1987).

THE FINAL SIX

Now your counselees should go for it! They visited some, didn't get to others. They talked with anyone and everyone about their top 20. They read extensively. They reflected on their values, interests, abilities, and career aspirations until their brains hurt. They weighed the hours of travel, the large school and small, the short dorms and tall, cities and towns, the ups and the downs. They are now ready to choose the six finalists. The envelope, please!

As in a beauty pageant, there may be striking similarities among the final

NUMBER OF DEGREES CONFERRED, 1983–84

COLLEGE		BIOLOGY	CHEMISTRY	PHYSICS
Albion	MI	61	12	5
Albright	PA	65	6	1
Allegheny	PA	43	23	9
Bates	ME	36	6	11
Carleton	MN	35	35	26
Dickinson	PA	29	31	3
Franklin & Marshall	PA	38	26	15
Kenyon	OH	23	12	8
Knox	IL	18	18	4
Luther	IA	39	6	5
Mary Washington	VA	36	10	5
Middlebury	VT	22	7	8
Reed	OR	36	12	23
Swarthmore	PA	41	6	8
Ursinus	PA	42	17	8

Figure 16-6

six, *but your counselees should make certain that these similarities do not extend to the level of selectivity*. Their six schools should be an assortment of reaches, targets, and safeties.

Various educators believe that today's youngsters are not sufficiently encouraged to "go for it." But, you could become a most positive influence by encouraging your counselees to think big. In a field of six, they might want to apply to two reaches, three targets, and one safety. Or they could chest their cards and go for 2, 2, and 2. *All* your counselees' final choices should be schools that they would be happy to attend.

If your students have done their homework well, they should be admitted to at least half of their schools.

Chapter 17

"Making a Difference" for Different Counselees

Think of how boring it would be if your counseling capacity were restricted to pumping students' SATs and GPAs into a computer system, receiving automatic admissions to college A or college B, and resting peacefully with the students' happiness assured. Fortunately for your well-being, today's young people provide you with a much greater challenge. You feel even more fortunate when your expertise is summoned to aide a damsel—or swain—in distress.

All your counselees can use your help in growing to maturity, but some of them have more formidable obstacles to overcome than others. Consequently, some will need your skills more than others. You will have to do additional digging, for example, as you search for that "best possible" choice for a handicapped or minority student. And you might have to do some extended research in assisting a female counselee to achieve her true potential in a male-dominated field of interest.

A "DIFFERENCE" FOR WOMEN

Brown University's Jacob Neusner was a feminist before feminism, "because I grew up in a family of intelligent and assertive women and never realized women were supposed to be dumb and submissive." This and other illuminating and provocative comments can be found in Neusner's 1984 work, *How to Grade Your Professors and Other Unexpected Advice*. The author's grandmother operated a store and a real estate business, his mother published a newspaper, and the women he found attractive were brilliant, interesting, striking, and lively. "I married the most interesting woman I ever met." But it was only when Neusner became a college professor that he discovered that other people did not see things the same way he did. Indeed, the reality took some time to sink in.

> Too many girls speak quietly, do not contradict boys, seldom argue, and listen carefully. Too many girls write everything down and simply repeat it. Boys talk loudly, contradict and interrupt girls, prove contentious, and talk before they listen. Boys propose theories, explain things. . . . I am too impatient to accept the intellectual timidity of the obviously brilliant woman, too cynical to accept the assertive ignorance of the stupid man.
>
> I make equal demands on my students, men and women both, and set goals for them just beyond where they are. . . . What this means in practical terms in the classroom is easy to say. Women have to talk up, speaking in voices that can be heard. They have to develop capacities for assertiveness in vigorous discourse and in their writing . . . saying what they think in a straightforward way. Intellectually in the classroom there should be no difference between men and women. The society we hope to build requires the best of both halves of the population. It's that simple.

Coeducation

How do we build that society? Some people argue that the best preparation is women fighting for their niche in a coed institution—sink or swim. They contend that attending a single-sex college becomes an artificial, sheltering type of situation—an unnecessary postponement of the inevitable female/male competitive shoulder-rubbing that will take place out there in the "real world." Others see a contradictory problem: many women are not staying afloat for long in coed institutions—indeed some sink rather rapidly—in part because of their background experiences at the secondary school level.

The National Association of State Boards of Education's 1987 study, *Female Dropouts: A New Perspective*, points to social and academic influences that make young women susceptible to low self-esteem and poor academic performance. Girls are encouraged to be passive and "excel in personal skills that do not include academic and career planning." Schools also give more positive feedback to boys and discourage independence in young women. "Stereotyping in teachers' treatment of boys and girls and in the selection of courses still exists. . . . Many teachers' methods and attitudes favor boys' learning styles and the development of boys' self-confidence and are correspondingly less attentive to girls."

In another study, researchers from the Association of American Colleges conclude that sexism prevents women from obtaining degrees in male-dominated fields (engineering, computer science, mathematics, physical sciences, for example). The researchers argue that girls' experiences in elementary and secondary schools are "a major determinant of whether they pursue nontraditional careers."

Girls take fewer math and science courses, giving in to pressure from parents, peers, teachers, [counselors?] and textbooks. By the time women reach college age, they don't have the inclination or interest—or encouragement—to major in science or technical fields.

Again, Neusner:

> Do I claim that on today's campus women will find freedom to be themselves—to be women when they want, students when they want, intellectuals when they want, athletes when they want, whatever they want to be, wherever and whenever they want to be it? No, the opposite is the case. Women will have to develop their own criteria for judging classrooms and professors, colleges and universities, teaching the teachers how to serve all of their students. So far we have episodic lessons and a lot of guesswork.

Neusner suggests that when your female counselees begin to examine coeducational options, they should (1) look for female role models occupying important positions in both faculty and administration, (2) determine whether curricular offerings include courses in women's studies, and (3) learn whether women are equal partners with men in such extracurricular activities as politics, sports, and so on. "These seem obvious and fundamental questions. Another generation will refine things."

Single Sex

It is a distinct possibility that your counselee might attend a single-sex college. Though somewhat on the down-slide in the 1970s, women's colleges seem to be commanding more attention than ever in the 1980s. (Enrollment figures are up by 25 percent in the past decade according to a study by the Women's College Coalition.) Maybe that's because the schools have been able to convince women that under their auspices they will "get a better shake."

At least, Chatham College in Pittsburgh, PA, thinks so. In its illuminating booklet, *Cost of Dreaming*, Chatham quotes a 1982 Association of American Colleges study that found that the classroom environment at coed institutions puts women at a significant educational disadvantage because of the chilling effect of either being ignored or not being encouraged. A Carnegie Commission study reveals that women in coed institutions are more reluctant to enter into class discussion, for fear of being perceived by male students as less feminine. And in *College*, Ernest Boyer remarks that on coeducational campuses, "even the brightest women students often remain silent."

Chatham believes that a big plus for women's colleges is that women "learn to lead in a supportive environment which expects hard work, self-discovery, achievement, and success." The booklet goes on to suggest that many female executives and leaders in our country graduated from women's colleges. (Ten of the 23 women in Congress attended women's colleges.) It also states that these young women who have chosen to be different, "will go to medical school at a rate 2 to 11 times higher than their coed counterparts, and will major in such 'male-dominated' fields as chemistry, economics, and mathematics at two to three times the national average for women." Clearly, these schools have a proven track record in providing an education that works well for many women.

Selling Women's Colleges

No one knows better than the college officials themselves the difficulties of selling the public on the numerous special advantages of a women's college. If it were just the singular task of sensitizing individuals toward the positives, it would be one thing; in their presentations, however, admission counselors have discovered that they have to plug away at breaking down the stereotypical images erroneously held by moms, dads, daughters, and counselors—yes, counselors!

The Women's College Coalition (an organization of 65 women's colleges based in Washington, DC) found, in an extensive national study of the college selection process as it applies to high school girls, that teachers and counselors are significantly biased about single-sex education. Much of this bias is unfounded, and secondary school educators are often misinformed as to the realities of the situation. Research indicates that when individuals have explored the topic in depth, they discover that women's colleges are indeed *not* finishing schools, monastic shelters, irrelevant in today's world, training camps for hard-core radical feminist activities, centers of elitism, or hot beds of lesbianism.

Point to Consider in Working with Your Counselees

- Perhaps the most significant: if you ever hope to work effectively with your students, you must face your own biases as squarely as possible, so as to keep your values separate from those of your counselees. Never let yourself forget that *each* of your counselees is a *one of a kind* person. And, as you self-assess, it might be important for you to think about the following:
    - Almost all teachers and counselors are products of coeducational institutions, and therefore have a limited frame of reference from which to advise.
    - Because of their biases, some counselors have problems dealing effectively with other basic selection criteria, like size of institution and religious affiliation.
    - Your own biases are continuously being refueled and/or tested by various segments of our society. And surmounting such influence isn't getting any easier.
- Another important point is to get your counselee to square 1—that is, getting her to even explore the possibility of a women's college. This is where you, the open-minded professional, can make a genuine impact. *Don't* be hesitant to broach the topic. You will be amazed at the number of young women who will display tentative interest. If your counselee is standing on square 1, or just outside of it, adopt an approach used by many successful

counselors: *strongly* encouraging the submission of applications to *both* coed and single-sex institutions. Why not apply to Smith College as well as to Tufts University? This kind of approach can buy time for sorting out feelings. Experienced counselors, keen on a "keeping doors open" philosophy, recognize that the many days between September and April can dwindle slowly—that the idea of attending a single-sex school can grow on an applicant. Things often "come together" after a campus visitation.

- Find the time to explore, with your counselees, some "special advantages":
  - That a large number of highly successful women in today's work force are products of women's colleges.
  - That the percentages of women majoring in mathematics and science at women's colleges are two to three times the national average for women.
  - That these institutions have an impressive success rate in placing their students in graduate programs.
  - That living in this type of environment can have a positive effect on a person's level of confidence and self-esteem.

    (One woman reported to the authors that after having graduated from a small New Jersey women's college, she found herself to be the only female in a male-dominated graduate program. "I felt totally comfortable and totally capable," she said.)
- If you discover that you have a goal-oriented counselee sitting in front of you, someone who has rather specific ideas as to the direction(s) of her life, you may well have a prime candidate for the submission of one or more applications to this type of school.
- Think about spending the same proportionate amount of time in learning about women's colleges as you do with coeducational institutions. Most counselors are not nearly as knowledgeable about the former as they are about the latter. Familiarity with the geographic locations of these schools can be most helpful and revealing. Through an understanding of proximity to all-male or coed schools, you can acquire a better feel for such things as male/female social interaction and cross-registration possibilities for additional courses. (Incidentally, since almost all women's colleges have cross-registration with coed or men's colleges, this might be something to look into with your students.)
- Examining the viewbooks is another way of acquainting yourself with the facilities and the academic and social life of these institutions. (Provided you can get through the glitz and glamor. At a conference seminar entitled, "Does It Really Look Like the Pictures?" you would hear the unhappiness of secondary school counselors with the overall quality of many of these publications!) As promotional literature, however, the Simmons College and Wellesley College viewbooks are excellent examples of content material that is down-to-earth, informative, substantial, and purposeful. Fine source material to improve your skills!

- Recognizing, as you do, that most 16- and 17-year-olds are not especially sophisticated thinkers and prefer not to be thought of as "different," you might encourage them to open up their thought processes to accommodate critical outcomes issues.

Sensitizing Projects That Worked

Four programs have been created by individual counselors or counseling organizations that have helped to dispel myths, correct false impressions, and orient the public to programs and activities of women's colleges:

Example 1: A Virginia counselor took a group of 13 girls to visit a nearby women's college. The group met with both admission officials and professors, toured facilities, and lunched in the dining room where they were able to communicate with attending students. It was an enlightening and productive experience. It also resulted in 4 of the 13 submitting applications to women's colleges in and out of the state of Virginia.

Example 2: At the 1986 PACAC (Pennsylvania Association of College Admission Counselors) Summer Institute, an annual program dedicated to enhancing the skills of college admission and secondary school counselors, attendees heard a panel of four women, graduates of or currently enrolled at women's colleges in the East, describe their experiences at the respective institutions.

Example 3: Smith, Mount Holyoke, and Wellesley colleges joined forces in hosting a breakfast meeting to update school counselors on the advantages of attending a women's college. The program was appropriately titled, "Why Go to a Women's College, or What Should You Tell Your Students Who Are Turning Their Noses Down at Women's Colleges?" It was an informal get-together with plenty of candid dialogue. Participating counselors were impressed with both the straightforward approach of the colleges and their total cooperative effort.

Example 4: A California high school developed a panel staffed with professionals from four types of collegiate institutions: private small college, large public university, technological institute, and women's college. The school's counseling department made two very wise moves with regard to program structure: (1) the program was held at night, so that parents, powerful influencers in the admission process but short on awareness, could attend and (2) the format was designed to keep the audience together for the entire evening. The end result was that all the parents heard all the panelists, *including the "tell it like it is" presentation by the women's college representative.*

A Final Word

Could we doing too much hand-holding with our young people these days? Many would say that we are. Historically, it has been the school counselor's job to help his students assume continued responsibility for their own lives. In today's world this can be a formidable task for the counselor, considering the sheltering type of society in which we live.

News articles indicate that colleges are getting in on a recent trend toward some of this hand-holding. The official term is "guiding": colleges guide the lives of their students. Women's colleges continue to resist this trend, however. In a February 22, 1987 *New York Times* article, Ann Burger, dean of Smith College, explains that the empowerment of students is an important educational objective at women's colleges. Sarah Sutherland, dean of studies at Mount Holyoke College, speaks to the article in a February 25 letter by stating that women have been guided long enough. "[Women's colleges] have consistently refused to hold more than one of a student's two hands. . . . they can have guidance without being guided. The distinction is more than semantic."

Interesting—especially since the lack of personal empowerment is societal, as well.

And, if "empowerment" is indeed a valid quest, might not your efforts to sensitize your counselees toward consideration of a women's college be a natural extension of your helping them to achieve greater self-direction?

A "DIFFERENCE" FOR THE HANDICAPPED

The implementation of the Education for All Handicapped Act of 1975 increased the school counselor's participation in the lives of disabled children. Counselors have always dealt with the gifted and talented, but most have been hesitant to deal with the handicapped: some welcome the opportunity to serve, others continue to see themselves as inadequate to the task. Lack of confidence due to a lack of formal training is the prime motivating factor.

Unfortunately, graduate training that would enable counselors to counsel with optimum effectiveness continues to lag far behind the demand for counselor services. Prior to 1977, when the 1975 Act was promulgated into law, very few individuals took any coursework in special education as part of a graduate program in counseling; even today, only a few states require a special education course of any kind for elementary and secondary counselor certification.

And, thanks to the 1975 Act, the needs of the disabled are becoming more fully addressed in an effort to maximize educational, social, physical, and vocational potential. Counselors presently work with a special services team to plan a counselee's yearly schedule, help develop an Individual Educational Program, consult with parents, and lend encouragement and support for postsecondary schooling or employment. They also find themselves consulting with a burgeoning number of special education teachers, hired because the federal statute has led to the identification of many more exceptional students.

Although the acquisition of special knowledge and skills is essential, many of the techniques you use for nonexceptional kids can also be used for the exceptional. You can utilize the same college counseling skills, except that special research might have to be conducted to uncover appropriate support programs for your counselee's specific handicap. Obviously there are differences for college placement of students with handicaps: for physical difficulties, the concerns will be largely physical (mobility, access, medical attention, etc.); for perceptual and neurological impairment, specific educational assistance might be necessary; for emotional impairment, you might look for a special counseling program.

Caution! Be aware that college programs specifically geared to the learning disabled can vary considerably in range and intensity of support services.

The Search

Handicapped youngsters have always had the same wide-ranging needs as their nonexceptional counterparts. A vital message that you can impart to your counselees is that *in spite of their disabilities*, they should participate in the same college admission decision-making process in which all other students participate. In the introductory comments to their valuable 16-page booklet, *How to Choose a College: Guide for the Student with a Disability*, the authors waste no time in making a salient point: "There are lots of guides and manuals available in bookstores telling the average student 'How to Choose a College'—*And All of Them Apply to You!!!*"

Published jointly by the Association on Handicapped Student Service Programs in Postsecondary Education and the HEATH Resource Center, the guide speaks directly to the individual student. It is an ideal publication to distribute to your disabled counselees. They can then use this booklet as a companion piece to regular guides. As for yourself, perusing the contents can help you sharpen your own skills as they relate to the handicapped and the college admission process. Single copies of the guide are available at no cost from:

HEATH Resource Center
One DuPont Circle, Suite 670
Washington, DC 20036

Multiple copies for expanded distribution can also be ordered through HEATH. The toll-free number is (800) 544-3284.

In summary, your counselees with difficulties shouldn't think of themselves as "handicapped": they are "*challenged*"! They should consider the same basic selection criteria as everyone else—they just need to handle a little bit more!

PAL

The year was 1970. It must have been a special year for Curry College officials, including Dr. Gertrude Webb, the founder of PAL (acronym for Program for Advancement of Learning). PAL is an individually designed service that affords conscientious, capable, but learning disabled youngsters who want to pursue a liberal arts education the support necessary for them to achieve their goals. Some 10 percent of the students at Curry (Milton, MA) are PAL participants. It would seem that the presence of such a program on a college campus could not help but enrich the lives of the other members of the college community.

Curry's well-written PAL brochure provides an excellent sense of what a substantive, comprehensive, and well-structured LD program is all about at the collegiate level.

St. Andrew's and the Physically Disabled

Tucked away between the beaches and the mountains of North Carolina sits St. Andrew's Presbyterian College. Although it was stated that the handicapped should consider the same basic selection criteria as their "ordinary" peers, some would not be comfortable being the "token" handicapped student on a given campus. For them there are schools like St. Andrew's where some 6 percent of the student body is so. Located on 600 beautiful, wooded acres in Laurinburg, 100 miles southwest of Raleigh, St. Andrew's has been making national news by treating their physically disabled as full-fledged members of the college community. Opportunity here literally knows no barriers. The campus, designed in 1958 to be completely barrier free, was one of the first institutions in the nation with a formal support program for the physically disabled. A rehabilitation center right on campus services students; a specialized career and placement counselor services these same students' "after-college" needs.

A "DIFFERENCE" FOR THE GIFTED AND TALENTED

Bright kids can be as confused about college admissions as anyone else. Most of these youngsters can handle the basic concepts, but they need specific help with specific problems at specific stages of the planning process. There is real danger in assuming that because some of your counselees are superdirected in most aspects of their adolescent life, they will be able to cope successfully with all the relatively new, and often confusing, tasks associated with college and career planning. The student who intends to apply to even one highly selective school needs sound advice on rather sophisticated questions.

Yes, the gifted and talented have their own unique problems. And, like the handicapped, they often suffer from an impaired self-image, caused in part by years of extreme anxiety and unrelenting pressure to excel academically. Some G&Ts, as they are called, attending our nation's private and special-admission high schools seem to be particularly stressed: competition for rank-in-class positions is unbelievable, and kids cry bitterly if they pull a 94.5 instead of a 94.6.

Counseling in one of these high-powered institutions is something that relatively few counselors will ever experience—so few, in fact, that some of the schools are pitifully understaffed. As a result, students are getting shortchanged on counseling, especially on much needed personal counseling.

Educators can dismiss such understaffing: "These kids are so self-directed, they don't need the same attention as typical preppies." Or "They're bright and talented—they'll pull it off." Nothing could be further from the truth! When high schools have to hold mandatory weekend retreats to help juniors and seniors deal with unusual amounts of stress, it gives a direct sign that our society is in deep trouble with its priorities.

A talented and gifted student needs a counselor as much as the next guy does—maybe even more. So do their parents. Academic talent is not synonymous with social maturity. These youngsters may have:

- Become so involved with their talent that they have not developed other parts of their personality.
- Found schooling so easy that they have not learned to face—and handle—a challenge.
- Been so pressured to excel that not winning is the ultimate defeat.

That they might:

- Experience a loss in enthusiasm for learning.
- Do poorly—or even fail—for the very first time.
- Be shunned for life by family and friends if they don't go to a "good" college.
- Be less viable as a candidate because they are too focused on the academics and not enough on the nonacademics.

You can be of tremendous help to these young people if you:

- Communicate frankly with parents who have unrealistic expectations. Not only can a youngster be misplaced in a particular course, she can be misoriented toward a particular school.
- Assist a student sort through his priorities so that he can keep things in perspective.
- Help a counselee who is not gifted in all subject matter areas work effectively with his weaknesses.
- Counsel someone on how to deal effectively with the pressure to get into a "hot" college, which is looked upon as a ticket to a "hot" career.
- Counsel a G&T who feels he has dishonored the family name and is contemplating suicide.
- Warmly—but candidly—bring reality to bear, and share with your counselee the real world of college admission: the rather heavy emphasis the "most" and "highly" competitive schools place on the "whole" person.

Being gifted and talented isn't easy. Then again, being exceptional in *any* way isn't easy.

A "DIFFERENCE" FOR A KID WITH A PAIR OF 400S

Counselors know full well that 1600 is the top combined SAT score, but they are confronted almost daily with counselees who have but half that total. Many of these students are out there searching for colleges, of course—and many colleges are out there searching for these students.

It is disconcerting to hear a parent refer to her youngster's SAT scores as "disgusting," "ridiculous," or "lousy." Your heart immediately goes out to the youngster, because you know that if the parent is that bent-out-of-shape talking with you, she must be doing a real job on her daughter at home.

As it is easier for a teacher to teach the "bright" student, so too is it easier for a counselor to counsel a student with a pair of 600's and top fifth ranking—but such is not always the case. How *does* one handle the Browns, who have the desire and the money to send son Harry to an "ivy"—but Harry has a 400 verbal score? Or the Smiths, who are both graduates of a "highly (+) selective" state university, to which they want to send their daughter, but daughter's combined SAT is 800? Or the depressed junior who has just gotten back a pair of 300's? Or the most difficult of difficult cases: the counselee who has a pair of 400's and is in the bottom quarter of his class. If he had earned average grades, at least you'd have *something* with which to work.

None of these situations is easily resolved—each is a case unto itself. If you are an experienced counselor, you've undoubtedly developed a certain amount of expertise in handling these special issues. If you are new at it, you'll want to search the alternatives so that you can be supportive, upbeat, "Let's get on with it," "There are plenty of other options."

Test Score Interpretation

A troublesome factor in your working with parents who must face a pair of 400's can be their misunderstanding of the particulars of standardized testing. It's a constant source of amazement to see parents, who year after year examine their offspring's average standardized test scores, somehow believe that he or she will nevertheless "come through" on the SAT's. Unfortunately, while parents see the progression of scores, they don't understand them—and sometimes don't make much of an effort to understand. Once again, it raises questions as to the practicality of mailing home test results, even with written explanations. It argues for the interpretation of scores *by* counselors to parents. And it further argues for having a counselor in every elementary school, for the purpose of *early* test interpretation and communication.

More than the average amount of confusion, unrealistic expectation, and emotionalism can be witnessed with parents going through the admission process for the first time. Remember: this may be *your* twenty-third season, but it's *their* first, and their *son's* one and only. Patience is of the utmost importance in counseling. And it most surely can be put to the test when one is repeatedly asked,

"Are these scores any good? Can I get in anywhere?" Keep reminding yourself that this is a "first" for this student.

Quality of Communication

Your making a difference with the average or marginal student virtually demands open and honest communication with parents—with special attention paid to parental expectations. There's no reason why communication can't be both frank and warm at the same time. Parents need to see that *you* are the professional. It is not only what you say and how you say it that matters, but also the whole aura of professionalism that you present.

Some counselors are too passive as they work with the admission process. A professional aura calls for a "take-charge" attitude, on occasion. There's nothing wrong in remarking, "This is the way we are going to. . . ." It's directive, but the "we" includes *student, parents, and counselor*.

Besides—a directive approach can convey an enthusiastic manner. (And the counselor's low level of enthusiasm is a major objection often cited by parents.) Nowhere is counselor enthusiasm more important than in working with average students. Many of them are already on their way "down for the count"; so your upbeat and willing attitude can help immensely. An additional trait for you: an innovative spirit (which isn't developed in the careers of some professionals, unfortunately) can also be a working plus.

The Two-Year College: A New Beginning

Your directive approach might call for making a rather radical (in parental eyes) suggestion: for example, "John should consider a *private* two-year college." You might see the junior college as the perfect spot for your not-so-mature counselee. What with the warmth, special attention, and reduced pace such a small setting can provide, a two-year school can be a great beginning.

Parents may see it as a "complete waste of time and money." Some continue to believe that starting at a two-year institution means lengthening the total undergraduate program—but not so! Most institutions of this type take considerable pride in the quality of their transfer programs. Some even publish special informative brochures that list those senior colleges to which their students transfer. You can do much to highlight these advantages to parents.

What you can do for yourself is to understand that not all two-year colleges are alike. Admission officers at these institutions are most concerned that counselors take the time to peruse the literature and become knowledgeable about the differences. For example, Dean Junior College in Franklin, MA, accepts but 65 percent of its applicants. As Steven Briggs, the dean of enrollment management, reminds us, "This is hardly open admissions. Further, the mission here is different from that of a community college. We are primarily a residential college with a student population representing twenty-five states and a dozen or more foreign countries."

When you recommend a junior college, consider suggesting to families that they be comprehensive in their approach to college selection, that is, that they apply to both four- and two-year institutions, public and private. Somehow, the whole business of the two-year college becomes more palatable to parents when cushioned by a recommendation to examine a certain number of senior colleges as well.

A "DIFFERENCE" FOR THE WAIT-LISTED

Occasionally you will hear someone exclaim that he wished his favorite college had rejected him instead of wait-listing him—it's a fate more cruel than rejection. Of course, colleges aren't alone in this process: the military uses alternates in its ROTC scholarship selection process, professional athletic teams use backups who sit and wait on weekends, Broadway theaters use stand-ins who stand and wait on weekends *and* weekdays.

While waiting for either thin or fat envelopes to arrive, many students do pause to reflect on the positives and *negatives* of being wait-listed. But even when students acknowledge the heavy odds against coming off of a waiting list, they hope against hope. For most, the hope is false and the agony is prolonged.

The Procedure Described

A waiting list provides an opportunity for qualified students who have not been admitted on or about April 15 to be admitted later in the spring, or early in the summer. Colleges and universities "go to" a waiting list to fill space in the freshman class not reserved by the first group of admitted students.

A "rolling admission" college has little or no problem here, but a "candidate reply date agreement" school must accept many more students than it can ever hope to accommodate. It expects a certain percentage of admitted students to decline its offer of admission—and the percentage might vary from year to year. When more students decline an offer of admission than the school expected, the waiting list is employed to fill the void. (When *fewer* students decline, the college must scramble to find space for its "largest freshman class"!)

At some schools, like the University of Richmond in Virginia, the waiting list is not numbered or ranked. In a 1985 memorandum to secondary school students and counselors, the University of Richmond states that it is able to determine how well the freshman class has formed a few weeks after the May 1 deadline. At this point, it uses their waiting-list plan: Richmond rereads the several hundred students on the waiting list to select the best qualified candidates. But not all schools operate in this fashion. Some do their homework ahead of time, and although they'd never admit it to their various publics, their waiting lists are not only in place, but rank ordered as well.

The fate of any waiting list is completely dependent upon the responses from the first group of students, and that is what makes the entire process such a "crapshoot." Over the years, some schools rarely have to go to the list; others find themselves periodically withdrawing it from file drawers; still others employ it regularly, if only for a few candidates.

Your Role as the Counselor

With a wait-listing announcement, there is not a college worth its ethical salt that does not advise applicants in a "holding pattern" to make plans to attend their next-choice school to which they have been admitted. And, speaking of ethics, this is an opportunity for you to remind your counselee to return her post card *only* if she would like to continue on a particular institution's waiting list, and *only* if she would plan to attend the institution once admitted.

With wait-listing, occasionally *both* you and the admission counselor can "make a difference" in a youngster's life—a *big* difference!

We have included the admission counselor even though much of the public doesn't believe that this person is genuinely looking for ways to admit students. This polished and affable rep is often jokingly referred to as a "rejection officer." How little the public knows! They should sit in on some of the admission committee deliberations or read Richard Moll's book, *Playing the College Admissions Game*, to understand more fully this difficult and complex process. But *you* know that these counselors, in spite of the numerous constraints placed upon them, do work hard to ensure that as many good candidates as possible get to attend their schools.

The Richmond memorandum goes on to state, "The University of Richmond will welcome your [the candidate's] visit to the campus, but your *personal visit will not become a deciding factor in your candidacy for admission from the waiting list*." The admission committee indicates that it will also examine the latest academic records, standardized test results, and other updated credentials for rereading.

Note that Richmond does not completely close the door to either an initial or an additional campus visit for wait-listed candidates. It's also important to notice the receptivity toward the submission of updated data. This should tell you something about your potential impact on *certain* wait-listed situations.

Specific Ways in Which You Can Assist

- Pick your cases carefully! Get involved only where there is a clearly demonstrated need to do so and the student is truly deserving.
- Your best approach is the tactful one. Inquire as to whether or not the college received *all* the information it needs to make an informed decision, for example, latest SAT scores, midyear grades, recent activities or honors. Never challenge the school on its decision!
- As you reach for the telephone receiver, ask yourself this question: "Did I *fully* and *completely* support my counselee's candidacy?"

- Make certain that your counselee does some of the work. The greatest gains are made where both counselor and counselee are involved in any appeal process.
- A returned post card is not enough! Your counselee should write a letter. (The college will respect him more for doing this.) If he did a less than adequate job in initially "tying" himself to the school, this is his "moment of truth"! You could follow up with a *brief* letter of your own—a letter rather than a phone call—because it (1) looks less spur-of-the-moment, more thought-through; (2) signals a greater seriousness of purpose; and (3) provides the "harried-in-May" admission counselor the chance to work conveniently with your communication.

In the letter shown in Figure 17-1, kept purposely brief, the *counselor* "ties" herself to the college. (Incidentally, she was successful. The admission director of this highly selective Pennsylvania school scribbled the phrase, "It worked!" on the counselor's copy of David's June acceptance letter.)

- Remember that both you and the admission counselor are working toward the same end. If a wait-listed youngster wants to go to a particular college badly enough to press the issue, the admission counselor will be looking for a way to admit him. Your extra effort can *sometimes* help.

> Dear Mr.
>
> I would like to further "go to bat" for my counselee, David Tinsmann. He was recently placed on your waiting list. David has been accepted to some very fine schools, but he really wants to attend ________________.
>
> Two years ago I visited your campus and participated in a one-day workshop. Needless to say, I was most impressed with both your school's facilities and its programs. Consequently, I have since been encouraging certain students to make application to ________________. I believe David would be an excellent addition to your campus community.
>
> Anything you might do concerning this matter would be most appreciated.
>
> Sincerely,
>
> Patricia Logan

Figure 17-1

- Person to person, counselor to counselor, can pay great dividends when it comes to your students and the college admission process.

"GREATER DIFFERENCE" SUGGESTIONS FROM THE COLLEGES

Here is an assortment of comments from admission representatives in the authors' search to learn how school counselors could make a greater difference in the admission process:

- "Counselors could answer our questions more honestly. We typically get counselor responses that do not appear to match the true ability, i.e., 'This student will do superior work. . . .' when he/she has a 'C' average in high school."
- "We require our applicants to write an essay. The more thorough and detailed the essay is, the better the chances are for serious consideration."
- "Department chairpersons should urge their counselors to participate in consortium tours."
- "Do more to encourage students to visit campuses. Even if a student can't fly out to CA to see UCLA, he/she can visit a large, urban university nearer to home to see what it 'feels like.' "
- "Is there any way you can convince students to apply as early as possible, as opposed to waiting until near, or on top of, stated deadlines? Many wait until the eleventh hour as though this were a painful process much like paying income tax. Many of these students receive less than full consideration because at any point in time we fill to capacity."
- "If no class rank, at least give us some indication as to how the student has performed in relation to other class members."
- "Talk about college with junior high students. Isn't senior year planning a bit late?"
- "I know it is difficult, but could you please make your recommendation for the college in question. We often receive the same recommendation the student would get to an open admission community college. Unless some discrimination is made, the recommendation is worthless."
- "More counselors for fewer students would help with communications!"
- "Wish we had more college *counselors* in the West. For example, in California, the role has been turned over to paraprofessionals, career centers, and volunteer mothers who seem only interested in their own children and where they will continue with their education."
- "Counselors can serve as important role models for those students who do not have a good support system at home."
- "Encourage students to *complete* their files with schools to which they apply. Let colleges know when they are no longer interested in them so we

can get these students off our system. This would save us considerable time in doing follow-ups on incomplete files."

- "Give us more counselors who can find the time to seek out and help us identify those well-hidden disadvantaged students 'toying with success,' to encourage and support them. If this could be an eighth or ninth grade project it would be wonderful!"
- "You could make us more aware of our own impact—positive and negative—on your counselees. What do people think of us? How do we do our work as professionals? Are there better ways to do what we do?"

IN CONCLUSION . . .

It would be so much easier to work with kids if they were all cut from the same cloth—but then we wouldn't need counselors. Young people are certainly different from each other. Even if you have seen innumerable students who look and/or act very much like the one in front of you, you must remember that this is a unique person. His problems are similar to those of other youngsters; he has a similar home life, lives in a similar neighborhood, and takes similar courses—but the combination is *his*. This is the only life *he* has lived.

Individuality—a most significant word in a counselor's vocabulary. There *is* something beautiful about being the only one in the world. Today's young person needs to be reminded that he is unique, one of a kind, and then have this message periodically reinforced. Who better to do this than you?

SUGGESTED READINGS

Female Dropouts: A New Perspective. National Association of State Boards of Education, 701 N. Fairfax Street, Suite 340, Alexandria, VA.

Looking for More than a Few Good Women in Traditionally Male Fields. Project on the Status and Education of Women, Association of American Colleges, 1818 R Street, N.W., Washington, DC.

NEUSNER, JACOB. 1984. *How to Grade Your Professors and Other Unexpected Advice*. Boston: Beacon Press. A delightful, crystal-clear, and thought-provoking piece. It reads like a personal letter to high school and college students. Don't miss Chapter 18 entitled "Sex."

Chapter 18

Working with Minorities

The less the student gets from other sources, the more he needs from you!

So true! And it is especially true if you counsel in a school whose enrollment is heavily black and Hispanic. An unwieldy caseload, typical of that kind of school, often means that you can't give nearly enough.

But what would it be like if you only had to counsel 100 students? How *would* you advise your minority students on college admissions? An entire volume could be written on this important topic, but, for the time being, here are a few points to consider:

1. If you are encouraging a student to attend a predominantly white college or university, you and she will want to explore campus support services. Statistics indicate that the high attrition rate among blacks and Hispanics at these institutions is usually due not to academic reasons but to general unhappiness with the overall situation. Transferees and dropouts cite such problems as low minority enrollment, the nonexistence of campus minority organizations, student attitudes toward minorities, the absence of institutional *and* community role models, weak academic counseling and tutoring programs, and the absence of a particular minority church within the com-

munity. You and your counselees will want to explore these issues carefully. Interestingly, one or two of them appear as selection characteristics on worksheets published by various computer search firms.

2. The bottom line is, "Will I feel comfortable on this campus?" On some campuses, yes; on others, no. The critical factor is the match between the *personality* of the student and that of the institution. A preliminary critical factor is your knowing your counselee *and* the institution intimately, so that you can properly advise him on his choices. At some colleges and universities, minority support services are strong and the welcome mat has been set out in full view.
3. Be alert to the fact that there are students who lack self-confidence and self-esteem and feel comfortable only with members of their own race. Some of them might profit from being with a variety of people. Being black in a predominantly white institution, for example, could foster greater self-confidence and develop a broader base of experience.

A few comments from *The Black Student's Guide to Colleges*, edited by Barry Beckham:

> 'Vassar,' says a satisfied sister, 'is an excellent place to grow.' . . . Support services at Vassar are described by many respondents as 'excellent'.
>
> No word is heard more on Brown University's campus than 'diversity.' It definitely is Brown's claim to fame, and the black student population here is a testament to it. Most black students who matriculate at Brown are informed in September of all support services at a pre-orientation Third World Transition Program.
>
> A black undergrad says that if you're an open-minded individual and interested in many things, Boston College will be perfect for you. . . . Most respondents comment favorably on the tutorial and study skills services available. The Afro-American, Hispanic, Asian, and Native-American Office (AHANA) supplies tutors and counselors. . . . Black alumns are looked upon very favorably by black students. They participate in Black Family Weekend. . . . Programs to encourage racial tolerance are few but students speak highly of the ones that do exist.
>
> Take note: you can be easily intimidated and discouraged by a university this large. But the word here is that the impersonal can be turned into the personal if you have a strong support system of black students, black faculty and administrators. Of course instances of commitment on the university's part—and there are sufficient examples at Ohio State—don't hurt either. . . . Expect to find an abundance of support services that receive high grades from the respondents of color: 'Counseling is exceptional, especially for coping with black-white relations,' assesses one undergrad. What Ohio State may lack in personableness may be compensated for in effort. The university's president has reportedly set the tone for affirmative action. . . . And high-level blacks hold positions as vice-provost for academic affairs; vice-provost for minority affairs; associate dean, College of the Arts.

SUBTLE DIFFERENCES

Although the size of minority enrollment and the quality of campus support services are top considerations for entering minority students, you will want to encourage certain students to examine a wider range of options. For example, there *are* youngsters who don't need substantial support services. They are so independent-minded, they have such a high level of self-confidence and self-esteem, that they don't care if people think of them as green, orange, or purple. These young people can handle almost any situation, even go it alone if necessary. Consequently, if they *wanted* to, they could be successful at a college that has 0 percent black and Hispanic students.

Moreover, if you only counsel toward schools with 10 percent or more minority population, then white schools will continue to remain white, won't they? Of course you'll need to have the right kind of counselee to do this kind of ground breaking. You won't want to break ground just for the sake of doing it, but you can't keep the old fences up, either. If a school has no Hispanic students, and your counselee *really* wants to go to that school, the fact that he is Hispanic should not be the deterrent factor. Your knowledge of him should enable you to advise properly on whether or not his is a realistic choice. Some youngsters can handle it, some youngsters can't. Some youngsters don't mind the aggravation; others have enough to deal with without it.

So, this is where you must exercise great care. Those who remain at a point where they *will* need varying amounts of emotional, social, and academic support at the collegiate level might drown on an all-white campus. Of course, the need for support is true of any student, isn't it. It doesn't matter what color he is. And, again, this is why it is imperative that you know each of your counselees well. The challenge, then, is to know whether a particular counselee can find success at a school with a low black or Hispanic enrollment and minimal support services, or whether he needs bigger numbers and more support.

HISTORICALLY BLACK—HISTORICALLY EMINENT

The 1954 Supreme Court decision to outlaw segregated educational facilities was certainly a landmark case. And it certainly has had a stunning effect on matriculation figures at historically black colleges and universities. Since 1954, the black student population enrolled at these institutions has plummeted drastically.

But there remain some 95 historically black colleges and universities in America, and they are a great national resource. The learning environments at these institutions might be best described as fruitful, caring, relevant, and divergent. They are, however, criticized for their inability to offer demanding courses, especially in the technologies; for having mediocre faculties and administrations; and for lacking proper library and physical facilities. Regrettably, some black schools with small endowments are being hit hard by inflation and governmental budget cutting, especially of the federal variety.

Obviously, there is more to college than the academics. Higher education is a total experience, no matter where one attends. Black colleges are not "good" or "bad" because they are black; rather, their quality rests on the job they've done to make the total collegiate experience a profitable one for the student. And, despite their financial and economic problems, black colleges and universities continue to attract students for the following reasons:

- A willingness to take a chance on a student who presents low admission test scores
- The broad presence of successful role models that helps to ensure a student's chance of succeeding both socially and academically
- A genuine promotion and encouragement of individual intellectual development
- A setting that fosters the individual enhancement of self-confidence and self-esteem

In the 1986 booklet, *Choosing to Succeed*, Frederick Patterson, founder of the United Negro College Fund, states:

> Academically, the Black college has a mission, to do for students something that is not available elsewhere. These institutions provide a Black perspective on history, introduce an African background and provide a particular attunement to the academic needs of Black students, including the remedial and preparatory. There is a willingness to go beyond the academic requirements, to provide a rapport that may not exist elsewhere.
>
> . . . At Black colleges, a student has the greatest choice of opportunities for self-expression and leadership without the racial factor coming into the picture. That freedom of choice is the hallmark of opportunity. Because of it, Black colleges are a training ground for leadership.
>
> . . . It is the process of selecting a college that is most important. Visit and see the school. Talk to students who are already there. Look at some of the outstanding graduates. In other words, select a Black school as you would any other school. Seek an honest evaluation, not a sentimental one.

DOWN-AND-OUT IN THE INNER CITY?

To put it bluntly, the condition of the public education of most of our urban youth is a national disgrace. One would think that, considering the immediacy and the severity of a problem with so many potentially negative consequences, public officials (in whose hands rest the educational lives of literally millions of disadvantaged youth) would have "moved out" on this problem by now. But, for the most part, they have not.

Positive educational advancement has been surrogated by negative criticism, stigmatization, and politicization.

With the public education of inner-city minorities in virtual shambles, it is no wonder that the few counselors in these schools find it difficult to think about, let alone become proactive concerning, precollege counseling.

In Newark, NJ, the state's largest school district at 52,000 students, a host of young people are ill prepared for such counseling. According to a September 3, 1987, *Trenton Times* newspaper article, only 26 percent of Newark ninth graders passed the 1987 state-mandated High School Proficiency Test (HSPT). Compare this figure to an overall 70 percent state passing rate or, better yet, to the 95 percent passing rate of many of the state's affluent suburban schools.

Let's look at it another way. There are 592 school districts in New Jersey. Fifty-six of them are considered "urban aid" districts according to the New Jersey State Department of Education. Twenty-nine of the 56 are considered severely "impacted" and contain 64 percent of the state's black and 75 percent of the state's Hispanic students. These 29 districts alone make up a whopping 25 percent of the students enrolled in New Jersey schools.

The gifted and talented urban youth aren't getting a much better shake. Of those who *don't* become discouraged and drop out, many get "lost in the cracks." In a joint project report issued by the National Education Association and the New Jersey Education Association, and published in the August 1987 issue of the *NJEA Review*, it was stated that in 1985, only 676 students in the state's 29 impacted districts were enrolled in advanced placement courses. Compare this with 1,640 students enrolled in AP courses in but four affluent suburban districts—which, taken together, represent barely 1 percent of New Jersey's students.

The disgrace of New Jersey is but a portion of the disgrace of the nation. The fact that one quarter of New Jersey youngsters are being largely ignored is nothing compared to what is happening nationally. Newark's problems are little different from those of such cities as New York, Philadelphia, Miami, Chicago, Detroit, St. Louis, Houston, and Los Angeles.

And you don't know whether to hope or despair. State legislators approve and fund mandated proficiency testing, on the passing of which hinges a student's high school graduation. Such testing has produced more than reading and mathematics scores! It has produced mass failure and unprecedented numbers of pupil dropouts, as well. At the same time, few of these same legislators do anything to properly fund the very schools from which these failures and dropouts emanate. Or, if they do, the monies are sometimes squandered or misappropriated at the local community level.

CAN SCHOOL COUNSELORS DO ANYTHING?

You bet! This is a grand opportunity for us to strengthen our position, morale, and numbers. Unquestionably, our great challenge is to become more involved in helping improve the quality of education for elementary and secondary school urban youth. The job *cannot* be done just with better facilities, teachers, class sizes, and programs. Urban youngsters need better counseling and support services, to deal more effectively with the adverse social, economic, and cultural pressures that impact on their education.

Historically, the educational community has been addressing these needs through the availability of special services personnel, such as school counselors. Unfortunately, in urban districts where the needs are the greatest, the counselors are the fewest.

The 1987 NEA/NJEA project report recommends that:

> Each school have at least one full-time guidance counselor and additional counselors on a ratio of 1:100 (K–12).
>
> Educational support personnel and high technology resources be employed to release guidance counselors, school nurses, psychologists, social workers, and other student support professional staff from clerical tasks and eliminate unnecessary paperwork which interferes with time to counsel students.

Local, state, and national counselor organizations can and *should* do more. But they cannot do it without you! If you haven't joined one or more of these organizations, *please* do so, so that your voice can be heard.

For, after all, can we counselors really afford to sit back and see that students do not shower after physical education classes because the showers haven't worked in years, or watch children attend schools in converted cheese factories and Civil War prisons?

> What we are doing to our urban children is not a black and white issue or a minority-majority issue, but rather a wealth vs. poverty issue. As a society, we need to redouble our efforts to teach [counsel] these children. Failure to provide the needed funding to urban districts now will surely cost more in the long run by placing an extra burden on society in terms of welfare, unemployment, adult training programs, drug rehabilitation, and the prison system.
>
> —Dr. Crosby Copeland, Jr., Superintendent of Schools, Trenton, NJ (from "The Urban Challenge," *NJEA Review*, August 1987)

If we don't do anything about this situation, accepting the notion that there will always be some winners and some losers among us, then that acceptance will inevitably make losers of us all.

SUGGESTED READINGS

BECKHAM, BARRY. 1984. *The Black Student's Guide to Colleges*. Hampton, VA: Beckham House Publishers, Inc. A great guide that takes 75 of the nation's most selective residential colleges; adds 24 historically black colleges; and then includes yet another 12 based on high black student enrollment figures, general popularity, and a view toward geographic diversity. The first 55 pages provide dynamite reading on precollege planning for both you and your counselees. The book is available in paperback and is well worth the purchase price.

Choosing to Succeed. P.O. Box 4702-B, Kankakee, IL. This thoughtfully prepared booklet, produced by the General Foods Corporation, would be an excellent piece to distribute to black high school students.

Chapter 19

Fish Farming and Other Unusual Majors

People sneeringly refer to them as "fads." Oh, a few might be, of course, but certainly not all of them. As a matter of fact, many (like psychobiology) are the amalgam of two sophisticated realms of study. Many are well known in some areas of the country and don't surface in others (like citrus horticulture). And while you might assume that Texas A&M offered a program in petroleum engineering, you might be surprised to find it at Marietta College in Ohio. The issue isn't the *peculiarity* of majors as much as it is *familiarity* with majors.

WHAT ARE THEY?

Just flipping through the "Career Curricula" section of the *Lovejoy* guide can give you a better sense of what is out there, and where it is. Some of the following two- and four-year majors and concentrations are more "unusual" than others; for some, only the location is a bit uncommon. Your creativity can evoke many more than are listed in Figure 19-1, but this is a start.

You are indeed a great "suggester"—especially when a student sends you signals that a "different" major might be perfect for him or her. Don't we owe it to our students to look beyond the big-six career fields?

INSTITUTION	STATE	MAJOR
Florida Institute of Technology	FL	Aquaculture (fish farming)—a comprehensive approach to the diverse and fast-growing field of fish farming. The program is designed to prepare students for entry into virtually any area of commercial fish culture.
Beaver College	PA	Artificial Intelligence/Cognitive Science—has two foci: to make computers more useful by increasing the complexity of their tasks and to understand human thought and the processes that define intelligence.
Russell Sage College	NY	Arts Management—offered jointly by Departments of Visual and Performing Arts and Economics; the intent is to prepare students to resolve problems in the relationship among artistic, administrative, and financial concerns.
Florida Southern College	FL	Citrus Horticulture—a study of the principles and practices underlying the propagation and growing of fruit, including the botany, utilization, processing, marketing, and management of citrus crops.
Philadelphia College of Textiles	PA	Color Science—the science of selecting and producing dyes, inks, paints, and other colorants that are both decorative and functional. Philadelphia Textile is the only college in the nation that offers an undergraduate major in this field. Careers in color science are limited only by one's imagination.
Evergreen State College	WA	Ecological Agriculture—examines options for viable, small-scale agriculture in industrialized and Third World nations; emphasizes practical skills in food production; students maintain demonstration and market gardens of Evergreen's organic farm.
Springfield College	MA	Emergency Medical Services Management—provides students with a broad-based education and prepares them for certification at various levels of Emergency Medical Services

		competency, up to the level of paramedic.
High Point College	NC	Home Furnishings Marketing—designed to prepare students to enter the marketing departments of home furnishings manufacturers or home furnishings industry suppliers, or to go into home furnishings retailing.
Georgia Tech	GA	Health Physics—a thorough grounding in the fundamental sciences to prepare students for a profession dedicated to the protection of people and their environment from the harmful effects of radiation.
College of Boca Raton	FL	Funeral Service—a study of the principles related to planning, computer utilization, implementing, and directing funeral services in accordance with the psychological, sociological, and theological needs of the family. Coursework includes study in service sanitation, funeral home management, embalming, and restorative art.
Manhattan College	NY	Nuclear Medicine Technology—educates technologists who can prepare radiopharmaceuticals, perform quality control tests, aid in medical procedures, and participate in research in the field.
Hiram College	OH	Psychobiology—allows students to combine training in biology, psychology, electronics, computer science, and mathematics to enable them to approach questions of how and why people and animals live and act the way they do.
Sterling College	VT	Rural Resource Management—develops qualities which encourage students to become responsible stewards of resources and personnel as managers of rural operations; courses focus on social, economic, and ecological consequences of management decisions.

Figure 19-1

ON THE OTHER HAND

Maybe an unusual major is not what your counselee is looking for. Sometimes colleges have a "different something," like Wingate College in North Carolina. Noting that few of its students had traveled to any great extent and therefore had limited cultural experience, Wingate instituted the "Great American Heritage" and "Winternational" programs. With the first, *all* sophomores who have at least a 2.0 average and are otherwise in good standing with the college spend a week in a city in another part of the United States. In the junior year, these same qualified students spend ten days in a European city. Prior to their visitation, students devote one hour a week during the fall semester boning up on the city itself and planning the projects to be undertaken once there (e.g., visiting Stonehenge in England).

Or how about Berea College in Kentucky, founded in 1855 by John G. Fee as an interracial college for low- to moderate-income students. (And Mr. Fee was almost lynched for his efforts.) At Berea there is no tuition; the students spend a minimum of ten hours a week working at a variety of jobs, including the maintenance of a campus hotel that serves as a training facility for the college's hotel management program. Students come predominantly from the Southern Appalachian mountain counties, but about 15 percent are from other parts of the country; 5 percent are international.

There are numerous other schools with "extras," of course. But with some, the differences are more striking. As one admission director stated, "Don't follow the crowd. Encourage students to look at unusual schools and specific experiences."

VERMONT 2, WASHINGTON 1

Not a hockey score—simply a reflection of three colleges in two states that exemplify an unconventional approach to higher education: Marlboro College and Sterling College in Vermont and Evergreen State College in Washington. While surely not the colleges for everyone, they might nevertheless serve the purposes of a few of your counselees who only need to be *exposed to different possibilities*.

And "unconventional" isn't necessarily a dirty word. It's not conventional to permit students to carry some or all of their coursework pass/fail, as some colleges have done. It's unconventional to eliminate SATs as an admission requirement, as Bates, Bowdoin, Middlebury, and Union colleges have. But Marlboro, Sterling, and Evergreen are primarily unconventional in their nontraditional approach to learning. As an important initial step, you should scrutinize the philosophy and objectives of a given institution, because unconventionality can take many forms.

Once you have ascertained the extent of the unconventionality, and appreciate it for what it is, it will be in your storehouse of knowledge for that candidate for whom such a school might be the prefect spot. As with the contemplation of a women's college, it's not just getting your counselee to the consideration stage; you have to be there first.

Marlboro College

At this small, academically rigorous college, Marlboro students are afforded a considerable amount of freedom, but structure *is* present to make the freedom work. The only requirement for the first two years of study is to pass a writing proficiency examination. Availability of, and close interaction with, *all* faculty (6-to-1 student/faculty ratio) makes for the finest sort of liberal arts education. The college offers all its upper-level students tutorial-based studies. Combined with small classes, tutorials are simply the way the faculty goes about teaching and students go about learning. It appears to work: one measure is that a whopping 60 percent of Marlboro graduates attend graduate school.

What is known as a "major" at most other institutions is known as a "Plan of Concentration" at Marlboro. The plan, often interdisciplinary, is designed by the student and his or her principal faculty advisor. After completing the plan, the student is examined by the plan advisors and an *outside examiner*, chosen for his or her expertise in the student's field of study.

Students sit on all committees, including admissions and faculty hiring and retention. Governance by the Marlboro College Town Meeting Association is decidedly different and is patterned after the traditional town meetings that continue to be a part of small-town New England political life.

Sterling College

An excerpt from its revealing brochure, *The Enduring Value of Sterling*:

> Sterling College has built a national reputation for its unique brand of demanding academic programs that involve the outdoors, the rural environment, and hard physical work. But the essence of Sterling's value—what it teaches most enduringly—is much more than just a set of skills. Sterling teaches an approach to life. Sterling builds an ability to do solid work; to make good decisions and live by them; to work with others; and to achieve a lasting self confidence.

The environment is isolated, but unlike the feeling students can acquire at other isolated colleges, students at Sterling don't feel closed in. On the contrary, the isolation seems to have a beneficial effect on concentration and commitment. If you have a counselee who is a bit short on self-esteem, a year at Sterling could do wonders for him or her.

Sterling has two basic programs: The Grassroots Project in Vermont, a one-year program combining hands-on work with classroom and laboratory learning in agriculture, forestry, and wildlife management, and The Rural Resource Management Program, a two-year course focusing on the social, economic, and ecological consequences of management decisions that culminates in an AA degree. A ten-week internship anywhere in the United States is included.

The programs sound fascinating. But what do people do with the education? According to the Sterling brochure—everything and anything. Dean of Students Stephen Wright states, "I don't care how many future biologists we turn out. If a student comes to Sterling and then decides to go into modern dance, I applaud. The principles we teach here can be applied anywhere and in any discipline."

Could Wright be right? One young woman from a private school in New York City focused on agriculture at Sterling, went on to pursue a degree in theater and management at Marlboro College, and then took a job in the theater while studying interior design and architecture at Parsons School of Design. It appears that her future will combine all her college learning—she plans to work in Africa on tropical architecture and the problems of modernizing societies. Wow!

Evergreen State College

Prior to the founding of Evergreen in 1971, the nontraditional approach to higher education was mainly the preserve of private schools like Bennington and Reed colleges. Evergreen, with its lush 1,000-acre setting on Puget Sound, differs dramatically from its earlier counterparts in that it is a *public* institution.

Studies at Evergreen are interdisciplinary in nature. The innovative academic program enables students to enroll each trimester (of ten weeks) in a single comprehensive program, called "Coordinated Studies." Groups of students and faculty get together to explore a single topic intensively from various perspectives. For example, the area of human development is studied by drawing knowledge from anthropology, biology, history, literature, psychology, and writing.

Cooperation rather than competition is the byword, and no grades are awarded. A student's academic progress is monitored through detailed written evaluations by faculty members. Evergreen officials are convinced that with their unconventional methods of undergraduate education, the 2,000-some students become better conceptualizers, analysts, and problem solvers. And all this for a mere "bag of shells." (The college is the cheapest accredited institution of higher education in the state of Washington.)

Those of your counselees who are active participants in their own education will feel comfortable at Evergreen. Although self-sufficiency is the thrust here, the independence is tempered by the close relationship between students and professors.

DIFFERENT DRUMMERS

Some students march to the beat of a different drummer, and some colleges provide the appropriate band. There are yet other schools with an unconventional approach to higher education, like Bard College in New York, New College in Florida, St. John's College in Maryland, or The Armand Hammer United World College in New Mexico.

Having a working knowledge of uncommon majors and uncommon approaches to learning can be most beneficial in your work with that "individual" counselee!

SUGGESTED READING

MALNIG, LAWRENCE R., WITH ANITA MALNIG. 1984. *What Can I Do with a Major in . . .?* Ridgefield, NJ: Abbott Press.

Chapter 20

The Application: No Ty½pos or Mispelings, Please!

Some people believe that attempting to sell yourself to a college is like merchandising jeans or toothpaste.

There is some truth here. Gaining admission to a college involves quality "packaging." But the quality depends not on how well a student *packages* herself, but on how well she packages *herself*. Yes, packages *HERSELF*. It's that simple.

As her counselor, you've worked to get this young woman to internalize the concept that she is one of a kind. If she wants to be accepted somewhere, especially at 1 of the 100 or so highly selective institutions in the nation, then she has to figure out what she's *really* got and who she really *is*, and let it come through, eccentricities and all.

The more selective the college is, the more it considers *nonacademic* qualities. If your counselee is up against someone whose academic record is equal to hers, the college will be searching to find which of the two can bring the most worthwhile "something" to the mix. She must find some quality that will make *her* more admissible than her competitor. Your counselee has a large (but workable) challenge.

Consequently, it is *very* important for students to be certain that *all* their submitted materials are prepared as thoroughly, thoughtfully, and creatively as possible. Is this kind of packaging dehumanizing? No more so than is a resume for a job.

While a rejected student might show little evidence of talent, leadership, involvement, or service, your counselee's activities could disclose considerable strength in one or more of these areas—*unless* she:

- Downplays them as trivial.
- Doesn't understand how to get them out and onto the table.
- Can't get the proper help in getting them out.
- Can get them out, but doesn't know how to present them well.

She would, in short, cause herself to become another look-alike applicant. There are many candidates who in fact are very strong but whose folders never get laid on the "possible" or "definite" stack because they have not presented themselves well. As this young woman's counselor, you can help her do some quality packaging.

THE APPLICATION ITSELF

All the months—even years—of preparation (the analysis of self, the minifairs attended, the campuses visited, and the interviews taken) come together with the completion of the application. Some seniors find the completion of a set of applications akin to having an additional course in their schedules. You, the counselor, might want to be sensitive to the pressures that "course" puts on these students.

Perhaps we should become more involved in advising on application completion, thereby enabling our counselees to do a better job in completing these two- to six-page documents. But, admittedly, advising isn't always that easy. So often students will write directly to a college for an application, complete it, and then return it to the college without your having seen it, much less having discussed it.

Most of the college application is cut-and-dried statistical stuff, but our involvement with students could center on such issues as the amount of completion time spent, the appropriate handling of optional questions, and the completeness of responses.

Several items need *special* attention:

The "Late Bloomer" Spot

As you know, the number of academically capable people who do mediocre or poor work prior to their senior year is staggering. American students are notorious underachievers. If your counselee falls into this category, he should take heart—it's not too late: colleges love to see an "improved" student. Obviously, the earlier he pulls himself up, the better, but even if he has bombed in his first three years, there's still hope. He might not get into Prestige U., but there will be many schools interested in his candidacy. Usually, the greater the academic ability, the greater the attraction. Your friend is going to need some very good senior midyear grades, however!

The student needs to find a spot somewhere in the application (or use a separate sheet of paper) to explain just why he had not been working to his ability; he *should not* waste the essay section for such an explanation. He should be thoughtful, objective, and upfront in his explanation, sounding as genuine as possible. Shoot for understanding, not pity! After analyzing the circumstances for his underachievement, he should conclude with a *sincere* statement of how his handling of this whole mess has made him a better person. He should never lay the blame somewhere else, for example, at the school's doorstep, saying that a particular teacher is famous for his tough grading practices. No complaining or making excuses!

The "Feel Free" Items

It is not at all uncommon for a college to ask its applicants to respond to the statement, "Please feel free to tell us anything else you believe we should know about you." The college will state that this is an optional item. Don't believe it! In fact, your students should *not* ignore any of the "feel free" or noncompulsory sections, except possibly material related to financial aid. The tackling of optional questions can demonstrate a sense of thoroughness, industry, and seriousness of purpose in a candidate. With applications that do not require an essay, disregarding these noncompulsory items is an even greater risk.

Tell Us Why You Want Us

At some point, either during an interview session or in a submitted short statement, a college may ask the applicant why she thinks that the school would be an appropriate place for her. Since colleges have their own personalities and your counselee has hers, she has carefully explored the makeup of both parties and found that they make a good match. So, if the student is offered the chance to "tie" herself in writing to a particular school, she should do it well!

Emory & Henry College, Emory, VA, addresses the question of "match" with an uncommon application—so uncommon, in fact, that that is what it titles it: "The Uncommon Application for Admission." E&H has placed the personal statement on the front page of its application, because the admission counselors believe that first impressions of their applicants should come to them through the personal essay, not by way of a bunch of statistics. Such a set-up gives more power to the applicant.

In Figure 20-1, note the question, "How do you think Emory & Henry will be able to develop similar experiences for you?" *The college is asking the student to make the tie.* (The figure is reproduced here with the permission of Peter L. Freyberg, dean of admissions, Emory & Henry College.)

There is a nice followthrough by E&H counselors at packet-reading time. In preparing an applicant's folder for review, the support staff "buries" all statistical information where it cannot be examined until well into the decision-making pro-

Emory & Henry College

The uncommon application for admission

Admissions Office, Emory & Henry College, Emory, Virginia 24327-0947 **Telephone (703) 944-3121**

Application Instructions: Please complete this form by typing the requested information or neatly printing in ink. Details about the complete application procedure are listed on the final page.

Personal Statement

Yes, it's that important. Your personal statement is important to us because we want our first impressions of your abilities, interests, and personality to come from you. The statement gives you the opportunity to tell us about your academic abilities and interests, community service, and values before we assess the more traditional statistical information such as grades, test scores, and high school curriculum. This section is crucial to us. Be sure to give it the attention it deserves.

Directions: Please write a personal statement, identifying one of your favorite classes or pastimes. Describe the activity itself and any personal relationships which you developed as a result of it. What made this class or pastime important to you? How do you think Emory & Henry will be able to develop similar experiences for you? [In addition to the written statement, you are invited to attach examples of your self-expression and creativity such as poetry, prose, photography, or other artwork. If additional space is needed, use the back of this form.]

Figure 20-1

cess. The E&H counselors believe that they learn more about the individual from material factors *controlled* by the candidate: the personal essay, letters of reference, and extracurricular involvement. Interesting!

As your counselees attempt to make the tie, please tell them *not* to use empty one-sentence comments such as, "I want to attend your school because you have a good major in elementary education." Or "I'd like to come because your school will best allow me to realize my academic potential." Or "I want to play football."

The following statement is a shade better. The student wisely includes *multiple* reasons for wanting to attend Drew University in New Jersey, but, unfortunately, the impression is given that the student has never set foot on the campus. How much stronger the statement would have been had he visited prior to writing the piece. (The word "excite" with all its derivatives is an overused word. This student uses it twice within a very short statement.)

> Having been born and raised in New Jersey and proud of it, I am excited at the prospect of continuing my education here in this State.
>
> Drew University is unique in that it offers an excellent education (particularly in my area of interest, political science) in what I understand is a beautiful, serene setting. Drew's close proximity to Manhattan would afford me the opportunity to experience the excitement of the city while still enjoying the tranquility of suburban living, a combination I have grown up with, and one I find most appealing.

The next statement is well written. Again, the author finds multiple reasons for wanting to attend George Washington University. Notice how he demonstrates what *he* might contribute to the university, even to the point of familiarity with the school's newspaper.

I have numerous acquaintances who have attended George Washington University, and their reactions to your school have been nothing less than enthusiastic. For this, as well as for several other reasons, I am eager to attend G.W.

As my interest in political science deepened, so did my desire to experience Washington, DC. This city is a vibrant, stimulating place in which to study. What other location affords the opportunity to observe the federal government in action? Moreover, G.W.'s international student body and multiracial environment will expose me to a variety of cultures and lifestyles.

Because I have thoroughly enjoyed my position as editor of our school newspaper, I look forward to working on G.W.'s *The Hatchet*.

I consider myself a mature, serious student, and one who would take full advantage of a George Washington University education.

X-ing the Box Marked "Race"

Up through the 1950s, colleges asked applicants to identify their race. Then came the 1960s. As a result, written identification and required submission of photographs became a thing of the past—all this in the name of lessening discrimination in applicant selection.

Today, we have a much different scene: colleges can't get enough of them—minority candidates, that is. And the situation has worsened since 1985. Some minorities are more "minority" than others. For example, although the black and Hispanic populations have increased, the number of black and Hispanic college applicants has decreased. On the other hand, in some areas of the country the oriental population is so great that a few schools don't count them as "minority" any more; so in certain instances, being Chinese can be as much a liability as it can be an asset.

Many adolescents tend to hide their heritage—particularly in predominantly white suburban schools. Why? Maybe it's an attempt to hide their "differentness." Or maybe because these young people would prefer (even subconsciously) to gain recognition and acceptance for *who* they are rather than for *what* they are.

You can be an encouraging force with your counselees on "disclosure" (properly identifying oneself on an application) if you point out a few things:

1. Your heritage can be an *acceptable* "edge" as many collegiate institutions avidly search to build cross-cultural campuses. If you are "cross-cultural," so much the better for you and for the school.
2. If your race or ethnicity is an issue and you're accepted, then you will know that the school *wants* you—it's not just luck of the draw.
3. Disclosure could mean special financial benefits.

4. And most important. You are what you are—*and you should be proud of it*! This is a land of differences and opportunities. Colleges don't like candidates who try to *use* their ethnic status—but they don't like students who try to hide it, either.

Thomas Hayden, director of college placement at Phillips Exeter Academy, says it well in his 1986 book, *Handbook for College Admissions: A Family Guide*:

> In applying as a minority candidate, students should not trumpet their minority status in front of the admissions committee. Nor should they obscure it. They should think honestly about the value of their minority status to themselves and to their own education, as well as their potential for contributing to the college they wish to attend.

HOW COMMON THE COMMON?

The common application group tries to reassure students and counselors with their front-cover statement:

> The colleges and universities listed above have worked together to develop and distribute the Common Application. . . . *All encourage* its use and no distinction will be made between it and the college's own form. . . . Students are urged to use this form, rather than writing to participating colleges for application materials.

In spite of these words, some counselors continue to believe that students will receive more favorable treatment if they submit a participating school's regular application. The fact that counselors even instruct their counselees not to use this material is mystifying, in that certain of the member institutions (for example, Bucknell and Franklin and Marshall) use *only* the common application.

If anything, we should be encouraging more standardization, not less.

SUBMITTING SUPPLEMENTARY MATERIALS

Supplementary materials come in assorted sizes and shapes. This is certainly the case with creative writing and visual arts pieces. The main purpose of submitting supplementary materials is to document a portion of one's life that cannot be fully presented by means of regular application materials. Some schools request that such things be submitted.

But the process can be abused. Colleges take pride in developing forms where the amount and depth of information requested reflects specific individual institutional needs. Therefore, your counselee should proceed with caution as he attempts to "stack the deck" in his favor. Admission folk still believe in the old adage: "The thicker the folder, the thicker the student." They can be a bit wary about a folder that takes up too much space in a file drawer or temporarily throws the entire applicant evaluation process into low gear.

Note: Students should be *judicious,* both in their selection of materials to be submitted and in the number of submissions.

What *not* to send:

- More than the number of letters of recommendation requested.
- Long essays, term papers, laboratory science reports, or original short stories.
- Documentation of scholastic or extracurricular achievement. It is not necessary for a youngster to rip the letter off his varsity jacket and send it in as evidence of his prowess on the gridiron. A college will usually take the word of the applicant as to awards and honors received.

What to send:

- A musical performance tape that *features* the applicant, a piece of original poetry, a small sample of artwork or a photograph of a larger sample, a newspaper article about or by the applicant, and a photograph that enlarges upon the descriptive text about a special project.

EARLY *WHAT*?

"Kenyon is it for me!" "I'd kill for Duke!" Each year, thousands of high school seniors make a decision to apply to their "very favorite" school under one of several "early" plans. It used to be just Early Decision. Now school counselors must try to keep Early Action separate from Early Notification, and Early Notification separate from Early Decision, with all the ramifications of each.

The EA and EN guidelines appear to be clear-cut and uniformly accepted, but schools can have slightly different policies concerning ED applications. And, as if it's not enough just to keep these different plans straight, schools such as Bates in Maine and Wesleyan in Connecticut even have Early Decision "rounds," where applicants can enter the "ring" at one of two different time periods.

Just as some other admission issues cry out for greater uniformity, wouldn't it be nice to have just one "early," with one application deadline date? But until that happens, it might help to have a handy reference guide to the three programs.

Early Decision

It's the oldest of the three "early" options. Under this plan, the student applies ED to *one* participating college or university, usually by mid-November. (The institution will generally render a decision by mid or late December.) There are really two forms of this plan: (1) the student *is not* permitted to apply to other colleges until the Early Decision school has rendered its decision, and (2) the student *is* permitted to apply to additional schools, but, once admitted by the Early Decision institution, he or she must withdraw all previously submitted applications.

If a student indicates a *strong* desire to attend a given institution by applying early, most schools will give them special consideration in the evaluation process. Indeed, at many of these schools, the acceptance rate of Early Decision candidates is a bit higher than that of applicants who choose the regular decision route. This phenomenon is largely due to the weight assigned Early Decision applications (colleges love to be loved) as well as to the strong credentials of the applicants. Nonaccepted applicants are almost always deferred to regular decision.

Early Action

Unlike Early Decision, this plan affords the applicant the luxury of applying early, but once accepted by an Early Action school, going elsewhere if he or she so desires. Applicants do *not* have to withdraw other applications. Wow! Of course this "best of both worlds" plan is only available at Brown, Harvard, Yale, Princeton, and the University of Notre Dame. Even so, it is comforting to know that at least at these schools one does not have to make a final commitment until May 1.

Also, unlike Early Decision, a student's application could be rejected and not deferred. Standards are exceptionally high with Early Action, so your counselees should explore all the ramifications of this option and exercise great caution in its use. For example, in their 1987 paperback, *College Admissions: Cracking the System*, the Princeton Review people urge students to stay away from Early Action unless acceptance is a virtual certainty. Why?

> Because applying early action doesn't really give you two chances to be admitted. The early-action pools at these colleges contain disproportionate numbers of very strong candidates. If your credentials aren't as good as theirs, your chances of being accepted will be lower than they would have been in a regular pool, because your application will look worse by comparison. . . . The admissions committee will remember you from the early-action pool, and they will remember you as a person they decided not to admit. They will also remember flaws and weaknesses in your application that they might not have discovered had they not encountered it in the early-decision period, when competition was tougher.

Early Notification

It's a kind of cross between Early Decision and Early Action—at least as far as Northwestern University is concerned. With this Illinois school, applicants apply by November 1 and are permitted to send out other applications. They do not have to accept the offer of admission as soon as they are notified, which will be about December 15. The kicker here, though, is that the final commitment to Northwestern must be made by *March* 1, as opposed to May 1. Northwestern finds this to be a sensible and convenient program for those of its applicants who also apply to Illinois state schools. Warning! Students must read the fine print. This is *not* a plan for anyone applying to one or more of the "highly selectives" who notify on or about April 15.

Gentle Reminders for Your Counselees

1. What will the applicant pool of a highly selective college look like in the spring? Who can tell. Certainly not the college. Therefore, admission standards for "early" candidates are purposely kept high.
2. To exercise the "early" option, your counselee should be *academically* well qualified. In selectivity levels, this translates into the school being no more difficult than a "target." If we adopt the Princeton Review recommendation for Early Action applicants, this means the school is no more than a "safety +."
3. Once admitted to an Early Decision school, your counselee *is going*! He signed a statement that if admitted, he would definitely attend and is thereby *obligated* to enroll at that college and *must* withdraw all applications to other schools. Even if your counselee refuses the school that has accepted him, he cannot ethically file applications elsewhere during that school year. (Exceptions might be made for serious problems, e.g., loss of parental income.)
4. Teach your counselee that "early decision" *must come from* "perfect match." He should not use the option unless he is totally convinced that the institution is a perfect one for him.
5. If a student plans to apply to an EA school that does *not* defer a portion of its pool, and if his credentials are marginal, he might wait to be considered with the total applicant pool when his credentials might appear stronger in comparison to others.
6. Another thought on the ED/regular admission decision: Will your counselee's record look more impressive in January than it does in November? Will his test scores be higher? Will his grades be better? Will he have achieved any awards? If the answer is "yes," it might be wise for your counselee to apply under a regular decision plan, when he will have more ammunition with which to influence an admission committee.
7. The stipulations of the ED program are signed by the applicant and *mailed back* to the institution. The student should make sure that *he keeps a copy of the requirements*. (Some secondary schools recommend that their students photocopy all their applications.)

A Gentle Reminder for You

You may have noticed that you are increasingly being seen as a major cooperating player in the Early Decision program. This is as it should be. A violation of an Early Decision agreement not only damages a student's chances of college matriculation, but the high school's credibility as well. More and more colleges expect you to both counsel on the early option *and* supervise the execution of it. For example, school counselors are asked to provide acknowledgment signatures, and departments are urged to track carefully those of their students who use one of the early options. That tracking implies that some code is used by the department to distinguish "upon acceptance, withdraw all other applications" from "submit *no* applications until you are accepted or rejected."

In the East, applicant abuse of the program has led some 40 colleges and universities to tie together via computer network. It is a relatively easy task for these cooperating institutions to identify which students are applying to which schools under the Early Decision plan. As one admission officer stated, "If we catch a student sending in more than one early decision application, he or she is a dead turkey."

Counselors are more frequently signing "on the dotted line"—but which one?

Oberlin places the commitment statement *in full* on the Secondary School Report Form. (See Figure 20-2.)

Franklin and Marshall puts its on a Supplemental Information Form, as shown in Figure 20-3. (F&M was one of the first schools to request that counselors join in encouraging students to adopt a more serious attitude toward early decision.)

Unfortunately, Cornell's statement of conditions is on the student's application, but the counselor is asked to sign on the Secondary School Report. Unless the counselor sees the student application, he does not know what he is agreeing to. (See Figure 20-4.)

If the applicant has indicated that he or she is applying to Oberlin as a First Choice–Early Decision candidate, please sign the following statement:

> I understand that above student has chosen to apply to Oberlin College as a First Choice–Early Decision candidate. If admitted under this plan, the student will 1) accept Oberlin's offer of admission by submitting the $200 non-refundable matriculation deposit within two weeks of acceptance (or notification of financial aid award); 2) withdraw all other applications; 3) initiate no new applications.

Signature of Guidance Counselor ______________________ Date ________

Figure 20-2

... An Early Decision candidate may initiate applications to other institutions; however, if offered admission to Franklin & Marshall, the candidate must withdraw the applications to other institutions and enroll at Franklin & Marshall. Early Decision candidates who live within a reasonable geographic distance from Franklin & Marshall College are required to have an on-campus interview.

If you wish to be considered as a candidate for the Early Decision Program, please indicate your acceptance to the conditions stated above by signing this statement. The signature of your high school guidance counselor is also required.

____
Signature of Applicant

I acknowledge that the applicant is applying for the Early Decision Program at Franklin & Marshall College and that the student understands the commitment to attend Franklin & Marshall College if accepted.

____
Signature of Guidance Counselor

Figure 20-3

If the student is applying under the early-decision plan, please read the following and sign below:

I have discussed the request for early-decision consideration with this applicant. If admission is offered in December, I will remind the applicant of the conditions of the agreement.

Signature: ______________________________ Date: ________

Figure 20-4

COLLEGES AWASH IN APPLICATIONS: THE MULTIPLE-APPLICATION GAME

Four! That's not a golf call—it's the number of colleges to which a student should apply, according to Bobby D. Schrade, director of school relations and freshman admissions at Baylor University in Texas. (And you thought things were tight with six!) Schrade's recommendation is especially timely, as the highly selective colleges and universities in the nation find themselves inundated with applications despite a shrinking pool of 18-year-olds.

In the July 1987 NACAC *Bulletin*, William Conley, director of admissions at Drew University in New Jersey, notes that the rather sudden rise in applications is partially the result of "spreading the recruitment net farther. We have successfully tapped new markets."

Others see it, however, as the great multiple-application game: prestige-conscious students "throwing in" applications to large numbers of institutions and often hurting themselves and their friends in the process. This shotgun approach can swell applicant pools and diminish the opportunity of all applicants. The more applicants, the more refusals! If a student applies to 15 schools and is accepted by 10, that means that nine other students were needlessly rejected—or maybe *she* was needlessly rejected by 1 or 2 of her other 5. Schools have always worked the percentages, but as the storm increases, acceptance is less and less meaningful.

Schrade has elaborated on his position:

> Early decision-making training is not rushing the student's maturity to adulthood. Reality is that in the fast pace of American life one simply must start making choices and decisions at an earlier point in the transition to adult responsibility. What better time to start than during the preparation for transition to higher education?
>
> Information and counsel are available. In fact, the student is force-fed by direct-mail pieces, at college information programs, in youth magazines, in various public service publications, and during high school counseling sessions. After all of these informational and counseling opportunities, the student who indiscriminately applies to every college or university that comes to mind has made a decision to do so, but in reality has made no choices.

Judith Guston, associate director of admissions at Sarah Lawrence College, is in agreement: "Too many students have unrealistic expectations as to their chances of admission. Besides, if a student applies to 15 colleges, he/she hasn't really made any choices at all." Students have not properly analyzed their prospects and/or have not learned to make meaningful decisions.

In more than a few secondary schools, implementation of a sound college planning process has given way to offensive consumerism: students overapply, violate Early Decision agreements, double-deposit, place themselves on more than one waiting list, all while ordering several final transcripts. All but the first are unethical. There are those who would suggest that the pervasiveness of the problem implies that school counselors are no longer able to accomplish their mission.

As counseling professionals, have we been losing ground? Shouldn't we work toward regaining it so that we can help our counselees better clarify their goals, aspirations, and thought processes? Has this not been our historical mission? But to take and hold the high ground we need courageous and energetic counselors with reasonable caseloads! We know the reasons for "energetic" and "reasonable caseloads." But we must become "courageous," because it is easier to acquiesce than to stand for what we believe to be the better course.

Consider the following:

- What *does* flooding the market with applications say about counselors' efforts to strengthen their role in the area of individual self-assessment?
- A department might not encourage overapplication, but it might not discourage it, either. Shouldn't we take our heads out of the sand? Put our money where our mouth is?
- If all secondary schools were to pull together on this issue, would we not make a "greater difference" in the growth of *all* our students?
- And to publicize the drawbacks of trying to "beat the system," should we not be doing more to get the message across to our most influential and *concerned* public—the parents?

It cannot be denied that counseling today's students on moral and ethical decision making has become a formidable challenge. Yet it is also true that unless we encourage young people to become effective members of society, society itself will have no future. There *are* departments that hold the line, tough as it is to do: they at least take both an oral and a written stand on such issues as the recommended number of times students should sit for an SAT or ACT and the recommended number of applications that should be submitted—all the while citing to families the disadvantages associated with exceeding such limits. There are departments that do a yearly monitoring of (1) numbers of applications submitted to individual institutions, (2) acceptances and rejections, and (3) final transcripts released. The first two years will be the hardest, but changes *can* be made!

SUGGESTED READINGS

HAYDEN, THOMAS. 1986. *Handbook for College Admissions: A Family Guide.* Princeton, NJ: Peterson's Guides, Inc. Chapter 5, "The Application Makes a Difference," is an especially worthwhile piece of reading.

ROBINSON, ADAM, AND JOHN KATZMAN. 1987. *College Admissions: Cracking the System.* New York: The Princeton Review, Villard Books. Overlook the fact that the editors are not especially kind to school counselors. Read Chapters 4 and 5; they are most informative.

Chapter 21

Visiting and Interviewing

The scenario is played out thousand of times each year: the family car goes over hilltops and around curves, its occupants strain at seat belts to get their first glimpse of Gothic U. And as you do your once-around drive of the campus, you see that it's all there—in three-dimensional living color. Just as you pictured it? Not quite. Just as it was pictured in the viewbook? Not at all. Nevertheless, as you and your family head toward admissions and a ten-thirty interview, you decide that even in the middle of winter it looks pretty good.

College visitation knows no season; families visit schools month after month, year after year. It's as if the smiles of ever-at-the-ready admission folk were frozen in place. And whether or not a candidate has an interview, the campus visit itself is extremely important for both him and his family. *Getting out and on to a college campus for that "living color" look is crucial to your counselee's eventually arriving at his best possible "match."*

Students have but a few hours to spend on a college campus, so how should they make the most of their time? One suggestion is that they do a little homework prior to their visitation. They should ask themselves what they hope to acquire from this firsthand visit. Lying behind the friendly faces and the physical facilities (that might include flag-hung fraternity houses) is the world of faculty-student relationships, co-curricular opportunities, social activities, and involvement with the surrounding community—all of which will positively and/or negatively affect your counselees' collegiate experience. The trick is for the candidate to look beyond the apparent, in order to gain a sense of how he or she would function on a particular campus. (See Figure 21-1.)

WHEN YOU VISIT . . .

1. If you have the opportunity to do so, by all means take a formal tour. Note which buildings are being shown to you. Is it a good cross sample? Make certain that you have a chance to see a typical freshman dormitory. And ask about off-campus housing. Check into what's available. Dorm living might cease to satisfy you in your junior or senior year. If you are athletic-minded, you will want to visit the gymnasium or field house.
2. Off tour, tap several students on their shoulder and ask them why they selected the school and how their expectations have been met. What do they see as the school's strengths and weakness? Listen hard to the answers. Most collegians will be only too happy to chat with you. Their perspective is not to be overlooked! So don't be bashful. Ask questions!
3. Try to have a meal on campus. What are the meal plans like?
4. When shown the student center, carefully check out its decor, physical condition, facilities. You could end up spending more time in this particular area than you think.
5. Pay attention to such telling things as posters, notices, and grafitti. Take home a copy of the campus newspaper, and then read it. This is a great way to "in-depth" a school, as to current campus social, political, and intellectual issues.
6. Stop by the counseling and placement office and see if you can pick up some placement brochures. Such literature can give you insight into student preparation for a career or graduate school.
7. If you know the discipline in which you want to major, you will want to visit that department and facility, especially if it was not part of the tour. Many departments are in fact housed in their own buildings. There just might be a department professor available to meet with you. You might even want to attend a class or two. Note the "culture" on the campus, including the rapport between students and professors.

Figure 21-1

Numerous colleges and universities offer overnight (weekday or weekend) programs for applicants or potential applicants. Naturally, the few youngsters who have the time to spend on this activity will see and hear much more than those who don't—and they should appreciate their good fortune. Figure 21-1, however, offers few tips on what students should look for if they have to squeeze their visits into "one-dayers."

THE WILLIAMSTON PROGRAM: AN UNUSUAL JOINT EFFORT

Taking a bus tour of college campuses is rather uncommon for high school students. Combining such touring with extensive classroom activity is a rarer phenomenon. Yet for more than a decade Williamston High School, Williamston, MI, has been doing just that: offering an integrated program that amalgamates college preparatory work in grammar and composition with extensive orientation in college admissions, including a two-day bus tour of Michigan colleges and universities.

Born in 1975, the program grew out of a cooperative effort among the school's administration, English, and counseling departments. Juniors who opt to take this English elective, entitled "College Preparatory Composition," reap the benefits of this joint endeavor: the development of appropriate writing skills to be successful in college freshman English and decision-making skills to deal effectively with the admission process.

A classroom group of 25 students lends itself well to discussion and question activity. Counselors "take over" the several composition classes on preplanned dates to work with students in five major areas: (1) general college orientation, (2) building decision-making skills, (3) specific admission information, (4) entrance examinations, (5) and financial aid. Michigan State University professionals are invited to address the students. For example, an MSU learning specialist might discuss study techniques and what students can expect in academic demands at the collegiate level. College admission counselors are also frequent visitors.

Of the five areas, decision making is afforded the most attention, partly because of the significant role it plays in college selection and partly because it has continued to be a neglected (and consequently underdeveloped) learning skill.

Undoubtedly the most important decision-making activity is the college tour—a voluntary overnight trip to several colleges and universities—conducted by Williamston counselors. All composition class students are encouraged to participate in this venture at a minimal cost of $25 per student. The school board provides bus transportation. A contrasting group of institutions is chosen each year, enabling students to compare big with small, public with private, and so on. If housing is available on campus, students spend the night in college dormitories. If not, efforts are made to stay at hotels where recreational facilities are available. Meals are taken in college dining halls to give students a taste of what college food is like. Students attend available cultural events, sit in on classes, tour campuses, work out in gymnasiums—all in the name of experiencing collegiate living firsthand. Composition teachers assign essays in which students are asked to compare and contrast the institutions visited.

Parents and *school board members* are invited to go along as *advisors*. The inclusion of parents (a "must," according to the counseling department) ensures program survival. Parents aren't at all hesitant to state on evaluation forms that the program is an excellent method of comparing institutions and that they recommend that the program be continued. "We haven't been flying by the seat of our pants and doing this each year because it's fun," remarked counselor Richard Brown to the press. "We do it because people say it helps them."

It's obvious that College Preparatory Composition is more than an English class at Williamston High School; it is also a concept and method that effectively prepares high school juniors to make a wide variety of informed decisions about their postsecondary education.

THE CAMPUS INTERVIEW: IN OR OUT?

June through December is interview season on college campuses. The admission people have no sooner announced their early spring selections for one class than they are thrust once again into the interview process with brand new candidates from another.

But a new question arises. Like the emblemmed blazers and rep ties that once characterized many of these sessions, is the individual interview *as a pertinent factor* in the admission decision going out of fashion? To some collegiate officials, it is. For example, many "highly selectives," suddenly inundated with applications, can't keep up with the numbers. As a result, to avoid creating a disadvantage for those who cannot be accommodated, some colleges disregard interviews by not writing up summaries for the evaluation of the applicant. *Here, then, is where an institution needs to be upfront about the weight, if any, it assigns to the process.* In other words, students need to know whether or not their interview will count.

Yet Another Excedrin Headache for the School Counselor

The fact that *The New York Times* ran a November 18, 1987, article entitled, "Increasingly, College Interview Is Out," is of little help to school counselors who must continue to worry about colleges where the interview is "in." Once again, the more dissimilarity there is among collegiate institutions as to the admission process, the greater the challenge to school counselors to remain optimally knowledgeable.

In view of the fact that the interview remains "in" at more than a few colleges and universities, we offer some suggestions on how you can work with your counselees on this rather perplexing issue.

Maxim 1: Make no mistake—the purpose of an on- or off-campus interview for the candidate is to "sell" him or herself. Just showing up for one of these "recommended" or "optional" conferences is a giant step in this direction. Such initiative can't help but send a signal of genuine interest to an admission official.

In addition to the positive thoughts a student furnishes in an essay, there is a certain advantage to presenting oneself orally—if, of course, one comes across well. Therefore, in your counselee's search for that best college, she should use the interview to convince the college that it's just right for her and she's just right for it. It sounds easy to do, but you'd be surprised how many "blow it," not by foolish comments, but by tepid presentations—presentations that end up going nowhere, with not much additional color being added to the portrait.

In his pamphlet, *Campus Pursuit—How to Make the Most of the College Visit and Interview* (Octameron Associates, Inc.), G. Gary Ripple, dean of admissions at the College of William and Mary, remarks: "Each year, I am always astounded by the number of candidates (nearly eighty percent) who waste the opportunities an interview can provide. This is particularly alarming when you think of all the arrangements required to make interviews possible."

Of course the question remains—how much of a difference can a 30-minute interview make? Undoubtedly you've heard more than one rep comment that the interview doesn't count for much; it is not an important factor in the total admission process. Yet after a decision is rendered, it is not uncommon to hear a rep mention that the applicant "didn't do well in the interview." It seems, then, that the interview is a risk factor: if you do it at all, do it well.

Maxim 2: Be careful how much credence and weight you give to the remark "the interview doesn't count for much." Virtually every secondary school has students who apply to selective institutions where the interview often counts for more than just confirming the recommendations of teachers and counselors.

Ripple certainly believes in the importance of face to face. So does the College Board. A 1982 study conducted by this Princeton, New Jersey, organization with nine selective private institutions revealed that interviews can be significant, especially for those *qualified but not exceptional candidates* who fall in the broad middle range of an applicant pool. For marginal students, this can translate into their "taking to the road" to interview at top-choice schools, that are often "reaches" or "target pluses." You can sense that interviews will count when you read such terms as "required" or "strongly recommended."

What Role for the Secondary School?

Being able to interview skillfully is not something one inherits from forbearers. It is something one can learn. And it is something that can be learned in school.

Enter the already beleaguered school counselor! Although snowed under with a myriad of assigned tasks, it is nonetheless critical for you to understand that for students, the interview can be the most intimidating aspect of the entire admission process and that these young people need a lot of help.

Some secondary schools approach the problem in a big way and hold mock interview sessions with their junior students. Some even do so through the medium of closed-circuit television. Others conduct seminars where various aspects of the interview process are examined. Naturally, the amount of time a department devotes to this topic is influenced both by the press of other counselor responsibilities and by the numbers of students who apply yearly to "interview" schools. (Most colleges do not require, or even recommend, an interview.) Whatever, counseling departments need to take stock of what if anything they are presently doing to help students improve their interviewing techniques, and then go from there.

Where and When to Interview

Interviewing is a process that your families will find time consuming, costly, and at times even nerve wracking; however, it is one that can pay great dividends if the candidate is successful in positively influencing his interviewer. But, except in cases of "required" interviews, if the candidate knows that he is not going to do it well, then he should not do it! Students who are very shy, buckle under pressure, or tend to be arrogant probably should avoid this type of experience.

If a school requires an interview, then of course the candidate should be there. If the catalog "suggests" or "recommends" one, then the statement should be taken seriously, and every effort should be made to comply. If it's "optional," then your counselee should consider himself off the hook a bit.

It is *very* important to interview at "reach" schools. It's important, but not as important, at "targets," and much less important at "safeties."

October, November, and December tend to be the busiest interview months for colleges and universities. If your counselee selects this particular time of year, she should make her reservations early! Although there aren't nearly as many collegians around, and contrary to the thinking of certain paperback whiz kid authors, summertime can be a great time for visiting and interviewing. It's much easier to get an appointment, and the whole situation can be less frantic for everyone involved. Many colleges even open their dormitories to families during the summer. It's a great way to sample dorm living. Take a picnic lunch along: some campuses are wonderful spots for picnicking, especially at lakeside at places like Colby, Furman, Wellesley, and Princeton.

Dress Up or Down?

Neither. Your counselees should wear plain nondistracting clothes. One's physical appearance *is* an additional important facet of the interview procedure—more important at some schools than at others—more important with some admission counselors than others. Rule of thumb: play it safe! A person's attire can be an interviewer's first impression, *and* first impressions *are* important.

Simplicity of dress prevents the interviewer from drawing unnecessary conclusions about your counselee's personality. No T-shirts, Reeboks, or jeans, please—even designer jeans. Making an exit with Jordache stamped on one's behind might not impress the interviewer. For women, a simple skirt and blouse or dress is always appropriate. For men, a sweater or jacket always looks nice; a tie is not really necessary. (It should be especially avoided if an individual is not used to wearing one.)

The bottom line is that admission folk want to know that a candidate has put some thought into his or her appearance.

Outer-Office Ritual

Arrive early! Your counselee will want to walk into her interview calm, cool, and collected—and smiling! (And one can't help but really smile at Quinnipiac College in Connecticut, where they personally welcome each interviewee with a big sign cut out of construction paper.) A private walk around the campus is always better taken before a session than after. (If done in the summer heat, however, allow plenty of time to get back into air conditioning before the introductory handshake.)

Your counselee should introduce herself to the receptionist and see if she can learn the name of her interviewer. Sometimes knowing a name ahead of time makes one feel more comfortable. While sitting and waiting for the host to make his or her appearance, a few deep breaths will help—so will a magazine of light reading to keep one's mind off what is to come.

Some authors would have the candidate standing a considerable distance away from her parents when the admission counselor makes his entrance, to present an air of independence. This is absurd. If anything, today we need to see more families standing together. There are those who even advocate leaving the parents at home. Nonsense! However, it is imperative that parents *don't* join their youngsters in the session—even if invited to do so—and this needs to be understood by everyone *ahead of time*. This is the *candidate's* "moment of truth," and after 12 years of formal education, and many more of parental guidance, she should be ready to deal with this new experience independently. (One young man went inside with not only his mother, but with his private counselor as well.)

And now, enter the admission counselor. When he announces your counselee's name, she should stand, shake his hand *firmly*, and then introduce her parents to him—loud and clear. (Believe it or not, some students have never had the opportunity of introducing their parents to anyone.)

Some suggestions for your counselees are given in Figure 21-2.

Keeping One's Name Alive

When the session has been concluded, your counselee should thank her host for his time. She should make certain that she has either written down his name or acquired his business card. Her next move (an often forgotten one) will be to send along a thank-you note within a week's time. The interviewer now becomes her contact person—an *important* individual with whom she can touch base for further information or for checking on the status of her application. When she writes the note, she might want to refresh the interviewer's memory as to whom she is by including a postscript like, "P.S. I did meet with the soccer coach as you had suggested."

Another controversial yet worthwhile tactic is to withhold a piece of information that one would have normally included with one's initially submitted application, for example, a newspaper clipping or a piece of writing. Send it *to the interviewer* with a brief note stating that you had forgotten to include the piece or that you now realize that it might be something that would be helpful to the com-

WHEN YOU INTERVIEW . . .

Do go prepared! You need to do plenty of advance study on yourself and the college! "Lack of preparation" is the number 1 complaint of college admission counselors. Tie yourself to the college here just as you did, or are about to do, on paper. Be prepared to discuss intelligently exactly why you are serious about Old Overshoe. Always state multiple reasons for wanting to attend: you're hell-bent on becoming a foreign service officer and Old Overshoe has a strong international relations major; you play men's lacrosse and you're aware that Overshoe has a dynamite team. These are valid and appropriate reasons for wanting to attend. But don't "come out" with a cute remark like, "I hear you have more women than men, and I wouldn't mind improving the ratio." A college interview is not the time for frivolity.

You might want to take an unofficial copy of your transcript along, that is, unless you have already applied, and your records are at the college. Don't present the document unless the interviewer asks for it.

Do set yourself an interview strategy: there will be some things you will want to know about the school and some things you will want the school to know about you. The strategy that you adopt should be consistent with the rest of your application.

Don't sit until you are directed to do so, and don't move any furniture. Keep your hands away from your face and your fingers out of your mouth.

Don't slouch in your chair, and don't fidget with your hair. If you don't know what to do with your hands, keep them folded in your lap. It's okay to cross your legs at the ankles or the knees, but make sure you are sitting erect when you do so.

Do take your lead from your interviewer, who might open the session with any number of questions, including some that are rather audacious: "Tell me about yourself!" "Why do you want to go to college?" "What do you expect to be doing ten years from now?" "Let's hear about your most valuable experience?" "What do you think about ... (a current issue)?" "What are your strengths? weaknesses?" "How would your friends describe you?"

Don't give disjointed one-word answers when asked a question. Provide your interviewer with complete responses. Be as concise as possible when the interviewer is simply trying to clarify a point. The dialogue should flow naturally. The best interviews are really just conversations.

Do open up, pose questions, and do a fair amount of talking. (You should carry about half of the conversation.) With certain less selective schools, there can be a tendency for the host to talk a lot, recruiting more than interviewing. If you find that your interviewer is doing most of the talking, redirect the conversation.

Figure 21-2

Don't say that you don't enjoy reading or that you read very little. Reading and college are practically synonymous terms. If you enjoy science fiction, admit it, but be careful with escapist romance novels. They are hardly serious literature. You will be doing extensive reading in college. Get used to it in high school!

Don't ask mundane questions. Put yourself behind the interviewer's desk. Would you want to hear the same insipid questions 30 times a week: "How many students do you have on campus?" "How many books in your library?" "Can I major in political science?" All this information is available in the school's catalog. So read it beforehand!

Do be genuinely enthusiastic about particular activities, but beware of a bragging tone. There is a definite distinction between enthusiasm and cockiness. If offered the opportunity, discuss those activities that fall near the top of your activity sheet.

Don't come on too strong or appear overanxious to impress—remember that "playing it cool" is almost always the preferred style. And while we're on the topic, don't try to impress the interviewer with your family and friends. The fact that your father is a noted heart surgeon, author, or politician may be important, but your college interview is not the time to bring this up. To a skilled interviewer you are the important one.

Do tell your host about the dedication and steadfastness you've developed on the playing field if you are an athlete and how all of this has had a salutary effect on your school work. However, if things weren't so salutary and the academics suffered a bit, admit it at once, but stress the importance of the "total learning experience"—on the field and in the classroom. If you're not sure you will play ball in college, then be "upfront" about it. After all, you are coming to Prestige U. to study, and you may not be ready to risk your legal career.

Don't get yourself caught in a heated political argument. As a high school junior or senior, you should be reading newspapers and magazines, for example, The New York Times, Newsweek, or Time magazine. A well-informed discussion of current events with your interviewer may win you a few points. One never knows when one might be asked about a recent Washington appointment. If you don't know something, say so. Sometimes difficult questions are raised just to test reactions.

Don't quiz interviewers about their backgrounds, and don't assume that they haven't experienced particular things. Aside from being their typical affable selves, college admission folk are almost always broadly educated, extensive travelers, and have eclectic tastes. They may be older than you, but most keep themselves current.

Don't "knock" your high school too much. You can be somewhat critical, but be mostly supportive. Telling your interviewer that your high school experience was beat, the education boring, the teachers uncaring, the stu-

Figure 21-2 (continued)

dents nerds, will only get you labeled a malcontent, a quality most admission officers dislike.

Don't play games (as some authors would have you do) with admission people, for example, pretending that this is your first interview so that you can be credited with your great social ease, or telling half-truths about your extracurricular record, or leading the interviewer to believe that his school is your first choice when it's not. Admission officers, particularly experienced ones, are very perceptive individuals who have been through it all before and can quickly spot a phony when they see one.

Don't be brutally honest. Your reasons for going to college might well be to earn a lot of money, improve your status, or make daddy happy, but these are not reasons that will sit well with an interviewer. You must have more reasons than those. Do some homework here, but state your reasons in your own words; your responses should sound as natural as possible. With regard to drugs, if an interviewer asks if you have ever tried them, and you have, a qualified "yes" may be the way to go, but never talk about more than a trial, and briefly mention your genuine concern about drug abuse. Today, most high schools have educational programs on drug abuse; therefore, knowledge certainly doesn't mean dependence. Only the phony would pretend total ignorance.

Do understand that on occasion your interviewer could be totally honest and propose that his school is not the right one for you. Your host might "counsel" you toward schools that might be better. It seems that the inability of some high schools to counsel for college has caused a few colleges to take up the slack. In a February 23, 1987, Time magazine article entitled, College Bound, Without a Map, John Ruohoniemi, director of admissions at St. Olaf College in Minnesota, states, "If the student is not right for us, we're going to suggest ways for him or her to find the right school."

Don't try to extend the conference unnecessarily. The length of a session is not a measure of its success. The length of an interview is often determined by the number of interview appointments for that particular day. You will get a message from your host that the session is coming to a close.

Don't judge the college by the interviewer. Sometimes students get "turned off" to a school because they didn't like the interviewer. It would be regrettable if an entire institution were judged on a 30-minute session. Keep an open mind.

Do practice your technique by interviewing at "safeties" and "targets" first. Save your "reaches" for last, when you've become more experienced.

Figure 21-2 (continued)

mittee in making their decision. This last bit of "keeping one's name alive" should be done about six weeks after the candidate has submitted her application.

OTHER KINDS OF INTERVIEWS

The Stress Interview

Admiral Hyman Rickover is reputed to have, on occasion, locked his nuclear submarine candidates in a closet to check their reaction. The pressures of living in close quarters, 20,000 leagues under the sea, however, are hardly the same as those experienced by a 17-year-old on a college campus (although high-rise-in-the-clouds dormitory life might just qualify!). Therefore, there would seem to be no need for such shenanigans at a college interview session. Right? Wrong!

Every once in awhile you get them: extraordinary sessions, popularly known as "stress" interviews. Supporters believe that such interviews reveal the real personality of the applicant under pressure. What it probably reveals is the personality of the interviewer. Asking teenagers to deal with long periods of deliberately provoked silence, or to visualize imaginary boxes on desks, is all part of this rather severe routine.

If a stress interviewer harshly broadsides your counselee with, "So! What can you do for this college?" she might get away with replying, "So. What can your college do for me?" But that is about all she is going to get away with, because she *doesn't* need to find herself sucked into a situation of attempting to top or outdo her interviewer. Her best move is to play it cool, real cool! Remember that the whole point of a stress interview is to get the interviewee flustered and upset. Again, coolness is the key. The less rattled a candidate appears to be, the better the opinion the "interrogator" will have of the candidate.

Above all, the candidate should not take a stress interview personally. She should view this off-the-wall session as a "game show" and play accordingly—by her wits and to win!

The Alumni Interview

Some schools require or encourage alumni interviews that are a substitute for, or a supplement to, those on campus. If students have already had an on-campus interview, they nevertheless might want to think twice before turning down the same offer from an alumnus. Often, the more people one has in one's corner, the better. With Reed College in Oregon, for example, applicants can decide if they want their conversation with a Reed alumnus to be considered an interview and, consequently, be reported back to the college.

The personalities of alumni are so different that it's tough to advise on specific interviewing techniques; alumni personalities can range from the friendly and genuinely interested in education types, to immature egocentrics, to outright bores determined to keep the wrong students out. However, you can suggest to your students that the preparation for this get-together should be similar to that of any on-campus meeting. Your counselees should move cautiously at first, examining for clues as to their host's character and personality. The power-hungry expose themselves with statements like, "So you think you have it to go to Prestige U." The interviewee should smile and be respectful, but express himself assertively. There is nothing wrong with his letting the interviewer know that he knows that this meeting *is* important and that competition for entrance to Prestige U. is stiff.

It wasn't that long ago that alumni were unapprised of what was happening on their campuses. Today, however, since alumni reports are of greater value to the home office, participating graduates, through periodic on-campus workshops, hone interviewing techniques and become more sensitive to the qualities that make interview reports helpful. And many schools (like Reed) have an extensive network of alumni who interview prospective students.

If for some reason a student is unable to have an on-campus interview, and he feels he can gain from such exposure, he might pick up a phone and call the college to inquire about the feasibility of an alumni interview in his area. Students seldom consider this option. You could help here.

While many admission offices believe that alumni reports are less likely to be as subjective as those from secondary schools, your counselees should *never* discount an alumni interview. A poor performance could mean a rejection letter.

SUGGESTED READINGS

OLIVEIRA, PAULO, AND STEVE COHEN. 1983. *Getting In!* New York: Workman Publishing. A popular bestseller that is lively and candidly written. Other than disagreeing with the authors' position that you should "visit colleges alone or with friends, *not* with your family," the work, including Chapter 4, "Campus Visits and Interviews," contains meaningful and practical advice for applicants.

RIPPLE, G. GARY. 1986. *Campus Pursuit: How to Make the Most of the College Visit and Interview.* Alexandria, VA: Octameron Associates. A concise, purposeful, and very readable pamphlet that lends itself well to use with groups.

Chapter 22

The Personal Essay

> In selective college admissions, applicants who fail to understand the importance of the essay and don't put forth the necessary effort, seriously jeopardize their chance to position themselves and lose the opportunity to enhance their academic credentials in the competition for a limited number of great opportunities.
>
> — G. Gary Ripple
> *How to Prepare a Great College Application*

At the National Association of College Admission Counselors' 1986 conference in Washington, DC, Jane Reynolds, assistant director of admissions at Tufts University, called the essay, "the glue of the folder . . . the point at which the student can pull together all the disparate elements that have been mailed to Box 4077, College Station . . . a piece that can create for me a sense of the individual, and sort of knit together all of those elements."

Reynolds is right. The essay tends to hold the folder together, but according to admission folk, the adhesive material is more library paste than crazy glue. Admission officers maintain that much of today's essay writing continues to be of average to poor quality.

If the essay is indeed an important part of the application package, in that it directly influences an admission committee's perception of a candidate, why aren't better essays being written? Year after year, at regional and national conferences, we continue to hear that most students misuse the essay, that their work is "tame, boring stuff," rarely giving a committee anything of value.

An admission official once remarked that students sometimes don't present themselves well, nor are they well presented by their secondary schools. The officer might just as well have added the word "counselor" to the end of the sentence. Let's not kid ourselves: the buck stops here. Counselors can, and most often do, have considerable control over the final submitted product.

Perhaps one reason for those poorly constructed essays is that we are not making enough of an impact on the writing process. What is *not* needed is "after-the-fact" involvement, whereby counselors, teachers, and parents give essays cursory readings, along with the "It sounds good to me" comments. What *is* needed is the approach talked about in Chapter 14, in which the counselor has gotten to know the student *well* and has worked with her on examining her own values, plans, and aspirations.

Doesn't this put the counselor in a favorable position for the first task: helping the student figure out what to write about? It's a natural. After working with his counselee on developing her self-perception so she can be true to herself on the printed page, all he has to do is sit back and pull it out of her. Then the counselor will have helped his counselee *write* a good essay because he has helped her *create* a good essay.

Actually, a skilled counselor should not only:

1. Know the young writer well, having worked with her over the years in developing greater self-awareness.

but also:

2. Be familiar with important approaches to, and techniques of, expository writing, particularly as they apply to the special demands of writing an essay for college admission.
3. Understand the different ways essays are utilized by colleges and universities and the ramifications thereof.

The first mandate presupposes that you have a reasonable caseload and are able to spend the necessary time on such self-assessment activities with your counselees.

The second charge does *not* mean that you have to advise on sentence structure and points of grammar, although some counselors possess the requisite expertise. And it doesn't imply that you should review a series of drafts and peruse the final copy, although you might want to. It *does* mean that you should counsel on such fundamentals as essay topics, including selection and focus, attitude, approach, and content organization. It also means that you should promote the feeling that a personal statement can, and should, breathe some life into an application.

The third requirement suggests that you familiarize yourself with the ways colleges might utilize essays: (1) to screen out less able applicants, (2) as a marketing tool (to attract specific constituencies to the applicant pool or, conversely, to widen the net), (3) to acquire autobiographical data on the applicants, and (4) to measure the writing skills and level of thinking of each student.

Playing the Devil's Advocate

On the other hand, is entirely too much being made of the essay as an admission factor? Since but 10 percent of the schools require an essay, and, of these, only 50 some scrutinize the writing to see whether or not all i's have been dotted and all t's have been crossed, would any demand for increased counselor assistance be worth it? Actually, one can't help but wonder (as one sits in national seminars, laughing along at paddling ducks, while presenters poke fun at actual essays) just what should be reasonably expected from a 17-year-old in the way of introspection, creativity, and sophistication of writing style. How many adolescents have the keen insight and necessary maturity to write as creatively as the highly selective institutions seem to demand?

Furthermore, there continues to be considerable concern at the secondary level about (1) the appropriateness of essay topics; (2) the qualifications of those who read the essays; (3) the overinvolvement of some parents, teachers, and counselors in the process; (4) the amount of attention that the "highly selectives" are paying to certain of the bright, but *underadvocated*, who are "at sea" with the whole procedure.

ESSAY POWER—WHAT TO DO WITH IT?

Some colleges spend as much as $100,000 on the flashy contents of viewbooks presenting their best qualities to prospective freshmen, they phone up high school counseling offices for an interpretation of the hieroglyphics of transcript course titles, they design their own application forms, and then they tell students what to put on them.

But the personal essay section of the application can become your counselee's "moment in the sun." Here's an opportunity for her to take control! This is her 8½" × 11" chance to appeal to the admission office and to position herself as a unique, but modest, individual. Or if she has decided that she is not all that unique, it's still her moment to compose a well-written, revealing, and caring piece—perhaps one that displays some vulnerability, as well.

So now the power is in her court. What is she going to do with it?

If she (1) uses the essay to whine about her SAT scores; (2) opens with the phrase "For as long as I can remember"; (3) grabs the space to laundry-list her activities, or repeats her application; (4) writes what *she* thinks the admission people want to hear; or (5) submits an illegible pizza-stained piece—she's doomed to failure.

On the other hand, success just might come her way if she (1) is natural, substantive, and specific, thereby causing the essay to be a more valuable piece to read; (2) writes in complete sentences; (3) demonstrates a good command of grammar, with *no* spelling or typo errors; (4) uses humor judiciously; (5) brings a little creativity to bear; (6) is a bit vulnerable.

Factors (1), (2), and (3) are *musts* for any writer to any college. The others must be used wisely—perhaps with a little help from the counselor. A student who uses them well just might out-talent the talented and get that other letter—a letter of acceptance.

Again, some would argue that few adolescents have the keen insight and necessary maturity to write as creatively as some of the more selective institutions would demand. Possibly so, but at the very least our students should be capable of writing substantively. Quite frankly, most colleges would be thrilled to see a bit more substance. Besides, any youngster who has lived for 17 years should have something of importance to say about herself.

Write! Write! Write!

If a student really wants to make an impression, then he *must* put a great deal of effort into his writing. No amount of drill, sentence diagramming, or using workbooks can overcome the uptight feeling that confronts a student when he has to write. But it's *only* through writing and rewriting, one draft after another, that he can gain control over expression and idea, thereby becoming a much more confident writer. It makes sense, then, in preparation for what many regard as one of the most important lifetime writing efforts, the college essay, to work long and hard at developing and refining one's writing skills. (See Figure 22-1.)

The prime source of your counselee's writing should be *his own experiences*, academic or nonacademic. Even when he writes about something objective, like a piece of literature, the work should reflect his own experiences. Never mind such things as character analysis, theme, literary style, and abstractions. The question should be, "What effect, if any, did the work have on the *me*, and why?"

Once again, note the emphasis on the individual. It is by means of the submitted essay that a college is able to examine additional *personal* qualities of its applicants. It can focus on some or all of the following: the depth of a person's understanding of certain intellectual, social, or political issues; quality and creativity of mind; sophistication of writing style; and level of grammar skills.

The better young people know themselves, the easier it is to talk and write about themselves. Encourage your counselees to "figure themselves out" as soon as you can!

With certain schools, particularly the highly selective ones, the essay can make or break a student; it can tip the scales in a close decision, depending on whether the essay is powerful or weak. And, if your counselee's credentials look good, it can be the icing on the cake.

WHEN YOU WRITE YOUR ESSAY . . .

Do write lean! A cardinal rule promulgated by former Cornell University professor William Strunk, Jr., is for the writer to omit needless words. Strunk, with noted author E. B. White, wrote The Elements of Style, a concise and practical "carry along" handbook on the art of writing. The two gentlemen maintain that "vigorous writing is concise." "A sentence should contain no unnecessary words, a paragraph no unnecessary sentences for the same reason that a drawing should have no unnecessary lines and a machine no unnecessary parts." Each time you use the passive voice, you add words to a sentence. "Bob struck Bill" is 65 percent leaner than "Bob was struck by Bill." The simple sentence in itself is active, moving from subject through verb to object.

Do start early. Leave plenty of time to revise, reword, and rewrite. You can improve on your presentation.

Do read the directions carefully. You will want to answer the question as directly as possible, and you'll want to follow word limits exactly. Express yourself as briefly and as clearly as you can.

Do tell the truth about yourself. The admission committee is anonymous to you; you are completely unknown to it. Even if you run into a committee member in the future, he will have no way of connecting your essay (out of the thousands he has read) to you.

Do focus on an aspect of yourself that will show your best side. You might have overcome some adversity, worked through a difficult project, or profited from a specific incident. A narrow focus is more interesting than are broad-based generalizations.

Do consider using the three Common Application form topics as early practice possibilities: (1) evaluate a significant experience or achievement that has special meaning to you; (2) discuss some issue of personal, local, or national concern and its importance to you; (3) indicate a person who has had a significant influence on you, and describe that influence.

Do feel comfortable in expressing anxieties. Everybody has them, and it's good to know that an applicant can see them and face them.

Do speak positively. Negatives tend to turn people off.

Do write about your greatest assets and achievements. You should be proud of them!

But . . .

Don't repeat information given elsewhere on your application. The committee has already seen it—and it looks as though you have nothing better to say.

Don't write on general, impersonal topics—like the nuclear arms race or the importance of good management in business. The college wants to know about you.

Don't sacrifice the essay to excuse your shortcomings unless you intend it to be a natural and integral part of your topic. If it's a question of underachievement, you should find a spot somewhere else in the application (or use a separate sheet of paper) to explain why you had not been working to your ability.

Don't use cliches.

Don't go to extremes: too witty, too opinionated, or too "intellectual."

Remember:

The personal statement is yours. If it looks like Madison Avenue, the admission committee will probably assume that it is your mother's or your father's or their secretaries'.

A "gimmick" essay rarely goes anywhere. The committee is amused, but unimpressed with your candidacy.

Write a serious essay, from the bottom of your heart, in the most mature manner possible.

Figure 22-1

A FEW SAMPLES FROM THE FILES

Let's take a look at some actual essays to identify some more do's and don'ts.

Note how well the student's essay in Figure 22-2 addresses the topic: the topic and selected experience are a perfect fit. The event is well described, and at the same time, we gain insight into the effect the stated experiences have had on the writer's development. The essay reflects the student's industry, sensitive nature, and selfless attitude. In structure and style, the essay is quite well written.

An essay does not always reflect the characteristics of the applicant. Note the differences between this essay and the one in Figure 22-3.

It's one thing to describe a humorous incident, and quite another to write humorously about a part of one's life: the latter is difficult at best. Here, the opening sentence is clever and attention getting, and the reader expects that a strong point will be made. Unfortunately, the rest of the essay is vague, confusing, and disjointed. There is no specific connection made between requirements presented for *Who's Who* and the student himself. The author states that he won an award, but the reader is left to surmise the difficulties involved in its acquisition and the effect it had on the student. "Realize" does not imply activity.

Now let's compare two "activity" essays.

PERSONAL STATEMENT

Required Essay 2: Individuals have the capacity to influence events and improve the situations in which they or others find themselves. Describe briefly an incident or event in which you played this role or one in which you hope to in the future.

There is nothing more gratifying to me than overhearing a child approach his parents with, "Mommy, look what I learned today!" or "Daddy, this is so much fun!" These comments, and other similar ones, are the results of the influence I have had on young children. For the past five years, I have in one way or another touched the heart of a child. As a magician, I have dazzled children with tricks and illusions. As a clown, I have prompted their smiles and laughter.

The children I entertain all look up to me. They like me and are always full of enthusiasm. They also listen attentively, forever curious about everything I do.

When I turned sixteen, I decided to extend this interest of working with children to teaching after-school classes at one of our elementary schools. I taught two of my specialties, magic and soccer. Some twenty children were enrolled in each of two classes.

The individuals in my magic class learned the concepts of this art and the basic techniques of performing it. Progress was easily measured as each child performed his own show at the end of the year. With soccer, the children were amazed to see the dexterity that I had with the ball, and became ecstatic knowing that they would have a chance to learn similar skills. What a pleasurable experience it was when one student hugged and thanked me for the instruction I had provided him.

Children continue to be a special part of my life. Maybe, later in their lives, some of my students will remember me. Just knowing that I have had some positive influence on their development is one of the most satisfying feelings I will ever know.

Figure 22-2

Although the essay in Figure 22-4 is fairly well written, the approach taken by the writer is typical of many students: the work is too broadly focused. The essay also repeats the activity portion of the application; the author misuses the opportunity by listing her extracurricular musical involvement. How much better it would have been if she had chosen to develop the sentence, "Over the next two years we worked to change it into . . . ,"thereby narrowing the focus of the essay

PERSONAL STATEMENT

In the space below or on an attached sheet, please write an original essay describing a humorous personal experience.

There's Who's Who in America, Who's Who in College, and I firmly believe in the establishment of a Who's Who in Summer Camp. After all, you have to start somewhere.

Literally millions of people have the misfortune to live in a country other than America. Some are unable to attend college for a variety of reasons, and in a smaller, much less important scale, some are unable to attend summer camp. If one is fortunate enough to go to a sleep-away camp, there should be something for which to strive.

It would be wonderful to earn a place in Who's Who in Camping. There should be specific requirements. One should be able to pass rigorous physical demands, specifically in athletics and outdoorsmanship. Just climbing the hills to one's bunk after a difficult day could be considered an accomplishment. There should be psychological requisites such as willingness to help, cooperation, initiative, dependability, and stability. Overcoming homesickness could constitute a major attainment. One should be outstanding in all phases of camp life.

In 1982, I was selected as the All Around Camper. I have had the privilege of attending Camp Weequahic for the past six summers. I accepted this award with pride and my name is now forever inscribed on a wooden plaque at camp. It is an honor I will always cherish. It has helped me realize that inspiration, aspiration, and perspiration are often rewarded. I can only imagine the feelings of those selected to Who's Who in College and Who's Who in America.

Figure 22-3

and making it a more vital piece. Perhaps the essay would have had greater strength if it had been written in the present tense, considering that the writer was a senior and still engaged in these activities.

The author of the next essay (see Figure 22-5) takes the same topic and nicely narrows his focus. He talks about his involvement and accomplishments in a positive, fervent, but controlled manner. It is an interesting piece with a most creative opening paragraph.

The author of this essay in Figure 22-6 has narrowed the topic nicely, and the piece is well written. He wisely writes on a subject that he knows something about, and one that is most important to him. The topic is explored in considerable

PERSONAL STATEMENT

In the space provided, please tell us about an activity that has been of special importance to you.

> Although I am not a music major I have been involved with our high school concert, marching, and stage bands. As a member of the concert band I gained an appreciation for classical music. The marching band offered me an exciting experience because I was part of a major change. During my first year in high school this band was only a pep band that played at football games. Over the next two years we worked to change it into a competition band, and this year won first place honors. I was also 1 of the 17 members of a stage band. Here I learned how to play the big band sound and jazz music. Since my high school has over 2,000 students, being a member of all of these bands has given me a sense of belonging. It has also given me a sense of accomplishment. . . .

Figure 22-4

depth, and at the same time the reader can gain insight into the student's character and personality. The work is an example of risk taking, because the writer is not fearful about openly expressing his opinion on an issue. The construction of this author's first sentence is relatively strong, far better than if he had said, "Music has always been a major part of my life."

Where is the *student* in the essay shown in Figure 22-7? Notice that she does not address the "why" of the topic, and consequently, we are not allowed into *her* world. The writing might satisfy the requirements of the academic essay, but personal essay "why" topics are designed to provide admission counselors with a glimpse into the applicant herself. The writer is improperly vague as to the identification and historical placement of Dwight Eisenhower and Fred Fischer. On the plus side, this student has a good command of grammar, and the writing style demonstrates a certain amount of creativity and sophistication.

And last but not least, Figure 22-8.

This piece is beautifully written; the content and style reflect both substance and creativity. Because the sentence structure is varied, the piece flows, and the reader is kept reading. More than that, because there is great depth to the work, the reader is able to learn much about the student's personality and character. Through her description of her development in Singapore, she leaves with the reader the conviction that she fully intends to see her college experience as a new opportunity for growth.

PERSONAL STATEMENT

In the space provided, please tell us about an activity that has been of special importance to you.

> I poise myself, ready to spring into action. As I look out across the playing field and see my team waiting for me to act, I push the noise of the crowd out of my mind. Raising my arms into the air, I count off. And as I lower them, my team reacts by moving about the field. I never have to worry that there's only a minute left and we're down by three. For, you see, it's half time, and I'm the Drum Major of the Medford High School Marching Band.
>
> Rising from sophomore clarinetist to Drum Major, for the past two years I have been responsible for organizing, arranging, and, of course, conducting the band. It is at games and competitions that I realize that all of the time and energy expended has been worthwhile. When I perform I fear falling off the podium, slipping in the mud, or generally looking silly. Nevertheless, I still pour forth enthusiasm, as if each performance is the performance of a lifetime. I guess you might say that I become not just a band leader, but an entertainer as well. The crowd and the band become spirited, and we have a good time. Quite frankly, I love hearing the applause for the band's presentation, and for my own personal performance. My work as Drum Major here at Medford has enhanced my leadership and human relations skills. It has also provided me with a greater sense of confidence, self-esteem, and accomplishment.

Figure 22-5

MORE TIPS FOR YOUR COUNSELEES

- A student can set up a file on himself, dropping everything and anything into it that might eventually help him in his writing.
- Ripple suggests that the student do two things in proofing his own work: "One. Use a ruler or a blank sheet of paper to cover the lines beneath the one you are reading. This will keep your eyes more focused. Two. Read your essay backwards. This will prevent you from skimming the text and force you to look carefully at each individual word."

PERSONAL STATEMENT

Discuss a local, state, or national issue that is of particular importance to you.

> Music to me is a universal language that offers countless means of expression. For this reason, I am constantly immersed in it. Whether I am helping customers at the record store where I work, playing my trumpet in a performance, attending a concert, or just relaxing with a favorite record at home, I find myself with music. This wide exposure has helped to broaden my tastes to the point where I am able to appreciate everything from rock to jazz to classical music. (It has also given me the opportunity to form opinions of musicians as people, especially popular musicians.)
>
> Pop music, like society in general, is saturated with unprincipled people–people who are eager to conform to any trend in order to achieve financial success. The majority of these recording artists build their careers around a peculiar gimmick or appearance; the increasing popularity of music video has provided an easily accessible medium by which these superficial qualities may be displayed. The music itself is usually nothing more than a watered-down conglomeration of currently fashionable sounds, and the lyrics are most often banal and trite.
>
> Luckily for serious music devotees, behind the glitter of the ephemeral top 40 superstars exists a smaller, but more permanent, group of uncompromising artists. These are artists in the true sense of the word, in that they probe their own respective musical and lyrical styles without regard to where the public eye is currently focused....

Figure 22-6

- Of course, it is imperative that the student have someone else proofread his work!
- Reading the essay aloud can also help one spot errors, because the ear gives the writer a second opinion on the piece.
- A student should set his essay aside for a few days, then read it again with as fresh and objective an eye as possible.
- If your counselee has access to a word processor, then he is really in luck.
- Students are probably their own best critics.
- Your cuonselees should start early! And practice! practice! practice!

PERSONAL STATEMENT

If you could interview a significant historical figure, past or present, who would it be and why?

I frequently wonder what motivates people to take the courses of action they do. Are they sincere or do they have sinister motives?

In the 1950s a demagogue by the name of Joseph McCarthy rose to power. McCarthy, a senator from Wisconsin, headed a witch-hunt which labeled many loyal Americans as communists.

He became powerful because, whether real or imagined, people were afraid of communism as a political force. Maybe it was because a few years earlier, Alger Hiss, a high government official, had been charged with being a communist spy, just as Ethel and Julius Rosenberg had been charged in the late 1940s. Or perhaps it was because China had recently turned communist and the Russians were now in possession of the atomic bomb.

The television and newspaper media also contributed to McCarthy's rise to power. Yes, the media, along with the American public, helped this man flourish. With the thought that communism might be taking over our government, Americans needed someone to turn to for assistance. That someone was Joseph McCarthy.

Like the Salem witch trials of the seventeenth century, McCarthy began pointing his finger at those individuals he "suspected" of being communist. Did he really believe that these people were communists, or was it some sort of personal vendetta on his part?

The demagogue's downfall came when he started pointing his finger at the wrong people, such as Eisenhower's army and Fred Fischer. Fischer's attorney destroyed McCarthy at the Army-McCarthy hearings in 1954....

Figure 22-7

IN CONCLUSION

If the essay is that vital a part of an applicant's folder, then it stands to reason that the better the quality of our advisement, the better the presentation. And since we *are* genuinely concerned about helping students gain admission to particular schools, then perhaps what is needed is a heightened commitment of time, en-

PERSONAL STATEMENT

Discuss a personal experience that helped form a belief or value that you hold.

"There is no way anyone is going to make me wear one of those ugly uniforms! I'll look like such a nerd!"

I can still hear and see myself three years ago, on my first day in the Convent of the Holy Infant Jesus. My long, skillfully manicured nails and hot pink miniskirt were obviously out of place amidst the myriad of blue pinafores and bowl-cut hairstyles: I was an oddity.

My parents' most difficult task upon moving to Singapore was enrolling me in a local school. They wanted to give me an opportunity to experience a new and different culture. My cloistered eleven years in New Jersey had left me unprepared for the shock of adjustment; I wanted only to attend the private American school where I would not feel like an outsider. As a result, I was unwilling to conform to the Singaporean society where I was initially unaccepted.

This obstinacy stayed with me for many months; I resented the innumerable rules of the Convent concerning attire and decorum. The highly demanding academic curriculum forced me to spend hours laboring over textbooks. My yearning for America made me hate the Convent even more.

Now, as I look back upon my Convent experience, I wonder when it was I started to like Singapore and to love my school. Perhaps it was the wonderful enthusiasm and support I received from the girls. The Convent girls were a united lot. They wanted, probably more than I, to see me as part of their togetherness. ...

Maybe the wall I had built gradually began to crumble as I unconsciously became involved in various school activities; we produced plays, arranged an elaborate trip to Malaysia, and organized functions with our brother school. My most tiring but delightful experience occurred when the school produced an official opening ceremony concert. ... I was elated as I listened to [my piece of poetry on love] being read before all the guests ...

My time in the Convent of the Holy Infant Jesus has contributed much to my life in its own special way. I worked hard to meet the rigorous demands of the examinations and was rewarded with an overwhelming feeling of satisfaction. I met foreign students who I initially felt were different from me; our differences have drawn us together in an exceptional bond of friendship. Learning about the culture and adjusting to life in Asia was undoubtedly one of the finest educations I will ever receive. My move back to the United States has given me an opportunity to appreciate all the people I have met and all the experiences I have encountered overseas.

"When you part from your friend you grieve not; for that which you love in him may be clearer in his absence, as the mountain to the climber is clearer from the plain."–Kahil Gibran

Figure 22-8

ergy, and dedication to an activity like essay writing. This is not to deny that at times the whole admission process seems like nothing more than a "crap shoot." But maybe we could and should be making a greater difference in loading the dice.

SUGGESTED READINGS

CURRY, BOYKIN, AND BRIAN KASBAR. 1986. *Essays That Worked*. New Haven, CT: Mustang Publishing. Yes, it's possible that students could end up mimicking one or more of these essays. Nonetheless, the 50 essays, divided into seven classifications, are real eye openers—well worth perusing for both you and your counselees.

RIPPLE, G. GARY. 1985. *How to Prepare a Great College Application*. Alexandria, VA: Octameron Associates. An excellent pamphlet that lends itself for use with groups.

Chapter 23

An Ever-Changing Financial Aid Picture

Remember the National Defense Education Act of 1958? Some do—they found employment through it. NDEA was once a powerful set of initials. The act was a major thrust to "increase our efforts to identify and educate more of the talent of this nation." And with increased identification came dollars to help the able, but financially less fortunate.

SHOULDERING THE RESPONSIBILITY

Now, 30 years later, we are still trying to identify and educate more of the nation's talented, but we're doing so with considerably less financial support from the federal government. Consequently, everyone else has been asked to shoulder more financial responsibility for the postsecondary education of our youth—especially parents.

College costs are skyrocketing, and they outpace inflation 2 to 1. The potential could hardly be greater for school counselors to render support to families in their quest to make that "best match" a reality. Simply doing an effective job of counseling on the basics of financial aid has taken on added importance for counselors. For example, today it is *critical* that families distinguish between the *price* of an institution and the actual *cost*. Often, if the initial price looks too great, families won't explore further. Parents need to know that many private colleges and universities in this country *have* some very innovative financial aid programs in place. And many of these same schools openly advertise that they *can* and *will* meet full need. It is vital that counselors become familiar with the *extensive* financial aid programs that many private colleges support.

In some institutions, as many as 80 percent of attending students now receive some sort of financial assistance other than family resources. Of course, to qualify for financial aid, a student must show the financial necessity: a family does not have to be *poor* to qualify for aid, but it must demonstrate a real *need* for it.

To assist them in their determination of financial need, most collegiate institutions use the College Scholarship Service (CSS) or the American College Testing (ACT) Program, or both. These national nonprofit need-analysis organizations employ a fair and uniform analysis system based upon family income, assets, and student resources to arrive at their final figures.

From UM to CM

As of 1988—89, the congressional methodology (CM) replaced the uniform methodology (UM) in determining eligibility for federal financial aid. The Higher Education Amendments Acts of 1987 mandates that CM must be employed to calculate students' needs for all Title IV funds, except Pell Grants and State Student Incentive Grants. Although there are marked similarities between the programs, the two methodologies can produce very different results for both dependent and independent students. Perhaps the greatest change is in how CM treats student income. While the UM ignores the earned income reported by the student, adds a standard "summer savings" figure to untaxed income, and permits the colleges to make adjustments, the CM bases student contribution on the student's total income from the prior calendar year. (Students are required to have 70 percent of their after-tax earnings available to meet college expenses.) Students are also expected to contribute 35 percent of their savings toward such expenses. Could this be a kind of double jeopardy if some or all of a youngster's yearly earnings find their way into a savings account?

"Package" Defined

Most families receive an aid "package," a combination of three types of financial assistance:

1. Grants and scholarships: monies that do not have to be repaid.
2. Loans: borrowed funds that usually carry a low interest rate and do not have to be repaid until after one graduates, and then over an extended period of time.
3. Work study: 10 to 15 hours a week of on- or off-campus employment through which one can earn money to help pay his or her way. (Freshmen hours are kept purposely light.)

Price Versus Cost

Financial aid and financial planning are areas in which a department's use of common terminology can pay dividends, as to the facilitation of communication. Your department might consider employing common terminology with such words as "price" and "cost." *Price* is the amount charged by an institution for tuition, fees, room, board, and miscellaneous expenses. *Cost* is the determined amount that a family must pay out-of-pocket toward these educational expenses. *Aid* is the difference between price and cost, which is determined by *need*. As you know, prices vary widely at different institutions. *But what a family can afford to pay doesn't often change.* In other words, the amount that the family is expected to contribute remains basically fixed, whether the college or university is priced at $5,500 or $13,000.

This can be presented simply and graphically, as shown in Figure 23-1.

Public Ivies: What Price Prestige?

Have you tried to get into the University of North Carolina at Chapel Hill lately? *You* might not have, but according to the January 13, 1988, edition of *The*

	COLLEGE Selective Private	COLLEGE State Midsize	UNIVERSITY State Large	UNIVERSITY Selective Private
Tuition and fees	$ 8,500	$2,500	$4,500	$11,500
Room and board	2,500	2,200	2,400	3,100
Miscellaneous (books, supplies, etc.)	1,200	950	1,100	1,225
Price	$12,000	$5,650	$8,000	$15,825
EFC (estimated family contribution)	4,200	4,200	4,200	4,200
Need	$ 8,000	$1,450	$3,800	$11,625
Grant (gift money)	5,000	–0–	1,500	7,000
Loan	2,000	1,450	1,200	3,000
Work study	1,000	–0–	1,100	1,625
Total Aid	$ 8,000	$1,450	$3,800	$11,625
Cost to family	$ 4,200	$4,200	$4,200	$ 4,200

Cost = price − aid

Figure 23-1

New York Times, 8,663 out-of-state high school students tried to do so in 1987. This figure was some 2,000 higher than the school's in-state applicant figure. And Chapel Hill only enrolled 552 (1 out of 15) from the outside that year.

There's a virtual stampede to public universities these days; families feel that one big reward for winning an acceptance to one of these schools for an out-of-stater is that tuition is substantially lower than at selective private colleges. But is it? Author Richard Moll *(The Public Ivys)* calls it "getting a first rate education without paying Ivy League tuitions." But do you? (See Figure 23-2.)

A tuition figure of $8,600 at University of Michigan is not exactly a bargain for out-of-state students. When you add $3,053 for room and board, $1,500 in miscellaneous/personal expenses, and $1,000 for travel, it brings the total cost to $14,153. New York students could well stay home and attend "highly selective" Colgate for nearly the same price. And New Jerseyans aren't necessarily being "cut a break" by the University of Vermont, either. At a tuition figure of $8,986, $3,646 for room and board, $1,200 in miscellaneous/personal expenses, and $200 for travel, New Jersey students could well stay home and attend "very selective" Drew U. for about the same amount of money. And the average dollar amount of aid awarded at both Drew and Colgate is considerably higher than that of UNC and Vermont.

Naturally, a student's "final six" are not based solely on financial considerations; however, it appears that we can no longer make such carte blanche statements as "tuitions are substantially lower at public schools than at private." Indeed, the phrase "What price prestige?" might be as applicable to the public sector

A SAMPLING OF PUBLIC INSTITUTIONS

Institution	Out-of-State Tuition	In-State Tuition	Average Amount of Aid
University of Vermont	$8,986	$3,118	$5,411
University of Michigan	8,600	3,000	4,300
University of Colorado	6,558	1,540	—
Penn State University	6,018	2,996	3,516
University of Virginia	5,800	2,390	3,150
University of North Carolina at Chapel Hill	4,447	850	2,258

Note: Tuition figures for 1987 obtained from each university. Average amount of aid figures extracted from the Comparative Guide to American Colleges, 13th ed.

Figure 23-2

of education as it is to the private one. In their ballyhooing of public institutions, journalists and specialty guide authors have helped hike tuition costs, raise academic standards, and swell applicant pools. You might want to explore this issue with your families, perhaps at an evening get-together, perhaps under the heading "Truth in Advertising."

Financing a college education is such a formidable task for some families that they get discouraged and overlook more costly but nevertheless potentially excellent "matches" in favor of inappropriate cheaper ones. We need to recognize that today's families are more or less caught in the middle between the federal government and the collegiate institutions. The federal government charges that colleges are charging what the market will bear; the colleges counter with the fact that they are simply doing "catchup" on faculty salaries and facilities from the lull of the 1970s.

But you can be there for your families:

- Don't let yourself become cynical about this topic. If you counsel in an affluent community, there *is* some danger of your becoming overly skeptical when you see, year in and year out, but a small percentage of families awarded any kind of substantial aid. Don't let cynicism take over! It is most important that you remain open-minded and maintain a positive attitude. Remember that each family condition is one of a kind. And you never know just where the "good aid fairy" will strike. A sound way to go with it is a "nothing ventured, nothing gained" attitude. If you haven't discovered it already, you'll find that many adults incorporated this philosophy into their lives long ago, and, for them, even $500 is better than nothing. Frankly, this is as it should be. A comment like, "The whole thing is a waste of time," will get you nowhere.
- Try a "mixed bag" approach and urge your families to submit applications to *both* public and private schools. Students *should* select colleges and universities without undue attention to price.
- If for some reason you cannot familiarize yourself with "many" financial aid programs, at least familiarize yourself with a "few." Exploring several aid programs in depth should provide a feel for what is out there at private institutions. And, once thoroughly oriented, you can quite accurately generalize from there.
- Parents are not expected to sell off little brother, but they are expected to make the maximum effort to meet education expenses. You can help them recognize that postsecondary education is a *capital* investment and that they should invest accordingly.

More specifically:

- Although parents have to request (reapply for) financial assistance each academic year, your reassurance that they will only have to complete the Financial Aid Form (FAF) or Family Financial Statement (FFS) once can be helpful.

- It is imperative that parents get the idea that in filling out a financial aid form, accuracy and completeness count! Anyone who is attempting to make sense out of another person's financial condition deserves to receive total and precise information.
- There are literally dozens of computer software packages that are aligned with uniform methodology. Parents can plug in the numbers and obtain nearly the same results as CSS does as to estimated family contribution.
- A college can interpret information received from a processing service somewhat differently, which can in turn cause the estimated family contribution figure to be lower or higher than that of the reporting service.
- Encourage your parents to seek *professional* help where needed. The financial information that they provide is always held in the strictest confidence by financial aid officers, bank officials, and other agency personnel. Reassure them that they are far from alone in this process.
- An increasing number of colleges are asking parents to submit a copy of their federal tax return (1040) in addition to the FAF or FFS. You might want to mention to your parents that such a request could be made of them.
- Just as college application submission deadlines vary according to school, so do those that govern the submission of financial aid information. Counsel your parents to be fully aware of all deadline dates and what they mean.
- Suggest to your families that in their campus visitation plans they might want to include a meeting with a financial aid official. Telephoning ahead for an appointment is a must! And how about dropping by another office—the placement office? Here you can find out about "life after college," or, to phrase it differently, "What return will I get on my dollar."
- Families need to understand thoroughly the terms and conditions of all financial assistance offered. No estimates or ballpark figures, please!
- Families should proceed cautiously if middlemen, like coaches and department heads, bear gifts. If and when an offer of financial assistance is made, parents should be certain that these particular college officials have the authority to do so.
- Stress to parents the importance of making and retaining a copy of all documents submitted and sending such documents by certified or registered mail.
- Students *should* inform their financial aid office of any and all additional "outside" awards received. Help them to understand that any additional award money that they report almost always reduces student loan, work study, or earning expectation first.

Costing It Out in Advance

Why is it important to settle on expenses ahead of time? There are several reasons: (1) once aid is received, a family can determine what percentage of the total price is covered by the award, (2) families can begin to budget early for

WORKSHEET FOR ANALYZING COLLEGE EXPENSES

Expenses	College A	College B	College C
Tuition	________	________	________
Room	________	________	________
Board	________	________	________
Required fees	________	________	________
Voluntary fees	________	________	________
Supplies	________	________	________
Textbooks	________	________	________
Insurance	________	________	________
Transportation	________	________	________
Personal expenses	________	________	________

Figure 23-3

unanticipated expenses, and (3) families can have a basis for making comprehensive cost comparisons among several schools. Parents need to comprehend that "price" can include many items beyond the large, obvious ones such as room, board, and tuition. Additional smaller expenses, identified in the handy worksheet in Figure 23-3, can mount quickly.

STATE INVOLVEMENT

Every state provides some type of financial assistance to qualified residents; some assist more than others. Most awards are need based, although some programs are based on other criteria, such as academic performance and admission testing results. According to Octameron Associates, Alexandria, VA, as reported in the November 25, 1985, issue of *U.S. News & World Report*, "1.3 million students received 1.2 billion dollars in need-based state aid and 249,000 shared 132 million in aid not tied to need."

In California (which, incidentally, operates one of the best state scholarship programs in the country), the student aid application (SAAC) can double for the FAF; that is, with certain California colleges and universities, students are free to submit either an SAAC or FAF form to the College Scholarship Service.

Guaranteed Student Loan Program

No longer will Mom and Dad be able to run to their local bank and borrow GSL money irrespective of family income. As of January 1, 1987, all GSL applicants must demonstrate financial need through the same system used to determine need for SEOG, CWS, and NDSL programs. Since the program is now strictly need based, families must file an FAF or FFS and indicate that they wish to receive Pell Grant money.

The formula:

Price of institution — cost to family — all other financial aid
= maximum GSL approval

To put it another way, GSL money can no longer replace expected family contribution. The impact on families, especially those of middle income, is potentially devastating. Some collegiate institutions are already writing in GSL funds as part of their financial aid packages, knowing that qualified students can borrow up to $2,625 per academic year as freshmen and sophomores and up to $4,000 per year as juniors and seniors.

FINANCIAL AID IS NOT FINANCIAL PLANNING

And the two "poles apart" terms should not be confused. *Financial aid* could be viewed as getting your hands on someone else's money, while *financial planning* is making the most of your own resources. There are many people wandering around the country calling themselves financial planners in order to sell a product. Financial planning is not a product; it is a process—a lifelong process.

Very little has been done to bring any kind of "planning" message to families with respect to the significance of *early* financial preparation for postsecondary education. (Studies continue to show that less than 10 percent of American families plan ahead for such education.)

Ah, but the picture is changing, as evidenced by the information-starved parents who can be seen flocking to the few school orientation sessions offered today. And, considering the times, why shouldn't these sessions be well attended? If parents know that they won't be getting financial assistance from outside sources, they can then shape their investment programs differently. Interest in these evening panel programs *is* on the rise, as more and more counseling departments sense that they should at least counsel parents on where to turn for proper professional advice.

An organization that is ready and willing to offer such advice is the International Association for Financial Planning. IAFP has a registry of some 600 members. In addition to the usual certification, candidates for membership must also offer three years of experience in the field, produce peer and client recommendations, submit a sample plan, and perform satisfactorily on a special five-hour examination.

For a complimentary membership directory, write or telephone:

International Association for Financial Planning
#2 Concourse Parkway, Suite 800
Atlanta, GA 30328
(404) 395-1605

COMPUTERIZED MATCHMAKING: CAVEAT EMPTOR!

Funds for higher education have become so tight that families are turning to financial aid "matchmakers" in greater numbers than ever before. The number of these computerized matching service firms has significantly increased, as well. Since the first company opened its door some 20 years ago, the advertising message has remained the same: "Big dollars are going begging. There are literally millions of unclaimed dollars just waiting for you and others like you."

But you might want to counsel your families: buyer beware! A study of over 50 firms by the California Student Aid Commission, utilizing a test group of high school students, revealed that not one firm provided effective matching. Researchers say that it is an unproved claim that significant amounts of educational monies are going untapped. However, if a family does not have the appropriate amount of time to conduct a meaningful search of its own, and wishes to engage a matching service, at the very least it should select a reputable firm, such as Dr. Herm Davis's National College Services Ltd., in Gaithersburg, MD. This particular company has a no-hassle refund policy if the family is not satisfied with the service.

Before plunging into a plan like this, your counselees and their parents might want to procure answers to a few questions. (See Figure 23-4.)

Remember, the financial aid picture is continually changing, but if you keep up with current trends, you and your families can be much calmer and more confident of success.

QUESTIONS TO RAISE WITH A FINANCIAL AID MATCHING SERVICE

1. What is the size of the financial aid source data bank?
2. How many leads will the company supply for the fee? How many of these leads are in the form of scholarships, grants, loans, work study programs, or contests?
3. In supplying its leads, will the company be duplicating state and national programs for which students will already be considered through normal financial aid channels?
4. Does the company periodically update its files as to eligibility requirements, application deadlines, and so on?
5. What has been the track record of the company? In other words, how successful have former participants been in securing financial aid from company-recommended sources?
6. What is the company's refund policy? Will it return all or a portion of the paid fee if the client is not satisfied with the services?

Figure 23-4

SUGGESTED READINGS

The College Cost Book. College Board Publications, Box 886, New York. A step-by-step guide to paying for college that also includes the costs at 3,500 colleges and universities. Revised annually.

DENNIS, MARGUERITE J. 1986. *Mortgaged Futures: How to Graduate from School Without Going Broke.* Washington, DC: Hope Press.

LEIDER, ROBERT. 1988. *Don't Miss Out: The Ambitious Student's Guide to Financial Aid.* Alexandria, VA: Octameron Associates. A fine source that covers a wide range of scholarships, grants, loans, and personal finance methods.

Chapter 24

Stress Factors That Affect the College Bound

"*I* had to handle things! Let them fend for themselves!"

Yes, that's one way to think about your students and the stress involved in the transition from high school to college. And there's some truth to it: young people should be learning to deal with difficult situations.

But a few other thoughts might cross your mind. First, in several ways things are more difficult these days. The world was much more "our own" back when we went to college 10, 20, 25 years ago. Now, global communication and instant news access make us feel like we're living in a fish bowl, so we can see thousands of people try for the same things we want. And that makes competition—and its stress—more urgent.

Then add to this the fact that parenting is a more complex process now (and is perhaps not learned as well); much of child rearing is neglected, pushed off to others—like the schools. Consequently, many youngsters have a hard time learning the skills they will need to survive *well*.

Third, most of us are in this service occupation because we feel that it is right and just that we help the next generation become stronger and more social than the one before it. The world is indeed much smaller, and the care of it is much more crucial.

You and your counselees have worked hard to set up appropriate programs of study, cope with extracurricular involvement, develop nonacademic interests, and (at last) apply to the "best matched schools" you could uncover. The question is: "What now?"

AFTER APRIL 15

Young people are vulnerable. They have not yet developed coping mechanisms to the point where they can rationalize or protest or circumvent problems as well as adults can. "Growing up" isn't easy, and the transition from high school to college involves a great deal of stress.

Many counselors are only superficially involved with their seniors come April 15. This is unfortunate, because there *is* an increasing need for counselors to understand the extent and depth of the anxiety these young people may be experiencing.

TELL-TALE SIGNS

Most students process stress very well. They get support from family, friends, and peer groups, all of whom can be very helpful. Some cannot deal with stress, so they make it known and get assistance. Others, however, mask their stress well: These are the students about whom we should be most concerned.

Counselees who are uncommonly stressed might telegraph signs. What should you look for?

- A precipitous drop in academic achievement
- Unexplained and nondistinctive illness
- A certain fanaticism about the admission process with consequent inability to relax properly
- Rapid mood swings
- Abnormal gain or loss of weight
- Unusual changes in personal attire
- A new and sudden reliance on drugs
- Exhibiting a rebellious and/or explosive temperament
- Displaying unusual excessive dependency
- Evincing withdrawal tendencies, including sleeping through classes (Because of their continuous contact with students, classroom teachers would be excellent sources of reference for you.)

MAJOR CONCERNS WORTH EXPLORING TOGETHER

School counselors are more aware than previously that effective counseling at the secondary level is an excellent way for students to (1) make a proper "match" so that they avoid becoming part of a substantial college dropout figure and (2) cope with the problems they will encounter later on.

The following are a baker's dozen of significant stress factors related to the college admission process. They address two major areas of concern: the planning process itself and the successful survival of the freshman year.

1. Concern as to what your peers will think and say about your acceptances and rejections. "Will I find myself involved in the acceptance/rejection comparison game?"
2. Concern about being asked to examine for and then expose your differences, when all along you might have been trying to hide them.
3. Concern that the decision making involved in the college admission process is more than you as a 17-year-old can handle.
4. Concern about doing well on admission tests.
5. Concern about the quality of advice offered: "Everyone appears to be an expert. To whom should I listen?"
6. Concern about pleasing parents: "How far do I go with their suggestions?"
7. Concern about living with the final decision: "Will I regret my ultimate choice?"
8. Concern about flunking out: "Will I be one of 10 or 15 percent of the freshmen who will not return for the sophomore year?" (Admission counselors at Elon College in North Carolina see this factor as one of the two greatest concerns on the part of college-bound students.)
9. Concern about roommate: "What will living in a dormitory and sharing space with someone else be like?" (The thought of who will be one's roommate appears to be the other great concern. This can be an especially difficult problem for an only child or someone who has never shared a room at home.)
10. Concern about alcohol and drugs: students might face frontal attack on already established morals and values. "Will I be ready for such an attack; will I be strong enough to adhere to my values?"
11. Concern about entering one of the "big six" career areas. "Just how important is it that I pursue a career in Engineering, Accounting, Business Management, Law, Medicine or Computers?"
12. Concern about leaving home.
13. Concern about doing well once on the campus. "Would I be better off attending a slightly less competitive school where I can be on top of the heap, as opposed to a more competitive one where I might find myself on the bottom?"

These and other factors can become the basis for group exploration activity involving students and/or parents.

SOPHOMORE YEAR AND STILL THERE!

It is heartening to see more secondary schools become more proactive as to the issue of stress factors. A few high schools and colleges have developed a variety of meaningful programs which you can emulate, purchase, or become a participant in, as you assist students to make as smooth—and lasting—a transition as possible from high school to college. As one collegian quipped, "It's my sophomore year, and I'm still here."

The Elon College Project

Recognizing the overwhelming need for additional information on individual student adjustment to college life, Joanne Soliday, dean of admissions at Elon College in North Carolina, has developed and "taken on the road" an inspiring, informative, and practical workshop entitled "How to Survive or Not Survive in College." The workshop is a high-energy presentation designed to encourage students to express and discuss their fears about going off to college. It has received rave reviews from counselors who have used it.

Since its development in 1983, over 400 presentations of "How to Survive or Not Survive'" have been given to some 8,000 students in North Carolina, Virginia, Maryland, and New Jersey, and it has been presented in workshop form at guidance counselor conferences from Georgia to Massachusetts. It is available in color on half-inch VHF video tape at a reasonable cost. Purchase of the tape enables you to "reach" your counselees year after year.

The Maret School Project

A significant and worthwhile evening program for families is that developed by the Maret School, Washington, DC. The project centers on the transition from high school to college, but with a twist. Parents and offspring are placed in separate rooms and are asked to brainstorm the same four questions; they are then brought back to review their responses together. The beauty of this kind of exercise is that families very rarely sit down to explore substantive and sensitive issues that relate to separation of family members. The evening can open the door to further discussion back home. Having the two parties meet separately gives young people the opportunity to be more free with their responses, knowing that parents will be unable to identify who made what statements. As is so often the case in group activity, parents and students learn from each other and—just as important—come to the realization that they share common, normal concerns. As might be expected, the young peoples' comments are more self-centered than those of their parents.

The four basic questions to which the Maret School asks parents and offspring to respond are:

1. What excites you most about the prospects of next year?
2. What do you fear most about next year?

3. What are the best aspects of your (child) going to college next year?
4. What are the worst aspects of your (child) going to college next year?

Parental comments can range from the forthright, "I'll feel less guilty when I work late," to the humorous, "Classical music will now be possible" or "My husband won't be as funny as the kids."

A culminating program activity, one that can translate into a moving moment between parents and offspring, is when both groups are asked to respond in writing to the following statement:

> If I could let my (child/parents) know one thing, it would be . . .

The statements are collected and then read quickly and in alternating fashion by the program leaders. A great way to close a great program! A great way to make a difference!

The Beverly Hills High School Project

Like other professionals, Patricia Henning, now a counselor at the Westlake School for Girls (Los Angeles, California), believes that counselors seldom adequately address the issue with their families: How do families prepare for, and consequently handle, the changes involved with the college-bound student's "breaking away" from the family unit? In fact, it was Henning's examination of her own role as a counselor in Beverly Hills that caused her to design a pilot program in 1985 for the Beverly Hills Unified School District. She realized that she was spending too little time in helping families cope with the stressful issues inherent in the separation.

Through an eye-catching letter of invitation, all parents of college-bound seniors are invited to an evening panel presentation. The program is conducted in May, after students have received their acceptance/rejection letters. The panel is comprised of four students and four parents and is led by a psychologist from the community. (Henning has found that having individuals on the panel who are willing to share and express feelings is paramount to the success of this kind of program. Consequently, it behooves the program developer to expend a considerable amount of time, thought, and energy on the selection of panel members.)

Henning sees three important goals accomplished with this type of presentation:

1. *Commonality*. Parents feel comforted by having the opportunity of sharing common separation concerns and by exploring issues that their youngsters are hesitant and/or unable to face.
2. *Communication*. Like the Maret School, the Beverly Hills project provides the stimulus for families to return home and to continue "dialoguing" on some of the topics introduced.

3. *Community*. Some parents find the evening so stimulating that they form groups to continue with the discussion and to assist one another to cope with certain ongoing issues of "breaking away."

Henning intends to use the project at Westlake School. A videotape of the program is available.

COUNSELING THE "REJECTED" STUDENT

In a fall 1986 article entitled, "What Do You Mean I Didn't Get In?" (*The Journal of College Admissions*, National Association of College Admission Counselors), James Coffey, director of guidance at Horace Greeley High School (Chappaqua, NY) remarks, "It is most important that the counselor be available and visible during this difficult period. Students need to know the counselor cares and is capable of playing a critical role in helping with feelings of damaged self-worth."

Coffey's focus is to "help the student feel good about the rest of 'self' separate from the identification with prestigious college placement. . . . Adolescents in this position easily lose sight of their wholeness, and the sensitive counselor can redirect their perceptions. If possible, a counselor should help the student understand the 'why' of the decision." If the reasons are not obvious, the counselor should discuss the case with the admission office. "Open, candid dialogue between the counselor and admission office serves to help the denied student understand."

This, of course, is where the establishment of a close relationship over an extended period of time between you and your counselee can yield returns. He or she will feel comfortable in coming to you. Now, for a change, you can counsel on feelings and *living*, instead of "getting in." As James Coffey suggests, you can "be there"—just being there will often suffice.

AS YOU WORK WITH YOUR PUBLICS

As you work with students and parents, it is possible that you contribute to their anxiety, just by the presentation of various admission topics at day and evening gatherings. There are a host of emotionally charged terms, such as "getting in," "deadline," "testing," and "rejection" that can send pressure indicators soaring.

To minimize the tension, be understanding of family concerns—and start early! If parents work *at the proper time on the appropriate issues* for their youngster's educational future, they will have gained a certain amount of ease in the process; panic is less likely to set in. Try to phase in precollege programs during the middle and/or junior high school years. Such programs should be broadly focused, with college admission topics carefully woven into the overall presentation. They should be well structured; for example, "We've done . . . so far"; "Our next step will be . . .".

(Many parents don't really want their "baby" to grow up. So you might find a subconscious resistance to early efforts to work on college planning; individuals try to put off the inevitable "leaving home.")

Having an extensive outside network of references at your fingertips is another way of relieving stress. Unable to provide an appropriate answer, students and parents are more than appreciative when you can steer them to those persons or agencies that can.

WHOSE STRESS IS IT, ANYWAY?

The youngster's, of course. And the parents'.

But there is another person sorely afflicted with college admission stress: *you*. You are conscious about how well you do your job, how well it *appears* that you do your job, what your spreadsheet of acceptances looks like. That's normal. But you (and there are many more like you) are also concerned about the welfare of your students: if they will indeed be happy with the schools you have helped them select, if you've provided them with the best advice on a difficult maneuver, if you challenged them enough.

Now that you've worked through the whole admission process with us, the amount of knowledge you have to utilize must seem overwhelming. Yet you need such knowledge to deal effectively with *each* youngster's application experience. Rest easy. You are but *one* of many adults involved in his maturational process. You do have a *special* role, of course, and in that role you furnish your counselee with the best information you can acquire and direct him where to go to obtain more. You help him grow so that he can accept the stress, the challenge, the failure, and the success and make them productive in his adult life.

Becoming a good counselor is the work of a lifetime! But you're closer today than you were yesterday, aren't you?

SUGGESTED READINGS

COFFEY, JAMES. Fall 1986. "What Do You Mean I Didn't Get In?" *The Journal of College Admissions*. NACAC, 1800 Diagonal Road, Alexandria, VA.

FARRAR, RONALD T. 1984. *College 101*. Princeton, NJ: Peterson's Guides, Inc. A most comprehensive, candid, and articulate guide in a question-and-answer format. Farrar is a professor of journalism at the University of Kentucky.

NEUSNER, JACOB. 1984. *How to Grade Your Professors and Other Unexpected Advice*. Boston: Beacon Press. Engrossing reading. An excellent buy!

RUPP, RICHARD H. 1984. *Getting Through College*. Ramsey, NJ: Paulist Press. A lively and literate work for both parents and students that comes complete with practical worksheets.

Index

a

b

c

d

e

f

g

h

i

j

l

m

n

o

p

r

S